Social Policy and

Social Work

Social Policy and Social Work: An introduction

STEVE CUNNINGHAM
JO CUNNINGHAM

Series Editors: Jonathan Parker and Greta Bradley

Los Angeles | London | New Delhi
Singapore | Washington DC

Learning Matters
An imprint of SAGE Publications Ltd
1 Oliver's Yard
55 City Road
London EC1Y 1SP

SAGE Publications Inc.
2455 Teller Road
Thousand Oaks, California 91320

SAGE Publications India Pvt Ltd
B 1/I 1 Mohan Cooperative Industrial Area
Mathura Road
New Delhi 110 044

SAGE Publications Asia-Pacific Pte Ltd
3 Church Street
#10-04 Samsung Hub
Singapore 049483

Library of Congress Control Number 2011944262

British Library Cataloguing in Publication data

A catalogue record for this book is available from
the British Library

ISBN 978 1 84445 301 6

Editor: Luke Block
Development editor: Kate Lodge
Production controller: Chris Marke
Production management: Deer Park Productions
Marketing Manager: Zoe Seaton
Cover design: Code 5 Design Associates
Typeset by: PDQ Typesetting, Newcastle-under-Lyme
Printed by: MPG Books Group, Bodmin, Cornwall

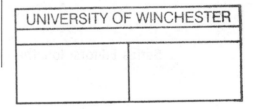

Contents

welfare • Service users' demands for greater autonomy • The
1996 Community Care (Direct Payments) Act • The benefits of
personalisation • A critical analysis of the personalisation agenda
• A social democratic vision of personalisation

Acknowledgements

We would like to dedicate the book to our parents, who have always provided us with inspiration and support.

We would also like to thank colleagues and students in the School of Social Work at the University of Central Lancashire for the encouragement they have given to us throughout the writing process.

About the authors

Steve Cunningham is a Senior Lecturer in Social Policy at the University of Central Lancashire. He has taught social policy at both undergraduate and postgraduate level for 17 years. His research interests are focused on welfare history, poverty and social security, the sociology of welfare, asylum and immigration policy, child labour and children's rights. Steve is the author of numerous publications in these areas.

Jo Cunningham is the Associate Head of the School of Social Work at the University of Central Lancashire. She has been centrally involved in the management and teaching of social work education for the past 13 years. Before commencing her academic career, Jo was a social worker in the area of children and families. Her research interests include childhood accidents, child death, asylum policy, and more recently the policy and practice context surrounding sex workers.

Series Editors' Preface

The Western world including the UK face numerous challenges over forthcoming years, many of which are perhaps heightened following the 2007 fiscal crisis and its lasting ramifications. These include dealing with the impact of an increasingly ageing population, with its attendant social care needs and working with the financial implications that such a changing demography brings. At the other end of the life-span the need for high quality child care, welfare and safeguarding services have been highlighted as society develops and responds to a changing complexion. National and global perturbations have continued to influence and mould social policy developments, which often determine the ways in which they are applied in social work practice.

Migration has increased as a global phenomenon and we now live and work with the implications of international issues in our everyday and local lives. Often these issues influence how we construct our social services and determine what services we need to offer. It is likely that as a social worker you will work with a diverse range of people throughout your career, many of whom have experienced significant, even traumatic, events that require a professional and caring response grounded, of course, in the laws and social policies that have developed as a result. As well as working with individuals, however, you may be required to respond to the needs of a particular community disadvantaged by world events or excluded within local communities because of assumptions made about them, and you may be embroiled in some of the tensions that arise from implementing policy-based approaches that may conflict with professional values. What is clear within these contexts is that you may be working with a range of people who are often at the margins of society, social excluded or in need of protection and safeguarding: the social policy responses designed to work with people marginalised within or excluded from society are dealt with in this book. This text provides important knowledge and information to help you become aware of these issues, and to respond appropriately when faced with challenging situations.

The importance of social work education came to the fore again following the inquiry into the death of baby Peter and the subsequent report from the Social Work Task Force set up in its aftermath. It is timely, also, to reconsider elements of social work education as is being taken forward by the Reform Board process in England and its implementation – indeed, we should view this as a continual striving for excellence! Reflection, revision and reform allow us to focus clearly on what knowledge is useful to engage with in learning to be a social worker. The focus on 'statutory' social work, and by dint of that involuntary clients, brings to the fore the need for social workers to be well-versed in the mechanisms and nuances of legislation that can be interpreted and applied to empower, protect and assist, but also to understand the social policy arena in which practice is forged.. This important book provides readers with a beginning sense of the realities of practice and the importance of understanding the history of social protection, welfare and policy as it impacts on the lives of individuals in the UK.

The books in this series respond to the agendas driven by changes brought about by professional body, Government and disciplinary review. They aim to build on and offer introductory texts based on up-to-date knowledge and social policy development and to help communicate this in an accessible way preparing the ground for future study as you develop your social work career. The books are written by people passionate about social work and social services and aim to instil that passion on others. The knowledge introduced in this book is important for all social workers in all fields of practice as they seek to reaffirm social work's commitment to those it serves.

Professor Jonathan Parker, Bournemouth University

Greta Bradley, University of York

Introduction

Most social policy textbooks begin by acknowledging the difficulties associated with defining social policy. The need to define the discipline stems partly from the fact that many students are encountering social policy for the first time and are often unclear as to the issues and debates that lie at its heart. One of the problems we face is that social policy is not taught as a distinct academic subject in secondary or further education. Consequently, students are often naturally quite apprehensive when first encountering it at university. Their anxieties are sometimes compounded by the fact that they may not be enrolled on a distinct 'social policy' course, and are wondering why, as students on social work, nursing, or other welfare-related courses, they are being 'forced' to engage with a discipline that they have not 'signed up' to. As lecturers who have taught social policy for many years, we are well aware of this reaction. However, many, indeed the vast majority of students have already been introduced to a range of social policy-related issues and debates prior to attending university – for instance, at secondary schools in their citizenship classes, or in sociology, politics, general studies or health and social care courses at college. In addition, of course, you will all have come across and been touched by social policies in your daily lives and this will have given you at least some knowledge about issues and debates covered by the subject. Indeed, it is frequently an interest in social policy-related issues that leads individuals to apply for social work and welfare courses in the first place. Hence, although many students have rarely studied social policy as a distinct academic discipline, we find that they are, sometimes unwittingly, already familiar with the much of the terrain that it covers. Indeed, when we ask students directly what they think social policy 'is', they are, without too much prompting, able to identify a range of themes, issues and debates that do relate to the study of social policy.

So if you are approaching this text feeling unclear as to what social policy is, or are questioning the relevance of the discipline to your course, then please do not panic. Firstly, you can rest assured that you are not alone. Many of your peers who are encountering the discipline for the first time will be experiencing similar anxieties. Secondly, we can reassure you that you will doubtlessly be underestimating the amount of knowledge about the discipline that you already possess. Thirdly, we are confident that having read this text you will understand the relevance of social policy to social work and welfare-related practice. Finally, we hope that the book will stimulate your interest in the discipline, and you come to see your social policy studies as not only a central, but also an enjoyable, engaging aspect of your training and education. Certainly, our own experiences suggest that once exposed to social policy, students are often keen to pursue this element of their studies further.

Structure of the book

Chapter 1 of the book introduces you to the discipline of social policy. As well as examining the historical development of the subject in higher education, it discusses the links between the academic subject of social policy and social work education. The chapter also explains how and why social policy can make an important contribution to your professional studies. We do so by assessing how recent public expenditure cuts have impacted upon service users and the ability of social workers to meet the needs of vulnerable people.

Chapter 2 adopts a historical approach and looks at the development of social policy and social work in the nineteenth century. It is often assumed that social policy and social work developments have, historically, been motivated primarily by humanitarian sentiment. However, such interpretations are partial, and fail to acknowledge the complex range of factors, concerns and forces that have shaped, and continue to shape, policy and practice. Our aim in this chapter, therefore, is to provide you a broad historical perspective, examining the respective influence of 'care' and 'control' concerns in framing nineteenth-century welfare developments. We also seek to draw your attention to the relevance of historical inquiry to helping us understand policy developments today.

Many social policy and social work textbooks include some discussion of the importance of political ideologies. Often, they contain brief chapters on the topic, which seek to summarise what the key principles of the different ideological positions are. However, although helpful, the student is frequently left with an inadequate understanding of how different political ideologies have, historically, shaped social policy and social work. The discussion is sometimes overly theoretical and somewhat detached from the policy-making process itself. In this book we deviate slightly from the 'norm', in that we locate our discussion of ideologies in four chapters – Chapters 3, 4, 5 and 6, which examine the historical development of the post-war welfare state. The advantage of this approach is that it helps illustrate how different ideological perspectives have exercised different levels of influence on social policy and social work developments at different times in British history. Hence, we chart a timeline of influence for different political ideologies, examining the extent to which each has influenced policy and practice. The main perspectives to be examined are social democracy (Chapter 4), neo-liberalism (Chapter 5) and Marxism (Chapter 6). These are important chapters of the book, and the theoretical perspectives examined here will re-emerge in subsequent chapters of the text, where we assess the political and ideological principles that have shaped specific social policies.

The remainder of the text is devoted to an analysis of how social policies impact upon citizens at different stages in their life course. The next four chapters therefore contain separate discussions on children, young people, adults and older adults. Chapter 7 examines how children have been at the forefront of social policy and social work practice developments over the past decade. Within social work, the inquiry into the death of Victoria Climbié and more recently the Baby Peter Connelly case have placed a very public spotlight on social workers attempts to safeguard children. However, our aim in this chapter is to show how an over-concentration on the issues of 'neglect' and 'child protection' can serve to divert attention away from the pressing need to address other factors that can impinge upon the life chances of vulnerable children, such as poverty, poor educational opportunities and health inequalities.

Young people have always been the subject of social policy and social work interventions. Chapter 8 will consider how policy initiatives contribute to and are in turn influenced by wider 'moral panics' about young people. We examine the growing evidence of youth exclusion in Britain today and question the effectiveness of recent policies. The chapter provides a broad assessment of the overall trajectory of policy, critically analysing the assumptions and concerns that have shaped it.

In their practice, social workers provide advice and assistance to a number of different groups of adult service users. Recent policy, in many cases shaped by user movements themselves, has focused upon the need to empower adult service users, by giving them more control over the services they receive. This is clearly a development to be welcomed, though concerns have been expressed about the direction of what has become known as the 'personalisation agenda'. Chapter 9 will provide a critical analysis of the potential of such initiatives.

Working with and providing services to older people can constitute a significant part of a social worker's role. As is the case with working-age adult services, the focus of some recent initiatives has been geared towards empowering service users, by providing them with the means to make decisions about their own lives. As well as examining these policies, Chapter 10 will also consider a range of other social policy developments that can contribute to or impinge upon the economic and social well-being of older people. In short, it will assess the relative ease with which older people are able to access the citizenship rights that other sections of the population take for granted, such as a decent income, appropriate housing and adequate access to health and social care services.

Finally, we hope that this book will help you appreciate the relevance of social policy to your studies. Certainly, the social work profession itself has acknowledged importance of social policy to social work. As the QAA Benchmark Statements for Social Work indicate: *Within the UK there are different traditions of social welfare (influenced by legislation, historical development and social attitudes) and these have shaped both social work education and practice*. Social work graduates, it states, must be equipped to *think critically about the complex social, legal, economic, political and cultural contexts in which social work practice is located*, and be able to comprehend the issues and trends in modern public and social policy and their relationship to contemporary practice and service delivery in social work. As social policy and social work academics, we passionately support these statements and have structured the book in a way that we believe will go some way to assisting you to meet these objectives.

PART ONE
THE HISTORICAL AND THEORETICAL CONTEXT

Chapter 1
Social policy and social work

Introduction

The discipline of social policy has a long been seen as a crucial element of social work education. Its links with social work training can be traced back to the early twentieth century, when concerns were raised about the overly moralistic training provided to social workers by the Charity Organisation Society (COS), which located the blame for poverty, squalor and other social ills in the 'inadequate' social habits of the poor. Attempts to promote the development of a broader social policy-based social work curriculum, which sought to acknowledge the wider structural causes of disadvantage, were, we will show, prompted by a desire to provide social workers with a more critical awareness of the causes of economic and social ills. The historical perspective we provide in this chapter will help you understand the development of the links between social policy and social work. However, we also want to stress the contemporary resonance of social policy to your social work studies. Hence, towards the end of the chapter we examine some recent, important social policy developments; in particular the cuts in welfare spending that are being introduced by David Cameron's coalition government. As well as assessing the impact of these upon service users, we will examine their implications for social work practice.

The origins of social policy

The origins of social policy as an academic discipline can be traced back to the early twentieth century, when a Department of Social Science and Administration (DSSA) was established at the London School of Economics (LSE) in 1912. The initial aims of this embryonic version of the subject were narrowly vocational and its syllabus was geared mainly towards meeting the perceived training needs of untrained voluntary social workers. *It is intended*, stated its syllabus for 1912, *for those who wish to prepare themselves to engage in the many forms of social and charitable effort* (Titmuss, 1966, p15).

Before this, social work training had been undertaken by the COS at the LSE's School of Sociology. We will look in more detail at the work of the COS in Chapter 2; however, for now it is just worth noting that its 'social policy' courses had contained an overtly moral undertone. In keeping with the prevailing philosophies of the day, as well as the COS's own moralistic philosophy, students were taught that poverty, squalor and other social and economic evils were a result of the ignorance or inappropriate behaviour of the poor. As Jones (1983) argues, at the core of the COS's provision was the notion that poverty and destitution were a consequence of a lack of morality or foresight rather than a lack of material resources. Accordingly, its courses focused upon the benefits of self-help and thrift, while bemoaning the idleness, profligacy and drinking habits of the 'lower orders'.

Those involved in creating the new DSSA, including the Fabian socialist Sydney Webb, were at least partly motivated by recognition of the failings of the COS's methods (Attlee, 1920). They felt that governments could and should intervene to promote citizens' welfare. In the context of the times, this was understandable. This was, after all, a period when the pioneering poverty surveys of Charles Booth and Seebohm Rowntree were laying bare the depths of urban squalor and poverty, provoking the consciences of politicians and social reformers. The failure of the COS's provision to acknowledge, as these exhaustive poverty surveys had done, the structural determinants of social problems was seen as a fundamental weakness and one which the new DSSA would seek to address. As Clement Attlee (1920, pp144–5), an early appointee to the Department's teaching staff put it, *The days are, it is to be hoped, past when people without any qualifications other than a good heart and the means of obtaining money plunged straight into social work without any consideration of ... what the effect of their actions were going to have, with the result that they only increased the evils they tried to prevent.* Or as Richard Titmuss (1973, p48), a leading post-war social policy scholar frankly stated, there was a general sense of *dissatisfaction with the existing methods of training upper-middle class girls in the technique of instructing the poor how to manage their poverty.*

That said, pathological, behavioural interpretations for social problems continued to find expression in the new DSSA's early social policy provision, which, like that of its predecessor, had a tendency towards the adoption of an overtly moralistic tone. *Academically speaking,* Titmuss acknowledged, *it was not perhaps a very respectable affair in those days.* Students continued to be seen as 'moral entrepreneurs', who would utilise their missionary zeal to put the 'lower orders' back onto the 'straight and narrow'. As Titmuss explains, *If poverty was a matter of ignorance then it was the moral duty of one class in society to teach another class how to live, and to lead them, through sanitation, soap and thrift to a better station in life* (pp18–19). Hence, for the princely sum of ten shillings and six pence, students enrolling in the DSSA could undertake a six lecture course on *The Household Economics of the Handworking Poor,* whereupon they be would taught how the working population bought their food, stored and cooked it. There was no recognition here of the fact that large sections of the labouring poor were simply unable to afford a healthy diet, and that it was this, and not 'ignorance' as to 'correct' eating habits, that lay at the heart of the nutritional problems they faced. Another course, taught by the renowned eugenicist Karl Pearson, focused upon the links between drink, alcoholism and infant mortality, while remaining silent on the impact that poverty, squalor and poor sanitation had upon premature infant death. As director of an influential national eugenicist organisation which viewed health, ability, crime and much else besides as 'inborn traits', immune to the influence of social reform, Pearson was perhaps hardly the best choice lecturer for a social policy course. Thus, provision at the DSSA, initially at least, continued to be shaped by more than the 'faint whiff' of individualistic, behavioural interpretations of social problems.

The quality of teaching did improve, though. Under the tutelage of a more radical generation of lecturers, such as RH Tawney, TH Marshall and Clement Attlee, a more progressive curriculum emerged; one which encouraged those intending to work with poor, marginalised individuals and families to understand the social and economic constraints that shaped their lives. Titmuss (1966, p18), an LSE student at the time, recalls being mesmerised by an inaugural lecture given by Tawney, a new appointee to the Department in 1913:

> *The problem of poverty, he said, is not a problem of individual character and waywardness, but a problem of economic and industrial organisation. It had to be studied at its sources and only secondly in its manifestations.*

The appointment of Clement Attlee to the Department in 1915 represented another significant milestone. His views of social work training, expressed in his 1920 book, *The social worker*, could not be further removed from those of the COS. Attlee used his book to condemn the COS's approach to social work education, accusing it of encouraging the adoption of *harsh and tactless methods*:

> *... a general assumption is made that all applicants are frauds unless they prove themselves otherwise, and this induces an attitude in the COS workers that is profoundly galling to the ordinary applicant, and is apt to bias those who receive their training from the Society.*

(Attlee, 1920, p65)

COS workers, Attlee argued, had *a tendency to clothe themselves in the filthy rags of their own righteousness*, and their *lack of sympathy makes their charity a hard and unlovely thing*. Attlee emphasised the need for social work students to be provided with a much broader, political education, which, when taught alongside their practical vocational studies, would better equip them to assist the people they would be working with. Rather than 'blaming' individuals for their predicaments, social workers should, he insisted, empower service users, and indeed even campaign for progressive social and economic change. Attlee argued that the social worker should be a *social investigator*, a *pioneer*, and indeed an *agitator, who has some clear conception of what society he wishes to see produced*. Those of you with a rudimentary grasp of political and social history may be aware of the future role Clement Attlee would play in transforming Britain's economic and social landscape, as the leader of the most radical, reforming, progressive government Britain has ever seen. For as the Labour Prime Minister between 1945 and 1951, Attlee presided over the introduction of the array of welfare services and programmes which we now know as the welfare state.

The reforming impulses of those such as Attlee, RH Tawney and TH Marshall did influence social work training at the LSE. By 1923, it was offering a two–three year course to welfare workers, which, as well as providing practical welfare work experience, offered a *theoretical grounding in economics, social history, local government, social and political philosophy, industrial legislation and 'current problems'* (Lloyd, 1923, p3). Similar social administration courses (social policy courses in all but name) also emerged in other universities across the UK, including Bristol, Birmingham, Leeds, Liverpool, Edinburgh and Glasgow (Attlee, 1920). This trend towards the incorporation of a greater 'social policy' element in social work training was prompted by a desire to move beyond individualised, pathological explanations for human misery, and to understand the wider structural causes of disadvantage that were largely beyond the control of poverty-stricken families. As we shall see in Chapter 2, social work 'in practice' prior to the Second World War (and indeed after 1945) may not always have lived up to these laudable ideals, but this shift in thinking did nonetheless represent an important change in attitudes to social work training.

The development of social policy after 1945

The huge expansion of welfare services after the Second World War undoubtedly contributed to the further development of social policy as an academic discipline. As new publicly funded services grew and absorbed more workers, so too did the demand for social policy courses and the discipline became established in higher education institutions across the UK. Initially, with a few notable exceptions, it developed on a somewhat narrow, relatively vocational basis, sometimes doing little more than providing welfare workers with descriptive information about the institutions they were employed in, as well as the legislation – or policy – that shaped their practice. However, as Brown (1983, p93) points out, social policy gradually developed into a *more lively and critical subject*, which began to ask more penetrating questions about the origins, values and shape of welfare provision:

> *A new generation ... looked at the services and asked: how far had they succeeded – and how far had they failed? Who had benefitted from them? Whose interests did they serve? What had influenced their operation and determined their outcomes?*

At the forefront of this shift were academics such as Peter Townsend and Richard Titmuss, who, as Brown notes, ensured that the discipline developed *an over-riding interest in the actual impact of social policies on individuals* (p94). The scope of the discipline thus became much broader, theoretical and critical, analysing the extent to which the post-war welfare state had succeeded in achieving its aims. Instead of simply describing social service structures, policy and legislation, social policy courses focused upon evaluating the ethos and principles that underpinned welfare, as well as assessing its impact on the social and economic well-being of citizens. The notion that social policies were motivated by altruistic, benevolent intentions – that they were, to quote one academic, *a good deed in a naughty world* (Donnison, cited in Brown, 1983, p95) – began to be challenged, as evidence of the failure of the post-war welfare state to respond to citizens needs emerged. Indeed, as we show in Chapter 4, by the late 1960s social policy academics were drawing attention to the disciplinary, controlling functions that welfare policies, including those related to social work, could perform. As Chris Jones (2011) points out, attempts to infuse this more radical social science perspective into social work education were not always welcomed by a social work profession that, in some cases, was still wedded to a conservative, vocationally orientated form of training. However, in the context of the civil rights campaigns and protest movements of the late 1960s, it was a perspective that many social work students themselves welcomed. Many had become disillusioned about the failure of their professional courses to tap into the critical and challenging insights provided by social policy/social science literature. Jones recalls his experiences of social work training around this time:

> *I remember all the professional lecturers promulgate views of poverty as though they were manifestations of pathological personalities and inadequate mothering; of how the well-functioning family with the mother at the hearth was the ideal and how clients were both devious and childlike. It really was so*

much stuff and nonsense and a million light years away from what we were discovering about class inequalities and the reproduction of poverty and disadvantage under capitalism.

(p30)

Social policy today

So what does social policy as an academic subject focus upon today? As Brown (1969, p12) states, *whatever are generally accepted as social problems, together with the complex human needs that underlie them, must be the first area of study* for the social policy student. Basically, at the core of social policy lies an evaluation of societal responses to social problems such as poverty, social exclusion, unemployment, homelessness, crime, health and education inequalities. Hence, the subject seeks to develop an understanding of the 'very real' policy issues and debates that affect people's life chances and opportunities. In this sense it is a dynamic and constantly moving discipline, at the cutting edge of policy debates which ultimately determine government and non-governmental responses to issues like child poverty and neglect, pension provision, asylum and immigration, as well as health, education and social service reform. However, it is perhaps the subject's dynamism, fluidity and breadth which make it somewhat difficult to define precisely. Because social problems and societal responses to them change and evolve, it is impossible to give a once and for all definition of 'social policy', or to provide a definitive list of the issues that it covers.

Traditionally, the curricula of social policy courses in the post-1945 period were geared towards analysing the way the 'big' publicly funded and publicly provided forms of welfare provision, such as social security, health, education, housing and social service, or social work provision, had responded to human need. In part, this reflected the context within which social policy as an academic discipline 'took off' in higher education after 1945. As we have already explained, this period was characterised by a dramatic expansion of state welfare, and a growing demand from public sector welfare agencies and workers for information about the problems that their organisations dealt with. In addition, at that time the state was the 'main' provider of welfare. Governments of all political complexions accepted responsibility for tackling economic and social ills, and social policy academics inevitably focused their attention on analysing the outcomes of public sector interventions.

However, from the late 1970s onwards governments have sought to reduce the state's role in the organisation and delivery of welfare provision, encouraging the development of a voluntary and private sector of welfare. We will examine the ideological principles that influenced this shift in Chapter 5, but for our purposes here it is sufficient to simply point out that today the state is no longer the sole, monopoly provider of welfare services, and a whole range of non-statutory organisations, as well as individuals and families themselves, are now involved in its delivery. Moreover, within public welfare agencies – including social service departments – market-led reforms have changed the nature of provision, profoundly altering its shape and organisation. This drive to reform and reduce the scope of state welfare has accelerated recently, as the coalition government has imposed drastic cuts to public expenditure (see Chapter 5). Allied to this has been David Cameron's much discussed (and contested) 'Big Society' agenda, which envisages a much greater role for the private and voluntary sectors in the welfare sphere. Hence, we are now faced with a much more 'plural', diverse welfare landscape than we were thirty or so years ago, involving a more fluid mix of state, private and voluntary sector interventions. In response to these changes in the way social policies are funded, organised and delivered, the academic discipline of social policy has inevitably had to adjust its focus, and its gaze now spans over a much broader, plural, eclectic field of welfare provision. So although the study of the 'public sector' still looms large in social policy courses, social policy curricula also seek to impart an understanding of the role played by private and voluntary sector organisations, as well as individuals and families, in meeting citizens' needs. Again, the intention is not simply to describe the changes that have occurred. Our aim is to critically analyse social policies and trends and assess their impact upon citizens' social and economic conditions.

In developing this critical analysis, new tools, methods and theoretical paradigms have been embraced by social policy academics. 'Traditional' social policy research, epitomised by its focus on particular services and problems, retains a strong hold on the discipline, though this has been accompanied by a more analytical approach, involving broader questions about the 'functions' of welfare and the role of the state. As we have already hinted, from the 1960s onwards, the 'social conscience thesis' – the notion that social policies are necessarily motivated by benevolent intentions – was challenged, and the search for alternative interpretations has led social policy scholars to focus upon the ideological influences that underpin welfare interventions. In doing so, social policy has shown a much greater willingness to draw from other disciplines, such as political science, sociology and economics. As Wilding (1983) argues, the marrying of the 'traditional' social policy approach with this newer 'theoretical' approach is a positive development; it represents a maturing of the subject and is in accordance with the aims and ideals of the subject's early pioneers.

The relevance of social policy to social work

Hopefully, our brief summary of the development of social policy will have given you an appreciation of the historical links between social policy and social work. In order to help you understand its relevance further, we will consider the consequences of some recent social policy developments; in particular the cuts in welfare spending currently being introduced by David Cameron's coalition government. As we will show, these will undoubtedly impact upon the economic and social well-being of vulnerable people, while at the same time constraining the options and resources available to social workers. In this sense, our discussion here will help reinforce the importance of including a social policy dimension in your social work training.

An analysis of the impact of the coalition's public expenditure cuts on service users and the social work role

In October 2010, George Osborne, the coalition's Conservative Chancellor of the Exchequer, announced £18 billion of cuts to welfare spending. He made it clear that welfare benefits (social security) would be affected, as well as local authority social care budgets. The coalition argued this was a necessary part of its deficit-reduction strategy, but many politicians and commentators claimed that the speed and intensity of the cuts were unnecessary and would create severe harm and hardship. The Labour Party, for example, proposed a more phased, moderate strategy of public expenditure cuts, while others argued that the deficit could be tackled through other mechanisms, such as tax increases, or a clampdown on tax evasion by major corporations and wealthy individuals. In short, political alternatives have been proposed, which if pursued would lead to different social policy outcomes. However, the coalition decided to press ahead with its rapid programme of cuts to welfare spending and it is the potential 'outcomes' of these that we turn to now. Here, we focus our attention solely upon cuts to local authority welfare budgets (we will examine the potential implications of recent social security reforms in Chapter 5).

Cuts to local authority welfare budgets

A significant proportion of the £18 billion of welfare cuts imposed by the coalition will come from reductions in the budgets given to local authorities by central government to support service users' needs. The government claims that efficiency savings can be made and that crucial front-line services will not be affected by the funding reductions. However, senior welfare services managers have expressed serious concerns as to the impact upon service users. The NHS Confederation, for example, has said that it is *deeply worried* about the cuts, with its chief executive predicting that they would lead to a severe restriction in social care availability:

> *It seems inevitable that we will see a significant withdrawal of support from some of the most vulnerable people in our society – before long we could see a majority of councils only supplying services to those with the most critical of needs.*

(cited in Samuel, 2010a)

ACTIVITY **1.1**

How might the Coalition's cuts impact upon the social and economic well-being of vulnerable individuals and groups? Here, it might be worth consulting:
- *Local media reports in your area about how the cuts are affecting levels of provision, especially 'thresholds' for care.*
- *National coverage of the coalition's cuts in* Community Care, *or 'broadsheet' newspapers, such as the* Guardian, Observer *and* Independent.

COMMENT

At the time of writing, the full impact of the coalition's cuts has not yet materialised and hence you may be in a better position than us to gauge their legacy. However, what is clear, even at this early stage, is that predictions that the cuts would undermine key social services have been proven accurate. Hundreds of thousands of service users are finding that their access to local authority-funded social care services is either being limited or entirely curtailed. Local authorities face an average 6 per cent cut in their social care budgets in 2011/12, and for some the percentage reduction is considerably higher. This has led many to:

1. tighten their eligibility thresholds for care;

2. Cut the funding they had previously provided to support crucial social care projects and local services.

Thresholds for care

In 2006, 53 per cent of English councils funded the social care of service users with 'moderate needs'; by 2011, however, this had reduced to only 20 per cent, the remainder providing support only to those with 'substantial' or 'critical' needs (Dunning, 2010). As Chapter 9 shows, many local authorities had already begun to ration care in this way prior to the coalition's cuts, but this process has greatly accelerated since October 2010. Indeed, the Local Government Association found that one in seven local authorities had responded to the coalition's cuts by increasing thresholds for care. Lancashire and West Sussex are two of many authorities to tighten eligibility. In Lancashire this will lead to approximately 3,900 service users and carers losing support they had previously been entitled to, while in West Sussex 4,500 will lose access to provision (Moseley, 2011; Lumley, 2011). These are but two of many other authorities that are increasing the thresholds for accessing social care, and it is likely that hundreds of thousands of service users and carers will be affected across the country. This has inevitably had an impact upon the ability of practitioners to meet service users' needs. One survey conducted by the British Association of Social Workers (BASW) in April 2011 found that three-quarters of social workers had reported that changes to qualifying criterion had resulted in their service users being denied provision that they previously had access to:

> *Services are being restricted to critical cases only, preventative services are being shelved and, overnight, people are being expected to find alternative ways of getting their needs met.*

> (BASW, 2011)

As well as introducing 'formal' mechanisms of restricting eligibility thresholds, it seems that some local authorities have responded to the cuts by utilising other, more dubious 'informal' methods of denying access to key services. Many social workers, for example, have reported being placed under pressure by managers to reassess service users and reduce their category of need in order to artificially restrict support. A *Community Care* survey completed in May 2011 found that more than half of all children's social workers had been pressurised to downgrade children from 'child protection plans' to 'child-in-need plans', thus reducing entitlement to support. Disturbingly, 40 per cent of respondents said they had also been pressured into prematurely returning accommodated children to birth parents in order to save money. The College of Social Work, BASW and the GSCC have all acknowledged that such practices are 'unethical', and contravene the social work value base, as well as well as the profession's code of practice (Cooper, 2011).

Other cuts in funding for social care projects and local services

As well as tightening thresholds for care, local authorities have also cut funding for certain key services. The discussion below illustrates how such cuts have impacted on two particular groups of service users – older adults and disabled children – through the reduction or withdrawal of funding from key services and benefits.

Older service users

Age UK (2011) estimate that services for older adults will be cut by £610 million (8.4 per cent) over 2011–12. In order to achieve these savings, councils have been forced to increase the costs of services such as day care and meals on wheels and close day care centres and residential care homes. Age UK's survey of 139 councils identified the following responses to the cuts.

- At least 61 councils (43 per cent of those surveyed) are increasing or imposing new charges on provision, such as home help or day care centres. The fear is that not all those who previously received these services will be able to afford to continue to pay for them.
- At least 27 councils (almost 20 per cent) are reducing personal budgets and/or domiciliary care packages, meaning fewer hours of help for those receiving support.
- At least 25 councils (18 per cent) are reducing the number of placements for older adults in care homes.
- Some 76 councils (almost 55 per cent) have reduced or frozen the support they provide for residential homes for older people, leaving many older people and their families having to absorb any price increases.

It is important to emphasise that levels of need among older adults in these areas remain the same as the previous year. The only changing variable is the level of funding available to meet those same needs. Again, what this helps illustrate is the extent to which national social policies have a very tangible impact both upon the life chances of service users, as well as ability of social services to meet their needs. Like other agencies that advocate on behalf of older people, Age UK has expressed real concern at the impact of these cuts on the lives of older service users:

> *Funding for social care is already inadequate and the system today is failing many older people at the time when they really need help. The consequences of cutting expenditure further to 8.4 per cent, indicated by our research, could be devastating. We are fearful that even more vulnerable older people will be left to struggle alone and in some cases lives will be put at risk.*

Disabled children

A number of commentators have also drawn attention to the negative impact of the coalition's cuts agenda upon the welfare of disabled children and their families. One estimate suggests that disabled children's services are set to be cut by 15 per cent in 2011–12, leading to the closure of many support services (Every Disabled Child Matters, 2011). Already, the availability of funding for short-break services and day care centres has been restricted in many areas, creating severe stress for parents with disabled children. Indeed, there is evidence that disabled children may be taken into care as a result of the cuts, partly as result of the increased pressure faced by parents, but also because accommodating children permanently is seen by some local authorities as a cheaper, less administratively 'burdensome' option than organising short breaks and respite care (Cook, 2011). Meanwhile, benefit cuts will reduce the income available to families with disabled children. If proposed changes to disabled children's benefits are made, it is estimated that they will cost 88,000 families with disabled children up to £1,358 per year. According to the charity consortium Every Disabled Child Matters (2011) this *will further confound the issues that families with disabled children on low income face and is likely to push many more families into poverty.*

Implications of the public expenditure cuts for the social work profession

Research has consistently shown that many of those who have chosen to enter the social work profession have done so out of a strong sense of social justice, or a more general desire to support and empower vulnerable groups (Hackett *et al.*, 2003). It indicates a clear desire among social workers to help address social problems; they want to 'help people'; to 'protect vulnerable groups'; to 'combat discrimination', and to 'enable people to reach their full potential'. Clearly, the policy developments we have discussed will have an impact upon the ability of social workers (and indeed yourselves) to fulfil these objectives and to perform their roles effectively. In the activity below, we want you to consider the potential implications of the reductions in funding we have outlined for the social work profession itself.

ACTIVITY 1.2

- *What impact might the current social policy environment have had upon morale within the social work profession? If you are on placement, you might already have had a 'hint' as to what its impact has been.*

- *How would you personally feel about having to implement the cuts imposed by the coalition government?*

COMMENT

All the evidence suggests that the cuts to local authority welfare budgets have had a direct impact upon the culture of social work teams, constraining and circumscribing the

Continued

---

welfare-related decisions that they are able make. Social workers, it seems, are being pressured into engaging in practices that they themselves know conflict with the needs of their service users, as well as their professional social work value base. Not surprisingly, a survey conducted by the BASW in April 2011 revealed deep concerns among social workers about the impact of the cuts of service users:

More than 95 per cent of social workers surveyed ... said the cuts they are witnessing would cause suffering and hardship, while over 90 per cent went as far as to suggest that lives would potentially be placed in jeopardy. The findings cast serious doubt over government claims that frontline services will be protected from budget-tightening across the public sector.

(BASW, 2011)

Such concerns inevitably lead to higher levels of frustration and stress among social workers. Almost three-quarters of respondents to a survey undertaken by the College of Social Work said that they expected stress levels to increase over the next twelve months, while over two-thirds predicted that already heavy caseloads and sickness rates would rise. In addition, six out of ten felt that their workloads would be more difficult to manage as a result of the cuts (cited in Children Now, 2011). Worryingly, the BASW (2011) found that over a half of the practitioners responding to one of its surveys stated that the cuts had been damaging enough to prompt them to consider leaving the profession due to the impact upon their ability to do their jobs effectively.

What conclusions can we draw from this discussion of the coalition's spending cuts about the nature of social policy and its relevance to you as a future social worker? What it does highlight is that the wider social policy environment has a profound impact not only upon the welfare of services users, but also upon the ability of social workers to perform their roles effectively. In this sense, it is crucial to understand that social work does not operate in a 'vacuum'; indeed, it is far more susceptible to the ideological whims of politicians than most other professions. What our discussion of the coalition's cuts has also shown is that social policies are often motivated by intentions that are often other than 'progressive'. In this specific instance, the desire to reduce public expenditure and reassure financial markets has been given primacy over the welfare needs of service users. In this sense, you can hopefully now see the importance of the need for you, as a future social worker, to have an understanding of the dynamics of social policy. It will provide you with a crucial insight into the causes of the difficulties that affect the service users you will be working with, and the barriers you might face in supporting them. The QAA (2008, p7) Benchmarks for Social Work require that students learn *to understand the impact of injustice, social inequalities and oppressive social relations,* and we hope that our discussion here, and more generally the book, will help you see how the social policy dimension of your studies provides just that opportunity.

CHAPTER SUMMARY

Throughout this chapter we have emphasised the relevance of social policy to social work education. As we have shown, the two have a long-standing historical connection. Indeed, the origins of social policy can be traced back to the pioneering work of those such as Attlee, Tawney and Marshall, who sought to transform social work training by infusing within the curriculum an appreciation of the social, economic and political constraints that shape the lives of service users. However, an appreciation of such constraints is no less important today than it was at the beginning of the twentieth century. As our discussion of the coalition's cuts to welfare spending illustrates, the wider political and social policy environment frequently does constrain and impede the implementation of what can be broadly defined as core social work values. As future social workers and welfare practitioners you will often face obstacles in putting your motivations, aims and values into practice, and an appreciation of the dynamics of social policy can help you understand the extent to which this is the case.

FURTHER READING

For those you who are interested in a 'first hand', historical account of attempts to promote a social policy dimension in social work education, Clement Attlee's *The social worker* is an interesting and worthwhile read:

Attlee, CR (1920) *The social worker*. London: G Bell and Sons.

If you are interested in a more thorough, wide-ranging introduction to social policy than we can provide in this short chapter, you may find the following texts useful. While not written with the specific needs of social workers in mind, they contain an appropriate mix of theoretical and issue-based social policy analysis:

Bochel, H, Bochel, C, Page, R and Sykes, R (2009) *Social policy*. Harlow: Pearson Education.

Lavalette, M and Pratt, A (2006) *Social policy: Theories, concepts and issues*. London: Sage.

Alcock, C, Daly, G and Briggs, E (eds) (2008) *Introducing social policy*. Harlow: Pearson Longman.

Chapter 2

The development of social policy and social work in the nineteenth century

Introduction

The study of history in the twenty-first century has become something of a form of popular entertainment. Supermarkets now stock a multitude of 'history' magazines, catering for a range of diverse tastes, from the family historian to the more serious academic historian. Mainstream, terrestrial television channels have responded to this growing interest in history, and their schedules are liberally peppered with history-themed documentaries and dramas. Indeed, there are now numerous television channels which are devoted solely to the broadcast of history-related material. As two people who share a passion for history, we welcome such developments, and can see the appeal of studying history for its own sake – simply because it is interesting! However, there are other reasons why you, as a current or future social worker, should take an interest in history. For example, a knowledge of specific periods of history can help inform us of how were got to where we are today, assisting us to understand not just the past, but also the present. Indeed, as we will see, academics and politicians often make reference to the past when interpreting more recent, and indeed future social policy and social work developments. This chapter examines a period of history that is often seen as being crucial in terms of the development of social policy and social work, covering the decades from the early nineteenth century to the early twentieth century. The chapter is interspersed with activities designed to encourage you to think about the links between past and current debates over policy and practice.

The origins of the welfare state: Care or control?

When contemplating the origins of the welfare state and the development of social work in Britain, there is a tendency to assume that the primary driving force has been humanitarian concern. It is often assumed that charities, social reformers and legislators were motivated primarily by a strong sense of social responsibility, and that as previously hidden social evils were exposed in the nineteenth century, philanthropists, charities and governments moved to stamp them out. Some historians do subscribe to this interpretation of history. Society, from this perspective, became increasingly sensitive to the needs of the poor, and as social evils were exposed, the harsh excesses of Victorian Britain were gradually curbed by progressive, charitable and state intervention.

This perception, that welfare has historically been about 'helping' the poor, also frequently shapes people's views of social policies in Britain today. Governments, it is often thought, provide welfare services, such as the National Health Service, free education, social security, as well the range of services provided by social workers, for altruistic reasons. They are moved, primarily, by a sense of social justice and a desire to 'assist' the less well off. Indeed, many of our students tell us that this is precisely the reason why they themselves were motivated to become social workers, or other welfare practitioners. They want to 'help' and 'empower' disadvantaged groups and make a positive difference to the lives of people who experience difficulties. In a sense, it is pleasing for us to know that many of our students are motivated to join what they see as caring professions by a strong sense of social justice and altruism. However, social policies and social work have, historically, not simply been designed to dispense 'care'. The welfare state has performed, and continues to perform other functions, and in this chapter we want to encourage you to think critically about both the origins of social policy and social work and the nature of social policy and social work today. In particular, we want to draw your attention to the extent to which both have also been shaped as much by a desire to discipline, control or modify the behaviour of disadvantaged groups as they have humanitarianism. We begin our historical analysis by looking at one of the most influential pieces of social policy legislation to find its way onto the statute books in the nineteenth century, the 1834 Poor Law Amendment Act (PLA Act). However, before looking at the main elements of the PLA Act, it is perhaps first worth giving some consideration to the key features of the system that it replaced.

The old Poor Law

Prior to 1834, families or individuals seeking welfare assistance, were dealt with under a locally administered system of 'relief', often known as the 'old' Poor Law. The types and levels of assistance offered varied by region, but by the end of the eighteenth century local parishes tended to provide assistance to able-bodied people via what was referred to as the 'allowance system' (also sometimes called 'outdoor relief'). With the allowance system support would be provided in the community (hence outdoor relief), and there would be no expectation that those seeking assistance would be punished for their predicament by being confined to a workhouse. The support provided included 'doles' (cash payments to unemployed labourers), payments in kind (such as food, or tools for work) and wage subsidies, all of which would often be adjusted to take into account the cost of living and size of families. While these systems of support were hardly generous (they were intended to provide only the most basic standard of living), they were influenced primarily by benevolence and humanitarianism, and a genuine desire to prevent the incomes of families falling below subsistence levels (Fraser, 1984). The relief was administered by autonomous local committees of parish overseers, who would inquire into families' circumstances before agreeing to give assistance. In some respects, this investigation was an early nineteenth-century equivalent of a needs assessment conducted by social workers today. If evidence of genuine need was found then some assistance would usually be provided. Of course, it goes without saying that cases deemed to be manifestly 'undeserving' would be refused, or any support provided made conditional. Moreover, because parish overseers had a good degree of autonomy, practices varied across the country and some parishes adopted a harsher approach than others. However, overall the system is said to have been administered in a relatively humane way (Rose, 1971).

Criticisms of the old Poor Law

By beginning of the nineteenth century this system of providing relief had become the subject of searching criticism. The old Poor Law had always had its critics, many of whom had long felt that it was too generous and laxly administered. Support, some had argued, was too readily available and this encouraged idleness and fraud. Rather than relying upon their own industry and hard work, individuals and families were choosing the 'easy' option of parish relief. In many respects, the arguments marshalled against the old Poor Law mirrored those used today by right-wing, neo-liberal critics of the welfare state. In short, welfare was said to have a morally corrupting effect, sapping independence and thrift, creating a dependent population, unable, or unwilling, to look after itself. Moreover, because the support provided under the allowance system varied according to family size, it was also said to have encouraged improvident marriages and a rapid growth of the population among 'undesirable' sections of the community who could ill afford to maintain themselves. Thomas Malthus, an influential political philosopher and opponent of the old Poor Law, expressed deep concern at the messages that this sent out to uneducated, 'feckless' sections of the community. There was, he stated, *no occasion for them to put any sort of restraint on their inclinations, or exercise any degree of prudence in the affairs of marriage; because the parish is bound to provide for all that are born* (Malthus, 1982, p66). Put crudely, critics such as Malthus argued that the system provided perverse incentives for 'worthless' paupers to breed more paupers, who would themselves become a burden and charge on the community. Again, we see here parallels with critiques of the welfare state today, particularly the often made claim that teenagers get pregnant 'just to jump the housing queue'.

The old Poor Law under pressure

The ideas of those such as Malthus had, before 1834, already influenced parish overseers in some parts of the country, and in these areas individuals and families requesting assistance were forced to enter a workhouse. The intention was to stigmatise relief in order to deter all but the most desperate from applying for support, and to force individuals to take responsibility for themselves and their families. In reality, there was little evidence of fraud or abuse of the allowance system in these areas. Indeed, the stigmatisation and punishment that occurred in some parishes seems to have been motivated primarily by a desire to cut the costs of supporting the poor, as opposed to any actual proof that they were not in genuine need. However, as the national cost of the old Poor Law grew (it had increased from £4.07 million in 1802/03 to £7 million by 1831), such claims were given added credence. Despite the fact that the vast bulk of requests for assistance were due to factors beyond the individual's control (such as bad harvests and trade fluctuations, or sometimes desertion or widowhood), the ideological climate had changed. Influential opinion began to embrace the views of prominent critics of the old Poor Law, such as Malthus, who had long bemoaned its 'insidious' effects.

The Poor Law Report of 1834

It was in such a context that in 1832 a Royal Commission on the Poor Laws was tasked with the responsibility of producing proposals for radical reform. Its recommendations, published in 1834, were infused with the Malthusian idea that indiscriminate, lavish levels of support were encouraging laziness and fecklessness. The Commission's report was primarily the work of two men – Nassau Senior and Edwin Chadwick – who, evidence suggests, had preconceived views about what needed to be done. Before commencing writing the report, both were already convinced that the old Poor Law created and exacerbated the problems that it was supposed to cure, and accordingly they only selected evidence which supported their preconceived views.

Hence, the report has been described by one influential historian as *in essence a piece of propaganda to support a predetermined case* (Fraser, 1984, p43). The report certainly makes interesting reading and it is packed full of 'evidence' which suggests that outdoor relief morally corrupted the poor, encouraging a whole range of dysfunctional, fraudulent patterns of behaviour. Relief, it was argued, was *mischievous and ruinous*, and corruptive of manners, character and civility. It was also accused of encouraging crime and disorder. Idle labourers were said to be *loitering about during the day, engaged in idle games ... or else consuming their time in sleep, that they may be more ready and active in the hours of darkness.* In addition, in language similar to that used today to condemn 'benefit cheats', the authors of the report argued that it was *utterly impossible to prevent considerable fraud*, claiming that even genuine cases were induced into indolent habits:

> From the preceding evidence it will be seen how zealous must be the agency, and how intense the vigilance, to prevent fraudulent claims crowding in under such a system of relief. But it would require even greater vigilance to prevent the bona fide claimants degenerating into imposters; and it is an aphorism amongst the parish officers that 'cases which are good today are bad tomorrow, unless they are incessantly watched'. A person obtains relief on the ground of sickness; when he has become capable of moderate work, he is tempted, by the enjoyment of subsistence without labour, to conceal his convalescence and fraudulently extend the period of relief.

(Poor Law Report, cited in Checkland and Checkland, 1974, p148 and pp116–19)

ACTIVITY 2.1

- *Can you see any links between the concerns outlined in the Poor Law Report and debates that occur today about the nature and impact of welfare on recipients?*

- *What are your views on the claims that are often made today about the 'extensive' nature of benefit fraud?*

- *How significant a problem is benefit fraud today, compared with other, related problems, such as non-take-up of benefit?*

- *As a social worker you will be working with a whole range of vulnerable people, many of whom will be dependent upon some form of welfare. Do you think the attention devoted to the benefit fraud debate might impact upon their self-imagery and their experiences of the welfare system? Might it discourage them from applying for benefits for which they are entitled to?*

COMMENTS

Many of the comments made in the 1834 Poor Law Report about the 'corrupting' nature of relief do have a contemporary resonance. Similar claims about the extensive nature of benefit fraud are made on daily basis in the media today. The benefit system, we are

Continued

told, is laxly administered, too generous and rife with abuse. This message is conveyed to us on a daily basis in lavishly funded benefit fraud campaigns, newspaper articles and television programmes. We even have a number of television documentary series dedicated to dramatically exposing the 'cheats' and 'liars' that take us, the unsuspecting public, for a ride. Frequently, stories of the 'sinners', that is the deviant, criminal scroungers, are juxtaposed with the narratives of the 'saints', the honest, law-abiding, genuinely needy claimants who lose out due to the actions of fraudsters. Through exposure to such popular representations of benefit fraud, our anger towards 'benefit cheats' is amplified, and it is hardly surprising, therefore, that most of us feel that this is a major issue that needs to be tackled.

Just how extensive is benefit fraud, though? More specifically, how significant a problem is fraud compared with a related social problem, such as non-take-up of benefits? Certainly, the amount of money lost through benefit fraud each year is not insignificant. Indeed, the estimated £870 million that was lost through tax credit and benefit fraud between April 2007 and March 2008 (Department for Work and Pensions, 2008) is a significant sum that could otherwise be spent on good causes, such as reducing pensioner or child poverty. However, this loss does need to be placed in context. During the same period, £1.1 billion was saved to the Exchequer as a result of underpayment of benefit. As Table 2.1 below illustrates, a further sum of between £11.35 billion and £18.03 billion was saved through people not claiming benefits that they were entitled to.

Table 2.1 Income related benefits: Estimates of non-take-up 2007/08

Benefit	Entitled not claiming (%)	Amount unclaimed
Income Support	12–22	£630m–£1,550m
Pensions Credit	30–39	£1,900m–£2,930m
Housing Benefit	13–20	£1,350m–£2,470m
Council Tax Benefit	32–38	£1,570m–£2,160m
Jobseeker's Allowance	40–51	£870m–£1,440m
Child Tax Credit (06/07)	17–21	£2,150–£3,420
Working Tax Credit (06/07)	41–45	£2,880–£4,060m
Total		£11,350m–18,030m

Source: Department for Work and Pensions, 2009; Inland Revenue, 2009

Why does so much money remain unclaimed? Some have argued that the disproportionate emphasis that has been placed upon fraud itself discourages people from making legitimate claims. As the Child Poverty Action Group (2009) has argued, *fraud is a demonstrably small problem and overestimating its extent ... may discourage genuine claimants from claiming for fear of being thought fraudulent* (cited in House of Commons Library, 2009). The evidence suggests that this may particularly be the case for pensioners, many of whom fail to claim their Income Support entitlements under the Pension Credit. The claiming process for the Pension Credit is extremely complicated, and fears about the consequences of omitting crucial pieces of information are reinforced by anti-fraud campaigns (such as the recent *No ifs, No buts* one), which emphasise the message that fraudsters will be prosecuted irrespective of their motives. Coupled with the stigma associated with having to respond to detailed, complex questions about personal finances and relationships, the overwhelming emphasis placed upon fraud acts as a deterrent to legitimate Pension Credit claims.

A number of commentators have sought to explain why so much emphasis is placed upon the issue of fraud in both media and political commentaries. Some, such as Golding and Middleton (1981) and Cook (1989), argue that the motives are very similar to those of yesteryear – as in the past, the intention is to discredit welfare provision, reinforce personal responsibility, and to justify the retrenchment of welfare entitlements. At the same time, the real issues, such as the poverty created by non-take-up welfare, are obscured by the 'scroungerphobia' generated by sensationalist reporting and political commentaries on the issue. This provides the rationale for politicians to justify retrenching welfare entitlements, even during periods of recession, when such policies would otherwise be seen as unpalatable. Golding and Middleton (1981) argue that it has always been thus, and they detect a remarkable level of continuity in past and current debates about the issue.

The Poor Law Amendment Act 1834

Despite the methodological flaws associated with the Poor Law Report of 1834, the solutions it offered were enthusiastically embraced by the political elite, and legislators set about devising a new Poor Law, which would discipline and control the poor, forcing them to make every effort to support themselves independently. The new Poor Law, which was introduced with the passage of the 1834 Poor Law Amendment Act, aimed to deter people from applying for support by making the receipt of welfare as uncomfortable and stigmatising as possible. Three basic principles underpinned the new Poor Law. These were, less eligibility, the workhouse test and centralisation.

Less eligibility

The Poor Law Report had argued that in order to deter bogus, unnecessary applications for relief, the position of those receiving support needed to be made considerably worse (*less eligible*) than that of even the lowest paid independent labourer. As the report stated, *let the labourer find that the parish is the hardest taskmaster and the worst paymaster he can find, and thus induce him to make his application to the parish his last and not his first resource*. Of course, at a time when the average age of death for labourers was in the mid-20s, it would, in practical terms, be difficult to reduce the condition of recipients considerably lower than that of the lowest paid independent labourer, without literally starving them to death. As EP Thompson (1972, p295) argues, at a time when many of those in work barely earned enough to live on, even the most inventive state would have found it difficult to create institutions which simulated conditions worse than those endured by large sections of the working poor. Such conditions were, though, created in the form of the dreaded workhouse. Henceforth this would be the means of putting the principle of less eligibility into effect.

The Workhouse Test

The PLA Act envisaged that all outdoor relief would be abolished and that the provision of support would be conditional upon recipients and their families entering a workhouse. The workhouse regime would be strict, drab, monotonous and intentionally cruel and degrading. The objective was to make workhouses places of dread and as prison-like as possible, thus guaranteeing the position of those claiming relief would be 'less eligible' (worse) than the lowest paid independent labourers. Inmates would be separated from relatives, be forced to wear uniforms, be fed rudimentary, often inadequate unappetising diets (see our comments on the Andover workhouse below), and required to engage in monotonous, meaningless arduous labour. They would be made to feel like moral failures and it would be made clear that the cause and solution to their destitution lay in their own hands, not that of the community. The workhouse regime, therefore, would ensure that only the most desperate – those genuinely utterly destitute and incapable of supporting themselves – would contemplate applying to the parish for relief. As one of the Assistant Commissioners tasked with overseeing the new Poor Law stated, *our object ... is to establish therein a discipline, so severe and repulsive as to make them a terror to the poor and prevent them from entering* (Thompson, 1972, p295). The 'offer' of the workhouse to those seeking help would be a 'self acting test' (hence *'workhouse test'*) of genuine destitution, since fear generated by the prospect of entering the workhouse would ensure that only those truly desperate would be prepared to accept it. According to Friedrich Engels, the Poor Law authorities were largely successful in this aim. *Can any one wonder*, wrote Friedrich Engels 11 years after the passage of the Act, *that the poor decline to accept public relief under these conditions? That they starve rather than enter these bastilles?* (Engels, 1845).

Centralisation and uniformity

It was also proposed that the new system would have a centralised form of administration, in the form of a new, national Poor Law Commission, which would ensure there would not be any variations in practice. In summary, all areas would be expected to operate the new Poor Law in a uniform, equally harsh manner.

The 'new' Poor Law in practice

The Poor Law Amendment Act was implemented across the country, and many areas built new workhouses, or used old ones to incarcerate those claiming public relief. The extent to which the 'workhouse test' was fully implemented is still a matter of debate among historians. Certainly, many areas ignored the efforts of the Poor Law Commission to encourage them to adhere to the 'spirit of 1834' (Fraser, 1984). However, in many others it was vigorously applied, and in those districts paupers in receipt of relief were often subjected to the most punishing, brutal and repressive regimes. The appalling conditions found in the Andover workhouse in 1845 (described below in a *Times* newspaper report), where starving inmates were found desperately gnawing on bones (including human bones), almost beggars belief:

> *Notwithstanding the horrors and atrocities to which the Poor Law has given birth, we could not have believed it possible that the measure ... could have led to anything so utterly revolting as the facts stated ... to have occurred in the union workhouse at Andover ... It appears from the investigation that has taken place into this truly shocking affair, that the paupers are employed in crushing bones collected from various sources, including frequently the bones of horses as well as other animals and occasionally some from churchyards ... and that while so employed they were engaged in quarrelling with each other for the bones, in extracting marrow from them, and in gnawing off the meat from the extremities.*

> (*The Times*, 14 August 1845)

A subsequent government inquiry confirmed these and other atrocities. It was found that the 'master' of the workhouse had acted as a dictatorial tyrant, bullying, intimidating and physically and emotionally assaulting inmates. He and his wife frequently denied paupers medical treatment, and food meant for inmates would be fed to the master's pigs, leaving paupers to scavenge from the bones they were supposed to be crushing to create fertiliser. This workhouse master made Dickens's fictional Bumble the Beadle (the workhouse master in *Oliver Twist*) seem almost tame by comparison. Andover, therefore, truly was a Dickensian workhouse of the worst kind. That said, while it was perhaps at the extreme end of the spectrum, such conditions were certainly not the exception in a system that encouraged contemptible treatment of the poor. As *The Times* (18 August 1845) argued, the practices uncovered were extreme, and technically illegal, but were *within the spirit and tendency of the law*.

In the light of what we have told you about the Poor Law Amendment Act, you may find it somewhat strange to find that its architects claimed they were genuinely interested in the welfare of the poor. The savage discipline of the workhouse may have seemed cruel, but it was, they argued, ultimately in the interests of the poor. As Fraser (1984, p47) has put it, its supporters claimed to be *acting like the loving parent inflicting sharp, painful punishment on the miscreant child – being cruel to be kind*. In the long term, paupers, like children, would benefit from short-term chastisement, learning from their errors, and once the crutch of relief was removed, they would learn to stand on their own two feet.

The Poor Law, the Charity Organisation Society and early social work

Clearly, the values and assumptions that shaped the PLA Act are far removed from those that underpin today's social work value base. However, this was not always the case. Indeed, as we hinted in Chapter 1, the values infused throughout the new Poor Law shaped and influenced embryonic social work, in the form of the Charity Organisation Society (COS). The COS, which was formed in 1869, was not, as its title may suggest, created with the aim of freely dispensing welfare to the poor. On the contrary, its leading figures, many of whom were deeply imbued with the Poor Law values and principles, were driven by the belief that too much indiscriminate charitable almsgiving was sapping initiative and self-help. Hence, at the COS's 1886 annual meeting, the Bishop of London described many charities as, *very little more than the refuge of imposters, who have failed elsewhere to get assistance* (cited in Evans, 1978, p208). The notion that 'crafty beggars' were taking advantage of the charitable assistance available was reflected in the original title of the COS; that is, the *Society for Organising Charitable Relief and Repressing Mendacity*. The word 'mendacity' is rarely used today, but in layman's terms it means deception, lies, dishonesty and deceit.

The COS saw itself as the voluntary equivalent of the Poor Law authorities, and its mission was very much the same – to prevent abuse of charity, force individuals to take responsibility for their actions, and rely upon their own efforts and industry. Was there any evidence that charitable support was rife with fraud? Certainly, by 1869, a multitude of charitable organisations had emerged to cope with the distress and need that the new Poor Law failed, or refused, to meet. In London alone, there were well over 1,000 charities with a combined income of somewhere in the region of £8 million, almost the equivalent to the amount spent on Poor Law relief (Mooney, 1998, p68). However, there was little real evidence that haphazard, overly sentimental charitable assistance was encouraging improvidence or fraud. Nonetheless, the COS's aim was to encourage as many charities as possible to adopt the same rigorous methods of individual case investigation as itself. Like its own caseworkers, other charities should seek to identify the 'deserving' and turn away the 'undeserving', leaving the latter to the vagaries of the Poor Law.

The establishment of the COS was, in short, an attempt to control and co-ordinate charitable activity and ensure that assistance was only provided to the truly 'deserving', in a way that would restore the spirit of independence, hard work and thrift. Its activities, therefore, were directed as much towards attempts to remoralise, regulate and control the behaviour of the poor, as they were to relieving their distress. The underlying philosophy was similar to that of the Poor Law and the assumption was that poverty, in most circumstances, was the result of avoidable personal failing, and could be avoided through hard work and foresight. As one contributor to the Charity Organisation Review stated in 1881:

> *There can be no doubt that the poverty of the working classes of England is due, not to their circumstances (which are more favourable than those of any other working population in Europe); but to their own improvident habits and thriftlessness. If they are ever to be more prosperous, it must be through self-denial, temperance and fore-thought.*

> (cited in Jones, 1976, p2)

The COS's interpretations for poverty, therefore, rarely acknowledged the structural problems that afflicted the working population, and poverty of 'spirit' rather than material poverty was seen as the main cause of social ills. To dispense charity to the indigent and morally culpable, and to provide for those who had chosen not to save for the predictable, temporary shortfalls in income, would, the COS insisted, be to reward improvident habits and fecklessness. It argued that such individuals should have no access to charity, and be forced to endure the discipline and rigours of the workhouse. Charitable provision should only be used to meet the exceptional, temporary needs of the genuinely 'deserving' poor who could be expected to show improvement. Theirs was, therefore, a particularly harsh approach. According to TH Marshall (1967, p167), its philosophy was *reactionary* and *morally repugnant to the modern mind*. As he points out, the 'hopeless' cases that were turned away included not only the 'idlers' the 'drunken' and the 'immoral', but also those affected by social problems over which they had no control, and those with physical or mental disabilities, the very groups who we today would deem most in need of welfare and social work services. The extent to which the COS was successful in persuading other charities to adopt an equally stern approach is a matter of debate, and our focus on the COS here is not intended to detract from the radicalism that infused the work of individuals and organisations who were motivated by more progressive intentions (see Ferguson and Woodward, 2009; Cree and Myers, 2008). However, the COS was certainly influential in London and a number of other major cities. Moreover, it also played a crucial part in shaping the national policy agenda, and it is often credited with developing the 'casework' method of investigation that social workers still use today.

The COS and the development of the 'casework' approach

Leading figures within the COS were insistent that charity should not be dispensed without a systematic investigation into the worth, merits and circumstances of each case. To this end, it pioneered the casework method of dispensing welfare that in some respects would be familiar to today's social workers. Before agreeing to provide assistance, no stone would be left unturned in the caseworker's attempts to ascertain the applicant's 'worthiness'. Visitors would seek to establish whether applicants were truly destitute by looking for evidence to suggest they were capable of supporting themselves. Homes would also be checked for evidence of 'indolence' or 'vice', with particular attention being paid to cleanliness of the environment and its inhabitants. A dirty home and dirty children would be seen as evidence of moral culpability and support might be refused on that basis alone. The possibility that the unkempt circumstances of people's homes may have been a result of chronic overcrowding, poverty and other factors beyond the control of individuals or families would rarely be considered, and the roots of distress were invariably located in their personal history or behaviour. As Helen Bosanquet, a leading member of the COS, commented in 1902:

If the narrow home makes family life impossible, it is because the family is already weak; where the deeper relations are strong they find a way either to ignore or control the difficulties arising from want of space.

(cited in Jones, 1976, p3)

Octavia Hill, another leading COS figure, had made much the same point in 1884. She argued that although workers houses were often *badly built and arranged*, they were *tenfold worse because of the tenants habits. Transplant them tomorrow to healthy and commodious houses,* she stated, *and they would pollute and destroy them* (cited in Jones, 1976, p3).

ACTIVITY 2.2

In an attempt to rescue the poor from their own 'depravity', Octavia Hill began to establish and manage a number of housing settlements, offering low-cost housing for poor 'deserving' families. Her legacy to social policy and social work has been a matter of considerable debate ever since. Some have described her as a heroine of the Victorian age; a philanthropist who devoted her professional life to improving the lives and homes of the poor. As Young and Ashton (1956, p. 115) wrote, Octavia Hill has sometimes been called the grandmother of modern social work, because her influence and her principles permeated all the later nineteenth century thought. *Others, however, have been less complimentary, highlighting Hill's dogmatic opposition to the development of publicly funded welfare schemes, as well as her authoritarian treatment of her own housing tenants. There can be little doubt that her views on both public and charitable welfare were shaped by her enthusiastic embrace of COS philosophy.*

These same, deeply moralistic values infused the administration of her housing settlements. The rent would not be the only cost of residence, and those prepared to become tenants would face curfews and a strict regime of intensive supervision. Regular inspections and instructional visits would be made by Hill's lady rent collectors, who would advise on cleanliness and moral rectitude. Hill was clearly seeking to do much more than provide housing to her tenants. Moral re-education was the broader aim, a strategy which was clearly based upon the missionary zeal underpinning the COS's broader philosophy. She acted as an all-seeing, omnipresent ruler and those refusing to abide by the instructions of her lady visitors were promptly evicted.

Social care or social control? Family intervention projects today
As we have seen, Hill's treatment of her tenants was shaped as much by a desire to regulate, modify and control their behaviour as it was to provide them with housing support. In this task we want you to think about the assumptions that underpin a recent flagship housing policy for disadvantaged families, Family Intervention Projects (FIPs). After reading the extract below, taken from a recent government published report on FIPs, try answering the questions that follow:

In some communities there are a small number of highly problematic families that account for a disproportionate amount of anti-social behaviour. Although much

Continued

has been done to tackle these problem families, it is clear that we need to go further, for their sake and the sake of the wider community ... Based on evidence, we now know that this small number of families need an intensive, persistent and, if necessary coercive approach. The Respect programme will establish a national network of family intervention projects ... This will ensure that the destructive behaviour which is so often passed from generation to generation, blighting not only these families but entire communities, is effectively tackled for the first time ... Family intervention projects use intensive tailored action with supervision and clear sanctions to improve the behaviour of persistently anti-social households. A key worker 'grips' the family, the causes of their poor behaviour and the agencies involved with them, to deliver a more co-ordinated response.

There are three distinct models of intervention which can be applied:

Intensive outreach programmes to families in their own homes ...

Intensive outreach programmes to families in dispersed accommodation. Families are provided with a non-secure tenancy by the project. Staff visit and provide/refer to structured individual and family sessions to work with the family on a range of issues identified as causing their anti-social behaviour. If the family complies with interventions and behaviour improves sufficiently then the tenancy can be made secure.

Intensive support programme in supervised accommodation. Families in this type of provision receive 24-hour support and supervision from staff provided by the project. Families are likely to be involved in many structured sessions comple- mented by daily unstructured observation. If the family complies with interventions and behaviour improves sufficiently then they will be able to move into one of the above ...

(Respect, 2006, pp2–5)

1. *Can you see any links between the methods adopted by Hill in her 'housing settlements' and the intentions of FIPs?*
2. *To what extent are FIPs based upon what one commentator has referred to as, behavioural, pathological interpretations for disadvantage?*
3. *Can you see any dangers in focusing so directly and publicly on what are perceived to be the 'problematic', 'destructive' patterns of behaviour of such a small number of families?*

By July 2009, FIPS were established in some 75 local authorities, and around 2,000 families had participated on them. Some are run and organised by local authorities, but many are provided by voluntary agencies. The previous Labour government was seeking to expand the initiative, envisaging that all local authorities would embrace it by 2011, by which time 20,000 families would have enrolled on them (Travis, 2009).

Continued

COMMENT *continued*

Ministers claimed that the projects were successful, and certainly evaluations commissioned by the government suggested that many families had shown some positive outcomes, with project staff reporting significant improvements in certain kinds of behaviour. The results of these initial evaluations, however, were tentative, and as the authors of one evaluation put it, should be treated with caution *(see, for example, White et al., 2008, p93). For example, findings tended to be based upon the subjective views of project staff, which may or may not have been accurate. Families volunteering to participate in the earlier stages of this initiative may also have been the most motivated and hence most likely to benefit from the scheme. Nor did any of the evaluations into the projects use 'control groups' to assess whether other kinds of intervention would be any more successful than FIPs. In fact, a recent re-analysis of these earlier evaluations concluded that the success rate of FIPs has been greatly exaggerated (Gregg, 2010).*

The assumptions underpinning FIPs, as well as their methods of intervention, have also been the subject of considerable academic debate. According to Garrett (2007), there is a danger that their narrow focus upon family pathology and biological metaphors (such as generational transmission of 'dysfunction', and the 'pollution' of the wider community), can act as an 'ideological smokescreen'. It can lead to the scapegoating of small, vulnerable sections of the population for problems that have wider, societal origins. The evaluation of FIPs conducted by White *et al.* (2008) found that many practitioners in the wider social work field expressed *resistance to the FIP ethos* for precisely this reason – they were *uncomfortable with the enforcing or 'punitive' element of the FIP model* (p34). Non-FIP practitioners also expressed concerns about a lack of qualifications and experience of FIP staff, and the emphasis such projects placed upon the personal qualities of their staff as opposed to formal professional qualifications.

Garrett argues that we should view FIPs with caution. When interpreting the techniques and outcomes of such projects, we should, he argues, look backwards at how historically similar coercive initiatives, such as the new Poor Law, have served to stigmatise recipients and popularise simplified interpretations of the causes of disadvantage. From this perspective, the ideological fallout caused by the behavioural focus of FIPs has the potential to impact upon all the poor, and not just those families directly affected. Newspaper headlines surrounding the FIP initiative, such as the *Daily Star*'s 'Sin Bins for Scum Families' (Hughes, 2009), do seem to suggest that such fears are not unfounded. Moreover, there can be little doubt that 'problem family' discourses, which, like the COS casework approach, focus the blame for societal ills on families themselves, have re-emerged in recent years after a welcome period of absence

The COS and its 'casework'

Before providing support, the COS's caseworkers would make detailed inquiries into the character of individuals. Poor Law officials, saving clubs, trade unions, the local clergy, landlords, employers, previous employers, neighbours and relatives would be contacted in an attempt to ascertain an applicant's true character. Once again, if there was a suggestion of impropriety, assistance would be refused, despite the fact that poor references may have been the result of personal grudges rather than accurate character assessments. Perhaps not surprisingly, many of those who came into contact with the COS's caseworkers resented their inquisitive, stigmatising methods of investigation, and many were deterred from applying for much needed assistance. This clearly happened in at least one of the unsuccessful applications for COS support outlined in Table 2.2 (Case 4). These cases, taken from the records of the Fulham and Hammersmith District of the COS, illustrate the sort of reasons for which families were turned down. As you can see, explicit moral judgements were made about the 'worth' of each candidate.

Table 2.2 Rejected COS applications

Date	Assistance requested	Decision
Case 1 14/01/80		*Labourer out of work for four weeks with young family, applicant earns well in summer and if he was more careful he would not require charity ... referred to Poor Law.*
Case 2 20/01/80	Arrears of rent	*Lodging house keeper with nine children (mostly grown up); she drinks, home dirty and there was a large piece of beef on the fire when I visited ... ineligible.*
Case 3 8/2/80	Temporary	*Bricklayer with young family out of work for seven weeks due to weather; RO says he is drunken lazy man but will give some bread for children; bad references from everyone; house dirty ... undeserving.*
Case 4 16/2/80	Temporary	*Pregnant 35 year old cook has been deserted by husband but does not give references, by 21/2/80, the applicant declines any help as she did not think so many enquiries would be made of her ... ineligible.*
Case 5 7/4/80		*Plumber with five children deserts his family and absconds to America; wife cannot account for his going away as they have always lived on the most affectionate terms ... referred to Poor Law*
Case 6 14/5/80	To be started hawking	*47 year old carman with family out of work for nine months due to illness. Mixed recommendations, RO says family are dirty, lazy, and encouraged eldest son to cohabit; children do not attend school; home dirty ... undeserving.*
Case 7 -/7/80		*56 year old governess (formerly employed by Lord Alfred Churchill) ... Former landlady says applicant used to tell neighbours that landlady was trying to poison her. Lord Alfred Churchill says she was highly gifted but he had to part with her as she appeared strange in manner. When visited by agent she was busy painting a likeness on a piece of china of Mr Plimsoll, late MP for Derby, and it was certainly beautifully done. She admits she was in a lunatic asylum for four years ... refer to Poor Law.*
Case 8 3/8/80	To get son into blind school	*38 year old widow with three sons, two of them blind. Good references, and children are indeed blind, but when women went before the [Poor Law] Guardians and they asked her questions she became so abusive she was ordered out of the room ... undeserving.*

Source: adapted from Whelan, 2001, pp101–36

When assistance *was* provided by the COS, it was not given unconditionally, and caseworkers would engage in further interventions with the families concerned. Hence, material assistance would be accompanied by strict moral guidance and super-vision, designed to ensure future self-reliance and independence. Indeed, for the COS, this casework element was the most crucial part of the assistance given, because it offered its visitors the opportunity to rehabilitate and treat the 'moral failings' that had contributed to destitution in the first place. As CS Loch, a leading COS figure, stated in 1910, *Treatment would take the place of mere relief. The class 'applicant' would become a supervised class, treated in connection with the home* (cited in Jones, 1973, p9).

The COS under threat and the emergence of the interventionist state

From the 1880s onwards, the assumptions that shaped the COS's work were increas-ingly challenged, and governments began to make tentative steps towards ameliorating some of the terrible social conditions that had previously been largely ignored. Indeed, the period 1870–1920 is often seen as heralding the beginnings of the 'interventionist state', when governments began to actively intervene to promote citizens' welfare. Over this 50-year period, a host of social policies were introduced, including free compulsory education, improved housing legislation, unemployment and health insurance and old age pensions. Legislation prohibiting child neglect was introduced, as were a range of other measures intended to promote child wel-fare, such as free school meals and medical inspection of school children. Indeed, many historians identify this era, and particularly the years of the reforming Liberal administration between 1906–1914, with the origins of the British welfare state (Fra-ser, 1984). Of course, as the social investigations of Charles Booth and Seebohm Rowntree vividly illustrated, these reforms were by no means adequate to meet need. They either used stigmatising means tests to target only the very poor, or failed to provide universal coverage (in the case of unemployment and health insurance). Nonetheless, the measures introduced did represent an acknowledgement that the state had a responsibility to look after the welfare of citizens, a recognition that had previously been largely absent.

In assessing this shift to a more interventionist stance, few historians now believe that legislators were motivated primarily by humanitarian concern. For example, the extent of poverty, and the problems caused by low wages, unemployment, under-employ-ment, child labour, poor housing and inadequate sanitation had already previously been well documented by commissions of inquiry, yet little had been done to alleviate them. Hence it seems unlikely that politicians were influenced by the sudden exposure of what, in fact, were well acknowledged economic and social evils. More important, it seems, were contemporary concerns over the impact of physical deterioration upon national efficiency. In the light of the economic and military competition from abroad that Britain faced at the end of the nineteenth century, it was becoming increasingly evident that the state could no longer ignore the appalling conditions experienced by the mass of the working population. By now, Britain's position as the foremost work-shop of the world and its place as the leading world economic and military power were under severe pressure, due to competition from Germany and the United States (Hall, 1984). The ill-fated Boer War campaign (1899–1902) in South Africa, where huge numbers of potential British recruits were unfit for military service, also provided a wake-up call to the political establishment. In Leeds, for instance, 47.5 per cent of volunteers were found to be unfit, whereas in Manchester 8,000 out of 11,000 (72.7 per cent) did not meet the relatively low standard of fitness required for service (Johnston, 1909). In 1904 William Taylor, the Army Medical Services Director General, bluntly told a Royal Commission on Physical Deterioration that up to 60 per cent of all recruits were *unfit for military service on account of defective physique. Is it not true*, he asked, *that the whole labouring population of the land are at present living under conditions which make it impossible that they should rear the next generation to be sufficiently virile to supply more than two out of five men for the purposes of either peace or war?* (Taylor, 1904, p96).

By the end of the nineteenth century, therefore, an ill-educated, over-worked, stunted, poorly housed and ill-fed population had become an economic and military liability, and there was a need to follow the example of other countries, in particular Germany, which had already introduced a raft of social legislation. In fact, leading Liberal poli-ticians who were responsible for many of the early twentieth-century measures of social reform were perfectly open about their motives for legislating, drawing atten-tion to the economic benefits of social reform. Rather than harming economic progress and encouraging dependency, progressive social legislation could, they insisted, contribute to the creation of a healthier, better educated population, pro-mote efficiency and foster the emergence of a more able, independent citizenry.

Reformers also felt that social policy could be used as a 'ransom' to prevent newly enfranchised workers from turning to the revolutionary creeds of the emerging socia-list political associations and parties. Certainly, Britain's political landscape had changed by the end of the nineteenth century. The franchise had been extended and by 1884 around 66 per cent of adult males in England and Wales were entitled to vote. New, radical political parties and movements had emerged to cater for this new electoral constituency, and they assailed the electorate with specifically working-class propaganda. As Hall (1984) notes, with the emergence of the Socialist League, the Fabian Society and the Social Democratic Federation, the 1880s saw the move-ment towards independent working-class political representation. Later, in 1893, the Independent Labour Party was formed, and this was followed by the foundation of the Labour Representation Committee in 1900, which subsequently became the Labour Party. In the 1906 General Election 53 Labour MPs were returned to Parlia-ment. At the same time new, more general, industrial trade unions emerged, which had at their heads a much more radical style of leadership. Many, such as John Burns, Ben Tillett and Tom Mann, were themselves socialists, and by the turn of the century were campaigning for increased state intervention. With the extension of the fran-chise, these new forms of political and industrial representation posed a significant electoral threat to the established political parties, and their demands could no longer be ignored (Thane, 1996). Conservative and Liberal governments, concerned about the working population's steady development towards political independency are said to have seen social welfare legislation as an anecdote to socialism, as something that would help to 'spike the socialist guns' (Mishra, 1977). To an extent then, sheer political expediency also forced otherwise reluctant politicians to recognise and act upon the demands of the labour movement to a far greater extent than before (Fraser, 1984; Gilbert, 1973).

The COS's response to state intervention

How did the COS respond to this growing propensity to introduce social reform? Perhaps not surprisingly, it was at the forefront of those opposed to government intervention, including the principle of free school meals for necessitous children, old age pensions, municipal housing, Poor Law reform, and initiatives designed to provide work for the unemployed (Jones, 1976, 1983). The position of its more orthodox stalwarts had hardly changed since its inception, and its leadership warned of the morally corrupting impact of state welfare on recipients, claiming it would deter self-help and promote dependence. The following comments were made by CS Loch, one of the COS's more prominent figures, in 1906, and they can be read as a response to the growing tendency for governments to intervene to ameliorate poor social conditions:

> *The individual should provide against hunger, nakedness, and want of shelter; the father against these things both for himself and his family. The ordinary contingencies of life, which fall within the range of ordinary foresight, should for the individual's sake, and for society's sake, be met by the efforts of the individual.*

(cited in Jones, 1976, p4)

Ultimately, the COS was unable to prevent many of the social reforms that it opposed from being enacted, but it did exert considerable influence in shaping the way many social policies were implemented. This is because its charity social workers were used extensively by local authorities to administer relief under schemes, such as those of medical and food assistance to children. According to Jones (1973), this was a particularly successful strategy, which allowed the COS to ensure that its principles continued to underpin most aspects of relief work.

The COS and the development of social work training

The COS's development of social work education at the beginning of the twentieth century was discussed briefly in Chapter 1. Its involvement in social work training also represented an attempt to ensure that its underlying philosophy would continue to be enshrined in both policy and practice. It is in such a context, Jones (1976) argues, that the COS established its School of Sociology in London in 1903. It was, he states, shaped by a *desire to reassert their claims of expertise in all the fields of social relief.* As the following comments, made by EJ Urwick, the first Director of the School, illustrate, at a time when the COS's philosophy was increasingly questioned, its efforts to formalise social work training did indeed seem to represent an attempt to reinvigorate and renew a message that seemed to many to be out of tune with the times:

> *The terms in which our truths are expressed often belong to a past age; have we not all been at times uneasily conscious that the mere appeal to fundamental principles of self-help, independence, thrift and the like, has lost much of its force, and that these principles must be recast, brought into new connections with current thinking, clothed in new language? For it is unquestionably true that the new generation is receptive enough, but, as always, demands a new preparation for its food.*

This was, then, a sophisticated attempt to ensure that the COS continued to play a decisive role in the future of welfare administration, constituting *an essential part of its strategy to extend its hegemony over the entire field of relief policies* (Jones, 1973, p19). The COS would, through its social work training programmes at the School of Sociology, seek to inoculate its practitioners from the corrupting influences of collectivist thinking, and, to quote one of its central council members, to *create a definite public opinion* upon the subjects with which it was concerned. According to CS Loch, the School had the potential to achieve much *more than Parliament or preaching, or books, or pamphleteering* ever could (cited in Jones, 1973, pp14, 20).

At the same time, the COS would use the School of Sociology to disguise the moral basis of its arguments and provide academic credence to its claims about the behavioural causes of social problems. In this respect, Jones cites Helen Bosanquet's attempts to explain destitution in terms of the individual's psychological malfunctioning. Dismissing social and economic explanations, she insisted that it was due primarily to their parents' failure to teach them *progressive interests*, such as thrift and self-help, at a key stage in their psychological development. Such theories, Jones argues, gave a cloak of academic and scientific respectability to the COS's insistence that it was the individual and not society that should be the object of rehabilitation. The whole aim of the project was, according to Jones, to *mobilise and organise its 'theoretical' works for the purpose of producing an enlarged cadre of trained social workers, who, it hoped, would come to have a major determining influence on social reform developments* (p20). Ultimately, the COS failed to stem the tide of reform, and as we will show in Chapter 4, the twentieth century saw the development of what we now recognise as the welfare state. However, the continued influence of the COS's moralistic casework approach to social policy and practice continues to be the subject of much debate and disagreement among academics today.

The legacy of the Poor Law and the COS on social policy and social work today

As we explained in the previous chapter, much has occurred in the spheres of social policy and social work since the early twentieth century. However, the period examined in this chapter is crucially important, and not just to those of us with an interest in social and political history. This is because commentators and politicians often refer back to late nineteenth/early twentieth-century developments as evidence to support their assertions about the nature of social policy and social work today. More importantly, proposals for the future development of policy and services are also often justified with reference to developments that occurred during this period (see Chapter 5). The 'lessons' to be learned from this crucial phase of history differ, depending upon the ideological predisposition of the commentators or politicians. However, the fact that it is universally seen as such a key era makes it important that you, as a future social worker, have a grasp of some of the key developments and debates that occurred.

CHAPTER SUMMARY

One of our aims in this chapter has been to inform you of some of the key developments and debates that took place in what is widely regarded as a key period in the history of social policy and social work. In doing so, we wanted to highlight some of the continuities in nineteenth- and twenty-first-century debates about administering welfare. As we saw, a theme that pervaded nineteenth-century policy and practice was the need to restore independence and self-sufficiency, influenced by the notion that moral culpability and not wider structural constraints were the cause of the problems that individuals and families faced. Some of the modern-day case studies that we looked at – for instance our discussions of benefit fraud and FIPs – show that such assumptions do, to an extent, continue to influence policy and practice today.

Our other main aim in this chapter has been to draw your attention to the relevance and importance of understanding historical debates about social policy and social work. You should now be able to appreciate their significance, and see that they have very real, immediate, policy-making relevance to social policy and social work in the twenty-first century. Academics and politicians do often refer to the past when justifying policies in the present, and in order to be in a position to assess the claims they make, it is crucial that you have an adequate understanding of the period examined in this chapter. We hope that this chapter has stimulated your interest in history, and that you will consult some of the texts we have indicated below for further reading.

FURTHER READING

If you are interested in reading a good general history of the welfare state, then we would recommend:

Fraser, D (2003) *The evolution of the British welfare state*. 3rd edition. Basingstoke: Palgrave Macmillan.

For the Poor Law, the following book combines some useful discussion of the topic together with a wealth of original documents:

Rose, ME (1971) *The English Poor Law, 1780–1930*. Newton Abbott: David and Charles.

For those of you who want to learn more about the activities of the COS, there are a couple of texts that we would recommend. For a positive interpretation of its activities, written from a neo-liberal perspective, see:

Whelan, R (2001) *Helping the poor: Friendly visiting, dole charities and dole queues*. London: Civitas.

For a more critical perspective see:

Jones, C (1983) *State social work and the working class*. London: Routledge.

Chapter 3

Ideology, social policy and social work

Introduction

From past experience of teaching social policy, it has become evident that the word 'ideology' can generate a certain amount apprehension among students. Students, perhaps naturally, gravitate towards topics and issues that they feel are more attention-grabbing, topical and relevant to their interests, studies and future chosen careers. As future welfare and social workers, many of you will doubtlessly feel that an understanding of the detail of how social policy affects particular groups of service users is more important to you than an appreciation of ideology, a concept that possibly succeeds only in sending shivers down your spine! Hence, you may feel tempted to skip the rest of this section of the book and jump straight into the next section, which contains chapters on children, young people, adults and older people. Needless to say, we would implore you not to do so, because we are firmly of the belief that it is crucial for you to have a basic grasp of at least some of the main political ideologies that have shaped the views of politicians, academics and commentators on social policy and social work issues. This chapter introduces you to the concept of ideology. The next three chapters are devoted to an analysis of how different ideological perspectives have influenced the development of social policy.

Ideology and welfare

As an incentive to encourage you to engage with our discussion of the merits of different ideological perspectives (and read this section of the book!), we list below a few 'benefits' that you will derive from gaining a basic understanding of some of the main ideologies of welfare.

- It will help you work out one of the most confusing, unfathomable quandaries that many new students to social policy and social work face

When writing an essay, you may have wondered why different academics and politicians who are discussing exactly the same issue seem to interpret it in very different, contradictory ways. Let us take the welfare state, the very subject of social policy. Some academics and politicians argue that we need to spend more on welfare, in order to more effectively tackle problems such as child and pensioner poverty, and to provide wider opportunities for vulnerable groups to secure 'inclusion' in society. Here, the solution to the difficulties faced by certain individuals and groups can be overcome by expanding and improving services. Others, however, argue precisely the opposite. They claim that the welfare state is already too generous, and that rather than 'solving' social problems it actually creates them by locking recipients into a state of passive dependency. The solution to social ills from this perspective is to cut welfare and contract service provision, forcing individuals to take more responsibility for their own welfare. Our students often find it odd that equally intelligent, esteemed, authoritative commentators on social policy issues can disagree so profoundly over such a fundamental point. An understanding of ideologies of welfare will help you why such major disagreements occur.

- You will be able to impress your friends with your powers of prediction

Unfortunately, we cannot provide you with the powers to predict this week's lottery numbers, football scores, or winning horses, but we can help you foresee how certain politicians and academics will interpret and respond to particular economic and social problems.

- Work out your own ideological predisposition

As Heywood (1998, p1) points out, *All people are political thinkers. Whether they know it or not, people use political ideas and concepts whenever they express their opinions or speak their mind.* You may not realise it, but your views and ideas on particular issues are likely to have been shaped by one or more of the ideological perspectives we discuss in the chapters included in this section of the book. Are you a social democrat, a neo-liberal, a Marxist, or a combination of all three? Read on, and you decide ...

What is a political ideology?

David McLennan (1986) has described ideology *as the most elusive concept in the whole of the social sciences.* Although this might not be a great starting point for our discussion of ideology, it does sum the concept up quite well, and partly explains the confusion that tends to surround it. One of the problems is that the term, 'ideology', has tended to mean different things to different people.

Ideology and ruling-class interests

For some, the term 'ideology' is seen to refer to the ideas of the ruling class. From this perspective, dominant groups seek to propagate a particular set of values (or ideology) that reflect their own interests, while at the same time justifying their dominance and rule over subordinate groups. In this sense, a ruling-class ideology seeks to 'reconcile the oppressed to their oppression' and is used to perpetuate a misleading and false view of the world. Karl Marx, a leading nineteenth-century political philosopher, used the term in this conspiratorial way to describe how ideology was subtly used by dominant groups to create 'false class consciousness' and to disguise from the working population the fact that their interests lay in the overthrow of the ruling classes. Ideology, therefore, was seen to act as a mystifying smokescreen, a vehicle through which the ruling class sought to promote and protect its interests, while 'tricking' the population into thinking that their rulers were concerned about the well-being of all the people.

Competing ideologies

However, since Marx's death in 1883, the term 'ideology' has lost some of this conspiratorial taint, and in much of the literature you will find reference to ideologies, rather than one ruling-class ideology. It is now generally acknowledged that there are different, competing interpretations of the world, some of which may reflect the interests of dominant groups and the rich, but others of which that might not. We use the term 'ideologies' in this sense to refer to rival, alternative sets of values and ideas that influence the way we think about events and issues. The three ideologies we intend to focus upon in this section of the book are social democracy, neo-liberalism and Marxism. Other 'ideologies of welfare' and theoretical approaches could have been chosen, and some of these – such as feminism, anti-racism and postmodernism – are referred to in other sections. However, as George and Wilding (1994, p7) point out, social democracy, neo-liberalism and Marxism are *major ideologies of welfare* and merit a detailed analysis in their own right. As we will show, each of these three ideologies is based upon very different sets of assumptions and values. Each offers competing explanations for and solutions to the social problems that you as welfare professionals will be responding to. However, before moving on to look at these ideologies, it is perhaps worth emphasising the link between political action and ideology.

Ideology and politics

Those who stress the importance of ideologies argue that politicians are motivated by much more than a simple desire to win popular support, elections and power, and that their political ideas and views have more deep-rooted, traceable ideological roots.

This is, of course, not to suggest that elections are not of considerable importance to politicians. Clearly, the aim of most politicians is to govern and without election victories they are confined to the wilderness of opposition. Nor is it to imply that politicians do not occasionally deviate from their ideological allegiances when particular circumstances demand a more pragmatic approach. However, politicians are motivated by particular sets of values, and ideas – ideologies – which shape their convictions about what needs to be done once power is achieved. In recent years, Conservative politicians are said to have been influenced by neo-liberal ideology, whereas the ideas and policies of Labour and Liberal politicians are traditionally said to have been influenced by variants of social democratic ideology. As we will show, these two ideologies contain very different values and sets of assumptions about a whole range of issues that are of importance to you as students of social policy and social work, such as:

- the causes and solutions to economic and social problems experienced by service users;
- the role of the state (or governments) in securing the needs of citizens and supporting vulnerable people;
- the role of the welfare state and social work in meeting the needs of service users.

ACTIVITY 3.1

The issues that we have listed above lie at the heart of debates about the nature of social policy and social work in the UK and they are the subject of much ideological disagreement.

In order to illustrate this point, we would like you to take time to explore how your own ideological preferences may differ with those of your student peers, by discussing your views on each of these of the issues listed. We suggest that you put all sharpened instruments to one side, because we predict a lively debate!

COMMENTS

As part of the above activity, you have presumably discovered your fellow students possess widely divergent views. This is hardly surprising. You probably each come from different family, social class and educational backgrounds; you may read different newspapers; watch different television programmes; and have very diverse interests and hobbies. Some of you may have taken an active interest in politics and welfare-related issues, while others will not have done. The point is, the contributions you and others made to the discussion will have reflected these influences, which themselves will have helped shape your value base, or, to put it another way, your own ideological predisposition. In short, despite what you may think, you are not a disinterested, objective analyst of the world around you, and your ideological disposition shapes the way you interpret the world and respond to particular issues.

Table 3.1 Summary of welfare ideologies

	Social democratic perspective	Neo-liberal perspective	Marxist perspective
The causes and solutions to economic and social problems experienced by service users	The economic and social problems experienced by service users result, primarily, from structural factors which are beyond their control, such as unemployment, poverty, poor educational opportunities, low wages and discrimination. Solutions lie in targeted interventions designed to address the root causes of these problems.	Well-meaning, but morally degenerative interventions have caused the problems they were designed to solve. Overgenerous welfare and an over-bearing 'Nanny State' have inculcated a range of dysfunctional patterns of behaviour, encouraging 'dependency', destroying self-help and voluntarism. Solutions lie in the reduction of state support and the promotion of self-help.	Capitalism is the root cause of economic and social ills. It is an economic system based upon greed, exploitation and an insatiable thirst for profit. Businesses rely on the fear of poverty to compel workers to engage in low-waged, exploitative labour. Until it is abolished genuine, fundamental social and economic improvement is impossible.
The role of the state (or governments) in securing the needs of citizens and supporting vulnerable people	Tackling the causes of economic and social ills is primarily the state's responsibility. Its economic and social policies should be geared towards expanding opportunities so as to ensure that all are able to achieve their potential. It should also seek to eradicate the 'barriers' that prevent marginalised social groups from accessing 'inclusion'.	It is not the state's responsibility to seek to secure the economic/social needs of individuals. It should merely seek to create an environment whereby individuals can secure their own welfare needs through work, or in a private 'welfare market'. Those unable/unwilling to look after themselves should rely primarily on voluntary/charitable provision.	The state in capitalist societies is not a neutral entity that objectively and compassionately responds to the needs of citizens. On the contrary, it always ultimately acts in the interests of business. Social policies are, in reality, geared towards meeting economic needs of business rather than the welfare needs of citizens.
The role of the welfare state and social work in meeting the needs of service users	The welfare state has a crucial, positive role to play in mitigating the difficulties experienced by service users. The post-war welfare state is seen as a hugely positive development, and one which should be celebrated and extended. Benefits should be improved and eligibility should be widened in a way that enhances people's opportunities to secure 'inclusion'. Social work has a crucial role to play in enabling service users, and in helping to meet their needs.	State welfare has 'seduced' service users into a state of passive dependency, and it needs to be drastically curtailed. A very basic safety net can be provided, but benefits should be cut, means-tested and eligibility tightened. Social workers should cease being politically correct, sentimental 'do-gooders' and should concentrate on 'correcting' dysfunctional behaviour, instilling appropriate norms and values, and stimulating self-help, hard work and thrift.	The welfare state (and social work) perform contradictory roles. On the one hand, they mitigate suffering, but on the other, they benefit capitalism. Welfare services that genuinely promote well-being should be welcomed, but the limitations of reform must be acknowledged. Social workers should seek to reduce suffering in the 'here and now', but they also have a 'political' role to play in fighting for a better society.

ACTIVITY **3.2**

In this activity, we want you to try to ascertain where you stand ideologically. In Table 3.1 we provide you with a summary of social democratic, neo-liberal and Marxist standpoints on each of the issues you discussed in the previous activity. It is a necessarily brief and somewhat simplistic summary of the three approaches (we look at each in more detail later), but it is sufficient for the purposes of this activity. Have a look at the table and try to identify whether you are of a social democratic, neo-liberal, or Marxist disposition.

COMMENT

When we have tried this activity with our own students, we tend to find that most tend to opt for a 'pick and mix' approach that draws from elements of each of the ideological perspectives. Some, for example, tend to agree that social problems are largely a result of factors which are beyond the control of individuals and families (a social democratic view), while also being sympathetic to the notion that 'generous' levels of welfare erode individual initiative and encourage idleness and dependency (a neo-liberal view). This apparently contradictory position is hardly surprising. On the one hand, research shows that many social work students are motivated to study social work out of a sense of social justice and a concern to help vulnerable service users (Hackett et al., 2003). Hence, aspects of social-democratic approaches to welfare do appeal to them. On the other hand, as we saw in Chapter 2, 'behavioural' interpretations for social problems have a long historical pedigree and they still feature prominently in media and political commentaries. Our students have clearly been exposed to this particular welfare discourse, and it is inevitable that this too will shape their views of welfare and welfare recipients. In this sense, it is not uncommon for people to hold a mixture of views on welfare-related issues.

However, unlike many of our students (and possibly you), many politicians and academics tend to gravitate towards one or other of the political ideologies we have briefly outlined above. Their ideological allegiances are often more fundamental and deep rooted, and there is a tendency for them to be either 'left-wing', 'centrist', or 'right-wing'.

RESEARCH SUMMARY

The left–right political continuum
Political ideologies are also sometimes located on what has been referred to as a 'left/ right' continuum. In its most simplistic form, the continuum can be visualised as a straight line, with ideologies located at particular points on the line depending upon how 'left-wing', 'centrist' or 'right-wing' they are. The usage of a continuum has been criticised for being an imprecise indicator of political allegiances, but the fact that it is so commonly used means that it worth devoting some attention to outlining its key features.

Continued

RESEARCH SUMMARY *continued*

The left–right political continuum continued

In terms of its origins, the 'left–right continuum' can be traced to the years preceding the French Revolution, when the aristocracy and those supporting the king sat to his right, while their opponents, or those considered more radical, sat on the left. In more recent times, 'left-wing' ideologies are seen to be those that are critical of capitalism and believe that it needs to be reformed, or even abolished, with the aim of creating a more equal, fair, socially just society. They therefore tend to advocate varying degrees of economic and social change in order to reduce economic and social and inequality. Put simply, the more stringent the criticism of capitalism is, the more 'left-wing' an ideology is perceived to be. Social democracy, therefore, is often described as a 'centre-left' political ideology, because although it is critical of the injustices generated by capitalism, it believes it is possible to gradually 'tame' it through piecemeal social and economic reform. By contrast, Marxism is portrayed as a 'left-wing' ideology, because its critique of capitalism is more fundamental. As we have seen, Marxists believe capitalism is incapable of reform and must be abolished. In the UK, the Labour Party has tradition-ally espoused 'social democratic' values, and hence is often referred to as a 'centre-left' party, though as we shall see in subsequent chapters, there is a suggestion that it has moved 'rightward' in recent years.

'Right-wing' ideologies are those which reaffirm their support for the existing state of affairs, and in particular capitalism. They tend to be supportive of free markets, as well as the notion that individuals should be responsible for meeting their own economic and social needs. In this sense, 'right-wing' ideologies have become associated with a de-fence of the status quo and support for tradition, privilege and inequality. As with the ideologies of the 'left', the more stringent and extreme the defence of the existing state of affairs is, the more 'right-wing' an ideology is said to be. Neo-liberalism is considered to be a right-wing ideology. It is fundamentally opposed to state intervention in eco-nomic and social affairs and promotes individualism, markets and free enterprise. In-equality is seen to be a natural outcome of effort and hard work and it is argued that government attempts to promote equality will reduce incentives to work and harm entrepreneurship, and promote dependency and idleness. In the UK, the Conservative Party has become associated with neo-liberal values, particularly since 1979. Since then, its economic and social policies have shifted 'rightward' and it now widely seen to have embraced an orthodox neo-liberal political stance.

The overarching influence of ideologies on the way politicians interpret and respond to welfare-related issues should not be underestimated. Indeed, it is frequently their dogged belief in a particular ideological framework that influenced them to pursue academic or political careers. Hence, they are not neutral observers of all that is around them, and their values and attitudes – their ideological predispositions – condition and shape the way they interpret and respond to welfare-related issues. These ideologies provide structure, or a 'lens' through which they view and under-stand social problems, providing them with a moral framework, a map, or point of reference which guides them in certain directions rather than others. Indeed, in the world of politics, ideologies can have an almost religious quality for some individuals, and the principles that underpin particular ideological perspectives become almost like articles of faith to their adherents. The former Conservative Prime Minister, Margaret Thatcher, for example, is said to have been particularly ideologically driven, in that she showed a determination to maintain an orthodox neo-liberal position on welfare-related issues. In this sense, there was a direct link between neo-liberal ideology and the responses of successive Conservative governments to the shape and delivery of social policy and social work. Similarly, many argue that the current Conservative-dominated coalition government is influenced by neo-liberalism, and this helps explain the strategy of public expenditure cuts that it is being undertaken at the time of writing this text. Similarly, social democracy is also said to have shaped policy and practice for considerable periods in the UK's history. For instance, the period 1945 to the mid-1970s is said to have been characterised by something of a political consensus over social democratic values and ideas, whereby politicians of all political parties tended to accept the basic assumptions underpinning social democracy. The next chapter is devoted to an analysis of the emergence of social democratic ideas and the development of this 'social democratic consensus'.

CHAPTER SUMMARY

In this chapter, we have sought to introduce you to the concept of 'ideology', and to encourage you to think about your own ideological predisposition. We have also provided a brief summary of three ideological perspectives – social democracy, neo-liberalism and Marxism – each of which has influenced the way commentators, academics and politicians react to social problems and welfare-related issues. The following three chapters provide a more detailed outline of each of these three ideological approaches, assessing the relative influence of each on the development of social policy and social work practice.

FURTHER READING

The following texts provide a good introduction to debates about the links between ideology and welfare:

George, V and Wilding, P (1994) *Welfare and ideology*. London: Harvester Wheatsheaf.

Lavalette, M and Pratt, A (2006) *Social policy: Concepts, theories and issues*. London: Sage.

For a discussion of feminist and anti-racist perspectives on welfare see:

Williams, F (1989) *Social policy: A critical introduction*. Cambridge: Polity Press.

Chapter 4

Social democracy and the development of social policy and social work after 1945

Introduction

This chapter begins by discussing the emerging influence of more interventionist, collectivist, progressive ideals on social policy at the end of the nineteenth century. It then goes on to examine the growing influence of social democratic principles, and in particular the way they shaped the development of the welfare state after the Second World War. This is the first of three chapters looking at how the three ideological perspectives we outlined in Chapter 3 have shaped welfare developments. As we stated in the Introduction to the book, we hope this historical, chronological approach to discussing our three ideological approaches will help you understand how each has exercised different levels of influence on social policy and social work at different times in British history.

Social democracy and welfare

As we explained in the Chapter 2, throughout much of the nineteenth century British governments did little to address many of the social evils that accompanied the Industrial Revolution. They pursued a strategy based upon 'classical liberalism'. A key principle of classical liberalism was that of the minimal state. Individuals and manufacturers, it was argued, were best left to pursue their own self-interests without interference from governments, and it was not seen as the state's place to promote economic and social well-being. Social problems like unemployment, poverty, ill health and insanitary housing were seen as having individual, behavioural causes – they were the result of 'thriftlessness', 'idleness' and 'drunkenness'. 'Laissez-faire' (leave alone), became the key defining principle of this era, and as we illustrated, this was reflected in nineteenth-century social policy and social work practice, which sought to modify the behaviour of the poor rather than relieve their distress.

The origins of social democratic ideology can be traced back to the latter quarter of the nineteenth century, when a new, emerging group of political philosophers, activists and organisations began to question prevailing classical liberal economic and political orthodoxies. They challenged the notion that individuals were necessarily responsible for their own misfortunes, drawing attention to evidence pointing to the wider structural, economic causes of social ills. The pioneering poverty surveys of Charles Booth in London and Seebohm Rowntree in York, which proved that poverty was extensive and largely beyond the control of individuals, provided plenty of ammunition with which to mount an assault on the assumptions underpinning classical liberalism. As Fraser (1984, p137) argues, *Together these surveys provided the compelling statistical justification for a more collectivist policy. Such a policy would have to take account of the growing acceptance that much poverty was the consequence of complex economic and social factors beyond the control of the individual.* Governments, it was increasingly argued, had a moral responsibility to intervene to assist people to overcome problems that were not of their making, and create conditions which would enable all citizens to achieve their full potential. Within social work, the challenge to COS methods of working with the poor was led by people such as Attlee, Tawney and Marshall, all of whom were passionate advocates of this 'new' way of thinking.

Many of those leading the challenge against classical liberalism, including Attlee, Tawney and Marshall, were influenced by socialism. They felt that collectivist social reform could be used as the means of not only alleviating the economic and social problems created by capitalism, but also as a mechanism of replacing unregulated capitalism with a fairer economic and social system, based upon the principles of equality and egalitarianism. Some socialists favoured a policy of violent revolutionary upheaval, but the most influential among them, within the Fabian Society, the Labour Representation Committee and later the Labour Party, believed that it was possible to reform society gradually, within the existing parliamentary system. Herein lies the beginnings of social democracy; that is, the attempt to transform society and create a more progressive, equal economic and social order through democratic, parliamentary means.

The creation of the Labour Party in 1906 was part of this social democratic strategy. It represented an attempt to secure the election of representatives of the working class to Parliament, so as to begin the process of securing the gradual reform of capitalism through the use of the democratic process. In Chapter 2, we discussed some of the social reforms that were introduced at the beginning of the twentieth century partly as a result of the challenge to the central tenets of classical liberalism. However, despite some progress, the period before 1939 continued to be largely characterised by an ideology of non-intervention. As RH Tawney, a key advocate of social democracy, pointed out, prior to this social policies were only reluctantly introduced, never sufficiently catering for the widespread unmet need that existed. They were designed more to 'manage' and 'preserve' unacceptable economic and social inequalities rather than to 'challenge' and 'eradicate' them. To cite Tawney (1964, p219), social policies *crept piecemeal into apologetic existence, as low grade palliatives designed at once to ... conceal the realities of poverty*.

Tawney's *Equality*

Tawney's classic text *Equality*, first published in 1931, provided an eloquent and compelling case for the adoption of social democratic ideas. Written during a period of economic depression, mass unemployment and widespread poverty, it set out a very different ideological path to that pursued at the time. By and large, governments of the period maintained a largely laissez-faire attitude to economic and social problems. Wages and unemployment benefits were in many cases insufficient to meet subsistence needs, secondary education was available to only a privileged minority, and health care was a commodity that millions could not afford to purchase. Governments, Tawney argued, should adopt a radically different approach, and seek to intervene in the economy and welfare sphere in order to create a more equal, fair society, where opportunity would depend upon aptitude and not ability to pay. Tawney set out a moral case for such intervention, appealing to common humanity and decency, but he also emphasised the economic and political benefits that would accrue from the adoption of a progressive welfare agenda. There was, for example, a pressing economic need (as well as a moral one) to improve the lamentable standard of schooling in Britain, which, prior to the Second World War, allowed roughly 80 per cent of children to leave school at 14, with no secondary education or formal qualifications whatsoever. As Tawney (1964, p146) argued, apart from any other consideration, *the mere economic loss involved in withholding from four fifths of British children the educational opportunities required to develop their powers is extremely serious. The nation*, he insisted, *has not such a plethora of ability at its command that it can afford to leave uncultivated, or undercultivated, the larger proportion of that which it possesses.* Similarly, there was both a moral and an economic case for providing free health care for citizens. Unnecessary sickness, he pointed out, accounted for the equivalent of the loss of 12 months' work of 560,000 persons, and cost the nation around £100 million. Hence, a national health service would not only enhance the life chances and opportunities of working-class people who at the time could not afford health care, it would also improve the health and economic efficiency of the community as a whole. Finally, Tawney also maintained that such 'civilising' policies would also serve to strengthen democracy itself. In the 1938 edition to his book he wrote that *democracy is unstable ... as long as it remains a political system and nothing more, instead of being, as it should be, not only a government but a type of society* (p30). Creating a fairer, more equal type of society, where all had the opportunity to achieve their full potential would add legitimacy to the British democracy, avoiding a repetition of events in 1930s Germany, where resentment of mass unemployment and poverty had generated disillusionment with democracy and propelled Hitler to power.

ACTIVITY **4.1**

Although the origins of the welfare state can be traced to the early twentieth century, substantive, genuinely progressive social reforms were not introduced on a large scale until after the Second World War.

- *Why do you think the Second World War was such a catalyst for change in terms of the development of the welfare state?*
- *Social policy historians have cited the Blitz, rationing and the evacuation programme as important factors contributing to a radical change in thinking on welfare. Why might this have been the case?*

The triumph of social democracy: The Second World War and the development of the welfare state

Many historians of the welfare state see the Second World War as a catalyst in the emergence of widespread support for the principles underpinning social democratic thought, and of the development of the welfare state. In interpreting these two trends, historians have pointed to how the peculiar circumstances of war fundamentally altered people's perceptions of what governments could and should do to tackle social and economic problems. As Derek Fraser (1984) argues, the Second World War was *perhaps the first 'peoples war', wholly dependent on the efforts and support of the whole population, not just the military prowess of the professional army.* Even more so than the 1914–18 conflict, it was reliant upon the efforts and sacrifices of the whole of the country, not just those involved in direct combat. Indeed, Titmuss (1950), one of the most influential writers on the post-war welfare state, estimated that the number of British civilians injured by enemy bombing raids was approximately the same as the number of British soldiers wounded fighting in all theatres of war. The very nature of this led to a feeling of 'shared sacrifice' and generated a momentum for social improvement after the war. As Paul Addison (1994, p130), another influential historian, points out, *The war effort ... hurled together people of different social backgrounds in a series of massive upheavals caused by bombing, conscription and the migration of workers ... The war effected a quiet revolution.*

A number of other developments occurred which also helped convince people of the merits of the social democratic case for government intervention. For instance, in the inter-war years, it was commonplace for politicians to claim that chronic unemployment was a result of the existence of a sizeable number of 'unemployables', who were unwilling or incapable of work. The 'solutions' that were proposed ranged from cutting welfare support in order to stimulate the 'lazy' and 'feckless', to the compulsory sterilisation of the 'residuum'. The war served to shatter this myth, because within a year unemployment had been all but eradicated. This showed that unemployment was a problem of lack of opportunity rather than motivation or ability. This realisation strengthened social democratic arguments for the development a proactive response to unemployment after the war, based upon governments providing people with genuine opportunities to work, rather than reducing benefits in a misguided attempt to incentivise the so-called 'idle'. The war years also saw the creation of an embryonic national health service, a development prompted by concern about levels of wartime casualties, but one that had been strongly resisted by governments before 1939. For the first time, free hospital care was provided to all British citizens on the basis of need, and again this reinforced the social democratic case for governments to accept responsibility for the health of citizens after the cessation of hostilities. Rationing also served an important precedent. It constituted a state guarantee for all citizens to be provided with access to a healthy, nutritious diet, a commitment previous governments had never been prepared to make (Addison, 1994). The experiences of the wartime evacuation programme, which involved hundreds of thousands of children being uprooted from poor, disadvantaged areas at risk of bombing and relocated in more affluent rural areas, was another significant development. As Fraser (1984, p210) argues, it *was part of the process by which British society came to know itself, as the unkempt, ill clothed, undernourished and often incontinent children of bombed cities acted as messengers carrying the evidence of the deprivation of working class life into rural homes.* Many of those who hosted evacuated children were genuinely appalled at the condition in which they arrived, and this did lead to much soul searching, and support for ameliorative measures to be introduced to combat the evils identified. Each of these developments and trends helped strengthen support for egalitarian policies and state intervention – key principles of social democratic ideology – both during and after the war. People began to question why, if governments could use their powers of intervention to secure these achievements amid the chaos and destruction of war, was it not possible to do the same in peacetime? It was within such a context, in December 1942, that one of the most important social policy documents in British history, the Beveridge Report, was published.

The Beveridge Report

The Beveridge Report, the brainchild of the civil servant Sir William Beveridge, was published on 2 December 1942. Beveridge had been tasked with producing recommendations on how to improve Britain's uncoordinated system of social service provision, but nobody, least of all the coalition government which commissioned the report, could have predicted the popular response to it. Arguably, never before or since has an official government report been greeted with such public enthusiasm or acclaim, or generated such a high degree of optimism. On its first day of publication 70,000 copies flew off the shelves of newsagents and booksellers, and altogether some 635,000 copies were sold.

When one considers what the Beveridge Report promised, it is easy to understand why it was so popular, and also why it has come to be seen as a classic social democratic blueprint. Basically, Beveridge argued that any post-war government should, as a matter of urgency, seek to use its powers of intervention to abolish what he referred to as the *five giant evils* that had characterised inter-war Britain.

- *Want*. By *Want*, Beveridge meant poverty. Poverty, he argued, was largely due to circumstances beyond the individual's control, caused by an involuntary *interruption or loss of earning power* or *the failure to relate income during earning to the size of family* (Beveridge, 1942, p7). Governments should, he insisted, accept their responsibility for eradicating poverty, by introducing a comprehensive system of social security (pensions, family allowances, unemployment insurance).
- *Disease*. *Restoration of a sick person to health is*, Beveridge argued, *a duty of the State*. The pre-war system of British health care was wholly inadequate to meet need, leaving millions responsible for the unaffordable costs of their own health care provision. Beveridge's report stated that governments should introduce *a health service providing full preventative and curative treatment of every kind to every citizen without exceptions, without remuneration limit and without an economic barrier at any point to delay recourse to it* (Beveridge, 1942, pp159, 162).
- *Ignorance*. In calling for the eradication of ignorance, Beveridge drew attention to the wasted talent that resulted from a system that compelled 80 per cent of children to leave school at 14, without any formal academic qualifications at all. There was, he insisted, a need for *an immense programme of building schools, training and employment of teachers ... to fit opportunity to young ability wherever it is found*.
- *Squalor* had created *bad conditions of life for a large part of our population* and needed to be the subject of a *planned attack* by government. *The war*, Beveridge (1944, p257) argued, *will leave a yawning gap* in provision which the state must ensure is *filled without delay by building more homes*.
- *Idleness*. By idleness, Beveridge meant involuntary unemployment. If governments could create conditions conducive to full employment amid the chaos and destruction of war, there was, he insisted, no reason why the same could not be achieved in peacetime. *We cure unemployment through hate of Hitler*, he wrote, so *we ought to cure it through hate of ... a needless scandal and wasting sore* (Beveridge, 1944, pp254–5).

Beveridge was well aware of the criticisms that his proposals for a massive increase in government responsibility for welfare would face from those still steeped in classical liberal traditions. *There are some*, he wrote, who may think his proposals were *inconsistent with initiative, adventure, personal responsibility*. However, he argued that there was *no economic or moral justification* for why Britain should not seek to tackle the five giant evils he had identified. *A revolutionary moment in the world's history is*, he insisted, *a time for revolutions, not for patching* (p6).

Critiques of the Beveridge Report

As we have already hinted, the levels of public support for the report were extraordinary. However, the reaction to the Beveridge Report was not one of universal acclaim. For example, senior figures within the Conservative Party were ideologically opposed to such a wide extension of state intervention. In addition, some feminist writers accused the Beveridge Report of failing to provide adequately for the social security needs of women.

Political opposition to the Beveridge Report

Although the Beveridge Report was welcomed by the Labour Party, which unsurprisingly welcomed the social democratic tone of its proposals, many Conservatives, including the Prime Minister Winston Churchill, were distinctly unimpressed with its recommendations for widespread government intervention and social reform. The Conservative Party's largely critical reaction to the Beveridge Report provides us with a good example of how a commitment to a particular ideological framework can shape the way politicians respond to particular social problems and issues. Many within the Conservative Party continued to be steeped in classical liberal traditions, believing in minimal state intervention and self-help, and this structured their response to the report. The ideological climate had changed as a result of the 'peculiar conditions' of war, but because the bulk of the Conservative Party remained wedded to classical liberal ideals, it failed to tap into this wholesale shift in the political environment.

The Conservatives' lukewarm response to the Beveridge Report was to prove to be a monumental political misjudgement and it would cost the party dear at the general election in 1945. For despite having the great wartime leader, Winston Churchill, as their figurehead, they were to suffer a humiliating landslide election defeat. Churchill was beaten at the polls by the leader of the Labour Party and former social worker Clement Attlee. His Labour Party took office, and immediately set about implementing what we now know as the welfare state. In the light of their crushing electoral defeat, and the popular support for the welfare state that emerged after 1945, most Conservatives came to accept the notion that the state had a responsibility for securing citizens' welfare. Hence, the period between 1945 and the mid-1970s has come to be seen as one characterised by a 'social democratic consensus', particularly over welfare-related issues. There were, of course, exceptions to the consensus, and some Conservatives continued to cling on to their classical liberal allegiances, but to varying degrees, both Conservative and Labour governments pursued interventionist policies designed to reduce inequalities and extend opportunity.

Feminist critiques of the Beveridge Report

In a much-cited pamphlet, written on behalf of the Women's Freedom League, Elizabeth Abbott and Katherine Bompas (1943) drew attention to the 'gendered' nature of Beveridge's proposals and its failure to acknowledge women's own individual social security requirements. *At present*, they wrote, *the Plan is mainly a man's plan for a man* (p20). As a number of more recent feminist social policy analysts have pointed out, Abbott and Bompas were right to suggest that the Beveridge Report was influenced by a pervasive 'ideology of motherhood' (Williams, 1989). The assumptions that marriage provided women with a 'meal ticket for life' and that a women's place was in the home did underpin the Beveridge Report. Consequently, it was assumed that most married women would not need any individual entitlement to social security in their own right.

As Timmins (1996) points out, the idea that a woman's place was in the home and that women would and should return to the domestic sphere following the end of hostilities, did seem to run contrary to contemporary developments, not least the fact that an additional 1.8 million women had entered industry alone between 1939 and 1943. In addition to this, many women had joined the armed services or undertook other work, trends that dramatically altered women's roles, status and indeed aspirations. Beveridge was not unaware of these trends, but he regarded them merely as a temporary aberration, assuming that once the war was over, the 'equilibrium' would be restored and women would return to performing their 'vital' household duties. For Beveridge, married women's unpaid work in the home was crucially important if the next generation of workers were to be socialised and reared effectively, and his proposals for social insurance were explicitly designed to reinforce 'traditional' gender roles. Hence, most married women were treated as dependents of their husbands, ineligible for social insurance related benefits (such as sickness benefits and pensions) in their own right, and if they did work they were in most cases only entitled to lower rates of support in times of need. As Williams points out, it is for this reason that Beveridge has since been seen as the *arch villain in much feminist writing* concerning the welfare state, with one such feminist commentator referring to his report as *one of the most crudely ideological documents of its kind ever written* (Wilson, cited in Williams, 1989, pp124–5).

It is not just the fact that Beveridge failed to acknowledge the possibility that married women's aspirations may have changed as a result of their experiences during the war that perturbs feminists today. Just as objectionable, they argue, was his failure to predict post-war social trends – such as an increased divorce rate and growing numbers of lone parents – which meant that marriage could no longer be relied upon as a principal means of economic security for women. Consequently, as we will see, those women who subsequently failed to conform to the 'traditional' family norm were, at best, forced to negotiate a social security system that was ill-suited to their needs, and at worst, subjected to discrimination and harassment. More serious still, the gendered assumptions underpinning the Beveridge Report are said to have had a *remarkably enduring influence* on social policy. According to Colwill (1994), *for many women the principles and assumptions around which welfare provision is constructed remain as intrusive, objectionable and oppressive as ever they were*.

More recently, some commentators have sought to defend Beveridge from his feminist detractors, claiming that he was a product 'of his time', and that he could not have predicted the far-reaching changes in family formation that would occur after the war. As Timmins (1996, p54) argues, *if he failed to foresee radical changes to come then that foresight was denied to many others*. For those such as Timmins, the real blame for the failure to adapt the post-war welfare state to changing social trends lies not with Beveridge but with post-war politicians who lived through those very changes. However, putting the question of culpability to one side, there is a general consensus that the gendered nature of Beveridge's proposals continue to shape the way in which many women today experience the social security system.

'Never had it so good?' The impact of post-war social policy during the period of the social democratic consensus

There can be little doubt that the commitment post-war governments made to maintaining full employment and to reducing social and economic inequality via the welfare state contributed to significant overall improvements in economic and social well-being. The 1950s and 1960s were decades of relatively full employment, and hence one of the primary causes of poverty in the inter-war years – unemployment – had been effectively removed. Health care and secondary education were now free to all, and better social security and housing provision helped alleviate some of the chronic levels of poverty and destitution that were a feature of inter-war Britain. In 1964, in the introduction to the fourth edition of RH Tawney's *Equality*, Richard Titmuss asked whether, in the light of these successes, the aims of social democracy had become redundant and outdated. *Have we in Britain*, he wrote, *reached such an equalitarian position that further substantial measures of collective redistribution are not called for, economically and morally?* (in Tawney, 1964, p15).

Certainly, many contemporary politicians and academics believed that the welfare state had largely achieved its aims, and that there was little need for measures to further reduce social class inequalities. As the Conservative Prime Minister, Harold Macmillan, famously said, it seemed as if the British population had *never had it so good*. Even leading social democratic intellectuals felt confident enough to proclaim that capitalism had been fundamentally transformed. According to CAR Crosland, author of the key 1956 social democratic text, *The future of socialism*, it was now manifestly inaccurate to call Britain a capitalist society. Capitalism, if not completely transformed, had been irreversibly greatly modified. Such optimistic assessments of the impact of the welfare state were reinforced by the findings of Seebohm Rowntree's third survey of poverty in York, published in 1951, which concluded that full employment and the welfare state had largely succeeding in eradicating poverty. His 1936 survey of York had found that nearly two persons in every 11 were in poverty, but by 1951 this had apparently fallen to two in every 118. As *The Times* (15 October 1951, p7) pointed out, it seemed that a *remarkable improvement – no less than the virtual abolition of the sheerest want – has been brought about*. Similar claims concerning the abolition of poverty and the creation of an 'affluent society' continued into the 1960s.

ACTIVITY **4.2**

In this activity, we want you to try to think about the imagery you associate with the 1960s. What feelings does that decade conjure up in your imaginations? Do you associate it with positive or negative developments?

COMMENT

When we ask our students about the 1960s, they almost uniformly associate it with positive imagery, linking it to technological breakthroughs (landing men on the moon), positive changes in popular culture, sexual liberation and progressive civil rights campaigns. This image of the 1960s seems to be in tune with how many of us think of the decade today. We tend to link it with great technological advancement, economic growth, prosperity and conspicuous consumption. This was, after all, the decade of the Beatles, the Rolling Stones, civil rights protests, the hippy movement, and, dare we say it, 'free love'. Even Preston North End (the preferred football team of one of the authors of this text) was a half-decent side in the 1960s, only narrowly being beaten by West Ham United in the 1964 FA Cup final! All this seems to point to a 'rosy' period of affluence and prosperity, and support for the notion that the objectives of social democracy – a more fair, equal and socially just society - had been achieved.

There can be little doubt that the material conditions of the working population in Britain did improve in post-war Britain as a result of the welfare state and full employment (Lowe, 1993). Certainly, when one compares social and economic conditions in post-war Britain with those of the 1930s, there had been huge gains. However, in the 1960s doubts began to emerge about claims that the five giant evils identified by Beveridge in 1942 had been conquered. A new, radical group of social policy academics began to draw attention to failings in welfare provision. Inequalities of wealth, income and power were, they argued, as firmly entrenched in the 1960s as they had been before the Second World War. Moreover, there were significant flaws and gaps in provision, which meant that many vulnerable people were not receiving the assistance they were entitled to and desperately needed. In addition, social work itself came under close scrutiny, as it became clear that pre-war, moralistic assumptions about the culpability of the poor remained remarkably resistant to change within social work practice, frustrating the adoption of a more progressive approach.

The rediscovery of poverty

In 1965 Brian Abel Smith and Peter Townsend published a study entitled *The poor and the poorest* (Abel Smith and Townsend, 1965), which succeeded in shattering the comfortable assumption that poverty was 'a thing of the past'. Their definition of poverty differed from the subsistence-level definitions which had traditionally been adopted in poverty studies, most recently in Rowntree's 1951 York inquiry. Abel Smith and Townsend argued that previous poverty research had placed too much emphasis upon assessing incomes needed to maintain subsistence, whereas more attention needed to be devoted to assessing relative needs. *People*, Townsend (1962, p221) argued, *are poverty-stricken when their income, even if adequate for survival, falls markedly behind that of the community*. Abel Smith and Townsend (1965) redefined poverty, using National Assistance levels (the then equivalent of Income Support) as an indication of an 'acceptable' standard of living. They argued that anyone with an income on or below 140 per cent of National Assistance levels could be seen as living on the margins of poverty. In redefining poverty they rediscovered it, finding that the numbers living in or on the margins of poverty had increased from 2.5 million people (7.8 per cent) in 1953/4 to 7.5 million people (14.2 per cent) in 1960 – 41 per cent of those in poverty were in work, but not earning enough to bring their incomes up to National Assistance levels. Three million older people and one in seven children were also found to be in poverty.

RESEARCH SUMMARY

Lone parenthood and poverty in the 1960s

Many of the children Abel Smith and Townsend found in poverty were living in lone parent families, and to an extent, they can be seen as victims of the 'gendered' nature of Britain's welfare system, which continued to see women as dependents rather than citizens with their own social security needs. By 1961, there were 325,000 'fatherless' families in Britain, but because they failed to conform to the traditional family norm, their needs were not catered for. Indeed, as one contemporary study showed, when they did seek assistance they often faced a hostile, harsh process that was geared more towards stigmatising 'deviant' lone parents than it was providing them with even a modicum of support (Marsden, 1969). Hence, for lone parents the claiming of means-tested support continued to be mired with the stigma of the Poor Law, and officials seemed to go out of their way to 'discipline' lone parents, making the claiming process as arduous and uncomfortable as possible. Mothers of illegitimate children were particularly targeted, but irrespective of the causes of 'fatherlessness', lone parents were constantly under suspicion and monitored in order to ensure they were not cohabiting with a male partner. Marsden's (1969) study found that almost 40 per cent of lone parents were failing to claim their benefit entitlements, which was hardly surprising given the treatment they received when attempting to do so.

The poor and the poorest was received sympathetically by the press and public. *There is*, acknowledged *The Times*, *concrete levels of evidence available that, at the lowest levels of wages, workers have not in fact shared in material affluence that is popularly supposed*. The Child Poverty Action Group was formed in the wake of the report's publication, and it called for the introduction of more generous family allowances, and for a more concerted effort to ensure people entitled to benefits (particularly pensioners and lone parents) received them. The screening of Ken Loach's hard-hitting docu-drama *Cathy come home* less than a year later served to reinforce doubts about the success of the post-war welfare state.

ACTIVITY 4.3

If you can, try to obtain a copy of Cathy come home. *Watching this film will help to give you an appreciation of the questions that were increasingly being asked about the nature of welfare provision in the mid-1960s. The film sensationally drew attention to the fact that more than 5,000 children were removed from parents each year, not through fear of neglect, but simply because their parents did not have access to adequate housing provision. It also highlighted the stigmatising, moralistic tone that continued to underpin welfare provision at the time (a theme we expand upon below).* Cathy come home *was watched by more than 12 million viewers, and repeated less than a week after its first broadcast due to popular demand. It is fair to say that its impact was significant. As* The Times *(3 December 1966, p9) noted,* the public conscience finds it unacceptable that in a relatively wealthy society so much bad housing is allowed to stand, that so many people live in unhealthy hovels, that so many live in hopeless overcrowding.

At the same time, inquiries in other sectors of the welfare state uncovered further problems. For example, in 1969 horrific conditions were uncovered at the Ely and Farleigh mental health hospitals, prompting widespread concern about the abuse suffered by patients in mental health institutions. At Ely, *Patients were knocked about, there was an unduly casual attitude to sudden death ... and there was pilfering of the food by staff* (*The Times*, 29 March 1969, p3). Meanwhile, at Farleigh, it was said to be *an everyday practice to punch people about* and casually increase the dosage of drugs to patients to keep them quiet (*The Times*, 12 August 1969, p2). The revelations prompted the Health Minister, Dick Crossman, to visit a number of institutions under his jurisdiction, and he was reported to have been *subdued and shaken* by what he witnessed. Following one such visit, he told one of his colleagues, *I am responsible for the worst kind of Dickensian, Victorian loony bin* (cited in Timmins, 1996, p259).

Social work during the social democratic era

There can be little doubt that the standard and level of provision of social work services improved after 1945, and that the social democratic era did coincide with a somewhat more progressive form of practice. Prior to 1939, many state and voluntary social work agencies would have railed against the idea that the causes of the problems faced by the poor were out of their own control. Likewise, the mere notion that state and voluntary welfare workers should show empathy towards such individuals and families, and devote considerable efforts to restoring and rehabilitating them, would have been seem as something of an anathema. On the contrary, throughout the 1920s and 1930s, the chronic poor were often described as a 'social problem group', written off as hereditary 'low grade defectives', incapable of rehabi-litation. The post-1945 period was to see the adoption of a somewhat more progressive approach, and cases that would previously have been ignored by social workers were now deemed worthy of intervention. As one prominent figure in the Family Welfare Association, the new name for the Charity Organisation Society, acknowledged in 1950:

> In the past, the families who today we are trying to treat with special concern and are calling problem families were probably written off as poor law cases or feckless and unhelpful.

(cited in Jones, 1983, p39)

However, individualist interpretations for poverty proved hard for some of those engaged in social work practice to shake off. For although the 'levelling effect' of the Second World War had led to considerable support for the notion that the state should accept responsibility for securing the welfare of its citizens, certain develop-ments also served to reinforce behavioural, pathological interpretations of social problems. Earlier we discussed the 'progressive' impact the evacuation programme had in changing attitudes towards social reform. However, evacuation also served to reinforce pathological interpretations for social problems. For example, public and professional opinion was not wholly sympathetic towards the parents of the often poorly clad, incontinent, malnourished evacuees. Indeed, there was a general feeling that much of the poverty could have been avoided if only parents of the evacuees had acted more responsibly, and brought their children up more effectively. Bad parent-ing, or more often than not 'bad mothering', was frequently seen to lie at the heart of the evacuees' problems. Mothers were, according to one account, invariably *dirty, verminous, idle and extravagant. They could not hold a needle and did not know the rudiments of cooking and housecraft* and *had no control over their children who were untrained and animal in their habits.* Many of the mothers were *foul mouthed, bully-ing and abusive, given to drinking and frequenting public houses, insanitary in their habits and loose in their morals* (Women's Group on Public Welfare, 1943, p3). Such anecdotal accounts of irresponsible parenting were widely reported in the press, adding credence to the notion that feckless parents were morally culpable for the condition of many of the child evacuees.

Many of the more lurid allegations made against working-class parents were baseless, and showed no appreciation of the poverty and deprivation that families had been forced to endure before the war (Macnicol, 1986). Nonetheless, they did help gen-erate an inaccurate, but pervasive image of morally culpable, irresponsible working-class parents. Accordingly, it was increasingly felt that improved welfare provision alone would not deliver the cure to the problems uncovered by evacuation, and that any solution must involve a process of 're-moralisation' and reform of the work-ing-class family. As Macnicol (1987) points out, what emerged was a discourse centred on the 'problem family', where emphasis was placed on the need for social workers to treat 'curable' poor socialisation, immorality and lack of social skills. So while intervention was to be different, and to an extent more humane than previously, as the following extract from the wartime *Our Towns* report, conducted by the Women's Group on Public Welfare (1943, ppxiii–xiv) illustrates, the language used to describe those suffering from a range of social problems was depressingly similar:

> *The ... submerged tenth ... still exists in our towns like a hidden sore, poor, dirty and crude in its habits, an intolerable degrading burden to decent people forced by poverty to neighbour with it. Within this group are the problem families, always on the edge of pauperism and crime, riddled with mental and physical defects, in and out of the Courts for child neglect, a menace to their community, of which the gravity is out of all proportion to their numbers ... Next to the problem families come those which may be described as grey rather than black; they are dirty and unwholesome in their habits through lack of personal discipline and social standard.*

The authors of this report, an influential group of leading voluntary social work professionals, were prepared to acknowledge a link between what they referred to as *the dark side of town life* and poverty (p103). In this sense they were at least partly in tune with the social democratic mood of the times. However, they saw *the problem of improving social conditions as one of education as much as of environment*, arguing that *more effort should be made to rouse and strengthen the human will ... for decent living* (pxiv). Thus, they continued to emphasise behavioural interpretations for the difficulties besetting what they referred to as *problem families*. Other voluntary social work organisations, such as the Family Service Units, which by the late 1950s could be found in a number of English cities, adopted a similar approach. They too often utilised disparaging language to describe 'problem families', but also believed that rehabilitation was possible through treatment and casework (Welshman, 1999). Their intensive family casework with 'problem families' would sometimes involve up to three supervisory visits each day, with treatment directed mainly at correcting the behavioural faults of the parents, usually the mother (Starkey, 1998). This blaming of mothers was to prove a common, recurring theme in post-war social policy and social work, and often it was they who were held responsible for the problems associated with families experiencing chronic difficulties. As Starkey (1998, p543) argues *The caricature of the typical 'problem mother' of a typical 'problem family', current in the late 1940s and 1950s, became firmly fixed in the minds of public health workers, social workers, housing managers and educationists as the central feature of an easily identifiable social nuisance.* Even the Archbishop of Canterbury accorded with this view, claiming in 1953 that the neglect of children in problem families was a result of *the heedlessness, the shiftlessness, the carelessness and ignorance of their mother*, and not the family's poor financial circumstances (cited in Starkey, 1998, p544).

As Welshman (1999) and Starkey (1998) note, voluntary organisations were hugely influential in terms of the development of social work after 1945, both in terms of their links to leading academics and policy-makers, but also the direct social work they performed for and alongside local authorities. Statutory social work was fragmented, uncoordinated and still very much in its infancy, and hence there was a continued reliance upon voluntary sector agencies, many of which continued to be steeped in pre-war attitudes and prejudices (Lowe, 1993). As late as 1959, the Younghusband Report estimated that there were only around 3,000 social workers employed by local authorities, and the vast majority of these (89 per cent) had no qualifications in social science or professional social work (cited in Hansard, 17 February, 1960, Vol. 221, c.). According to Eileen Younghusband (1978, p22), training was not considered a priority by local authority welfare departments. More important, she suggests, were the perceived virtues of *taking a firm line, standing no nonsense and not allowing people to get away with it*. Moralistic judgements about the causes of family difficulties therefore prevailed in the statutory and voluntary sectors. The job of the social worker, it seemed, was to supervise and control service users, and few attempts were made to include people in discussions that affected their lives. As late as the mid-1950s, some senior social service officials were still of the view that their main role was to *ensure that people do as they are told and to make them realise that they will be punished if they don't* (cited in Younghusband, 1978, p23). Medical Officers of Health, who also had a key role in shaping and delivering social work to vulnerable families (through the health visitors, home helps and other welfare workers they employed), also uncritically embraced the discourse of the 'problem family'. Indeed, as Starkey has shown, a number of Medical Officers of Health continued to believe social problems were a result of defective genetic inheritance, and feared that 'unfit', genetically determined weaknesses would be passed on to succeeding generations. For this reason, many local authority health departments would seek to target their family planning services at 'problem families', a policy that was supported by central government. Hence, in 1968, the government's Chief Medical Officer called for such services to be targeted at families characterised by *squalor, ill-health, an inability to cope and limited intelligence* (cited in Welshman, 1999, p468).

Of course, by no means all social and welfare workers subscribed to such claims, and by the 1960s academics and social workers had begun to question the validity of 'problem family' discourses. The publication of Barbara Wootton's (1959) *Social science and social pathology* represented a challenge to moralising approaches, which, she argued, failed to identify the structural origins of service user difficulties. She was particularly critical of contemporary casework methods, which concentrated upon psychological maladjustment rather than material need. *Always plumbing the depths of her client's personality*, Wootton wrote, *the social worker all too easily ignores the glaring evils on the surrounding surface* (p286). Modern social work had, she argued, found it difficult to divest itself of the moralistic, individualised casework approach, and was still in the habit of *confusing economic difficulties with personal failure or misconduct* (p291). There was a need, Wootton insisted, to *put the social back in social work*; for social workers to reject pathological interpretations, and to acknowledge and address the poverty and deprivation that continued to structure the lives of those suffering from a multitude of social problems.

It is partly because of the continued emphasis on family pathology, that Jones (1983, p40) has questioned whether the development of social work during the period of the social democratic consensus constituted a gain for working-class users of services. *A clear cut and unambiguous answer*, he concludes, *is not possible*, though he does identify a difference between the more progressive approach adopted by qualified statutory social workers in children's departments and the more 'traditional' practice found in other areas of the welfare state. Lowe (1993, p263) agrees, describing the 1940s and 1950s as a *far from heroic period* for the personal social services, when the implementation of a more humane policy was impeded by *the persistence of pre-war attitudes and institutions*. It was not until the publication of the Seebohm Report, which led to the introduction of social service departments and greater co-ordination and professionalism within social work, that more progressive attitudes would begin to prevail within policy and practice.

The emergence of more progressive thinking within social work should be seen in the context of the more general realisation that the welfare state had not succeeded in achieving its aims. Within social work, this manifested itself in the emergence of a new, more radical group of social workers, who began to question psychological, pathological explanations for the difficulties faced by service users. The focus instead moved towards combating the structural problems that contributed to individual and family difficulties though community work and welfare rights approaches. We there-fore began to see the emergence of what has become known as the *radical social work* tradition, a trend accelerated by the growing influence of left-wing (particularly Marxist) ideas, as well as organisational changes to social work which helped generate a collective sense of identity (Ferguson and Woodward, 2009). However, the emer-gence of radical social work coincided with the growing strength of right-wing, neo-liberal critiques of welfare, which were also challenging the assumptions that under-pinned the post-war 'social democratic' consensus.

CHAPTER SUMMARY

In this chapter we have examined how social democratic principles shaped the development of the post-war welfare state. As we explained, out of the ashes of war grew a new sense of social purpose, and a determination to use state intervention to eradicate the social and economic problems that had beset pre-war Britain. Never again, it was thought, would Britain be stalked by the giant evils of Want, Idleness, Squalor, Disease and Ignorance. The 'social democratic settlement' that characterised Britain's political landscape between 1945 and the 1970s undoubtedly wrought enormous benefits to British citizens. As Lowe (1993, p294) argues, there was *by any historic standard, a dramatic and sustained improvement in the rate of economic growth, the absolute living standards of the poor, the standards of health, the attainment of educational qualifications, the quality of housing and the care of traditionally neglected groups*. However, post-war Britain was no 'New Jerusalem' and it continued to be beset by a range of economic and social problems. Moreover, the welfare state itself – including social work – never fully managed to rid itself of the legacy of the Poor Law, and often welfare continued to be dispensed in a grudging, judgemental, stigmatising way. As we have already indicated, by the end of the period examined in this chapter, calls were being made for governments to reaffirm their commitment to a genuinely social democratic project and to redouble their efforts to address the nation's economic and social ills. These calls, though, had to compete with two alternative, competing 'solutions' to the crisis affecting social democracy, both of which were based upon radically different ideological principles. The next two chapters look at each of these in turn. Chapter 5 focuses upon the challenge posed by neo-liberal critiques of welfare, and Chapter 6 examines the influence of Marxist perspectives on social policy and social work.

FURTHER READING

For a couple of classic texts written from within the social democratic tradition, we would recommend:

Tawney, RH (1964) *Equality*. London: George Allen and Unwin.

Crosland, A (2006) *The future of socialism: 50th anniversary edition*. London: Constable and Robinson.

The latest version of Rodney Lowe's well known text provides a good, thorough analysis of the post-war welfare state:

Lowe, R (2004) *The welfare state in Britain since 1945*. London: Palgrave Macmillan.

Barbara Wootton's now classic book constitutes an excellent contemporary critique of the nature of social work in the 1950s:

Wootton, B (1959) *Social science and social pathology*. London: George Allen and Unwin.

For an analysis of the continued influence of behavioural pathological interpretations of economic and social problems during the period of the social democratic welfare state see:

Welshman, J (2006) *Underclass: A history of the excluded, 1880–2000*. London: Hambledon Continuum.

Chapter 5

Neo-liberalism and the development of social policy and social work after 1979

Introduction

The realisation that all was not well with the welfare state led social democrats to call for more funding for welfare and for the implementation of better, more progressive provision. However, in the light of the apparent failings of post-war social policy, social democratic values themselves were increasingly challenged. In particular, the general feeling of malaise that surrounded social welfare served to reinvigorate the critiques of social democratic values generated by those on the 'right' of the political spectrum. These critics, who included many prominent figures within the Conservative Party, were seeking to rehabilitate classical liberal values of individualism and self-help and utilise them to explain the problems that seemed to be besetting Britain. They claimed that too much rather than too little welfare lay at the heart of the nation's economic and social ills, and the country needed welfare retrenchment rather than expansion. The term that is most commonly used to describe this new, emerging ideology is neo-liberalism. In the discussion below, we examine the key themes of neo-liberal critiques of state welfare and consider their influence upon policy and practice.

Neo-liberalism

Neo-liberalism is most commonly associated with the economic and social policies pursued by Conservative governments between 1979 and 1997, but attempts to promote neo-liberal values and ideas began well before 1979. Indeed, the principles underpinning social democracy had been subjected to a sustained ideological attack since the inception of the welfare state, yet the 'crisis in welfare' described in the previous chapter gave neo-liberalism a renewed vigour and resonance. The political 'right' saw this as gilt-edged opportunity to undermine support for welfare and to advance their proposals to roll back the frontiers of the state. Neo-liberals argued that the economic and social problems the country faced were the result of benevolent but misguided attempts on the part of government to 'help' the poor. The post-war welfare state, with its range of free benefits and services, had sapped individual initiative, creating a state of 'helpless dependency'. Rather than relying upon their own efforts and initiative in the workplace, and making provision for their own welfare needs, people were choosing the 'easy' life of welfare. The 'Nanny State' was providing a seductive featherbed, luring people into a life of fecklessness, fraud and deceit.

ACTIVITY 5.1

Can you see any parallels here between neo-liberalism and the principles that underpinned the 1834 Poor Law Amendment Act (examined in Chapter 2)?

COMMENT

The language used by neo-liberals was (and still is) reminiscent of that used by the architects of the 1834 Poor Law Amendment Act. Generous state welfare was said to erode work incentives, encourage idleness and scrounging, and there was a need to return to the Victorian principle of less eligibility. Indeed, as the following comments made by Margaret Thatcher illustrate, prominent neo-liberals made no attempt to disguise the Victorian origins of their ideas:

> The other day ... I was asked whether I was trying to restore Victorian values. I said straight out, yes I was. And I am ... I believe that honesty and thrift and reliability and hard work and a sense of responsibility are not simply Victorian values. They do not get out of date.

> *(Thatcher, 1983)*

Of course, when appealing for a restoration of Victorian values, Margaret Thatcher and other neo-liberals said little about the chronic poverty, destitution, poor health and other social problems that were a characteristic feature of the latter half of the nineteenth century. As we showed in Chapter 2, the portrayal of the Victorian era as a bygone age of humanitarianism and philanthropy should not be viewed uncritically. Nonetheless, this appeal for a shift 'backwards', to a mythical 'golden age' of individualism and self-help was not without its electoral appeal in the late 1970s. Firstly it was reinforced by contemporary negative media campaigns, which portrayed welfare as being rife with dependency and fraud. Sensationalist, often inaccurate, stories about social security abuse were commonplace, strengthening neo-liberal claims that welfare was sapping initiative and self-reliance. Secondly, as is still the case today, people often look to the past through rose-tinted spectacles; they neglect to see, or are unable to appreciate, the 'darker' side of history and are attracted by the nostalgic notion that 'things were better' in the past. For some reason, the distant past always seems more palatable and appealing than the frenetic dangers and pace of life in the present, and this gives political appeals for a return to a supposed 'golden age' added resonance. In fact, as we will discuss in Chapter 7, historical research suggests that the Victorians were just as anxious about moral and social breakdown as we are today, and like us, they looked backwards to a supposed pre-Victorian age of virtue and responsibility (Pearson, 1983).

The neo-liberal critique of social work

Social workers also became a target for neo-liberal critics of the welfare state in the 1970s and 1980s. Keith Joseph, a prominent Conservative politician, argued that social workers had become seduced by perverse left-wing ideologies. They were too willing to *abuse their power and authority to urge or condone anti-social behaviour either on political grounds – against and 'unjust society' against 'authority' – or as 'liberation from the trammels of the outmoded family'* (cited in *The Times*, 21 October 1974). They had become one of the principal causes of social ills rather than one of the solutions, too prepared to excuse deviant behaviour, and unwilling to use their powers to discipline dysfunctional individuals and families. For those such as Joseph, social work needed to go back to basics, to rediscover its role in controlling recalcitrant families and individuals and restoring moral discipline.

Keith Joseph's critical comments about the nature of social work formed part of a wider, orchestrated political and media attack on the profession. This was partly prompted by a number of widely publicised child abuse scandals, which undermined support for social workers. To a certain extent, it also represented a backlash against the radical social work movement (see Chapter 6 for a discussion of radical social work). However, it should also be seen as part of a wider strategy being waged by neo-liberals within the Conservative Party to chip away at the social democratic consensus and weaken popular support for the principle of state welfare generally. If welfare professionals could be portrayed as ideological zealots, more interested in attacking liberal democracy and initiating political change than the welfare of those they were supposed to be serving, then it would be easier to persuade the electorate of the merits of cutting services and provision. In this sense, it is worth acknowledging that social workers were not the only welfare professionals to be attacked by neo-liberals. Those employed in other areas of the welfare state – doctors, nurses, teachers – received the same hostile treatment, as did the services within which they worked. Then, as is often the case now, such claims were embraced by a sympathetic right-wing press, which utilised its sensationalist powers of persuasion to reinforce neo-liberal critiques of welfare.

From critique to policy

From the 1970s onwards, neo-liberalism provided an increasingly influential critique of the post-war social democratic welfare state. However, as well as criticising existing welfare practices, its adherents also sought to provide an alternative future for welfare; one which would be based upon the key neo-liberal principles of minimal government intervention, self-help and the supremacy of the private market. Neo-liberals argued that the solution to the country's social and economic problems was for the state to withdraw from providing most forms of welfare. The considerable reductions in national insurance and taxation generated by this would leave citizens with the income needed to make provision for their own social security, education, health and social care needs in the private market. *Legislation and state interference*, wrote Rhodes Boyson, *should be cut back and limited to a requirement that all should insure against ill-health, misfortune and old age* (1971, cited in Butterworth and Holman, 1975, p386). Boyson was but one of countless prominent contemporary thinkers and politicians seeking to influence the future direction of social policy within an increasingly confident Conservative Party, and each shared a common ideological trajectory. State assistance, it was argued, should be maintained at a basic minimal level, designed merely to provide for the most needy, leaving all others to purchase their own care needs:

> It is not the job of the Conservatives to run an indiscriminate, improvident welfare state ... Our aim must be to increase personal independence, to spread private insurance, and to encourage true charity – by individuals not by institutions financed by involuntary taxes ... The Conservatives must actively work for the welfare state to wither away as personal prosperity and independent provision take its place.

(Boyson, 1978, p123)

The promotion of the virtues of private welfare was a key feature of the neo-liberal approach to welfare. State services were dismissed as unnecessarily costly, inefficient and overly bureaucratic. In the absence of any effective competition, welfare providers – for instance, the NHS, or local authority social service departments – had no incentive to cut costs and seek efficiency gains. They were, neo-liberals alleged, self-serving fiefdoms, more concerned with their own size, status and prestige than the welfare of those they were intended to serve. State welfare was also said to deny choice, enforcing a one-size-fits-all model, which was insensitive to service users' needs (Harris, 1971).

By contrast, neo-liberals argued that a competitive, private welfare market would lead to greater cost efficiencies and contribute to improved standards of provision. The need for providers of health, education, social care and other services to remain financially solvent would force them to keep a constant watch on costs and efficiency, driving down the overall expenditure on welfare. Meanwhile, competition for business would drive up standards of provision, as packages of care would need to be attractive to newly enfranchised welfare 'consumers'. In this ideal-type private welfare system, power would thus be transferred from the welfare agency to the consumer – that is, to the patient, the pupil, and the residential care patient, who could choose from a wealth of individually tailored packages of care best suited to their needs and desires. As well as empowering service users, such a system would be morally beneficial, promoting initiative, self-reliance and personal character. It appears to be a 'win-win' situation.

Neo-liberal welfare

Despite vigorously promoting private welfare, neo-liberals did accept (and continue to accept) the need for some limited, minimal form of welfare, but they maintain that this should be restricted to providing a very limited form of security. We outline some of the key features that might characterise an 'ideal-type' neo-liberal public welfare system below.

It should be based upon needs and not rights

Neo-liberals are deeply sceptical of universal, as-of-right benefits and services, and believe they should be replaced by means-tested welfare, based upon strict eligibility criterion. This should be designed to restore incentives to work, and to deter dysfunctional patterns of behaviour that are said to contribute to social and moral breakdown. It should, therefore, be proactive in weeding out what David Marsland (1996, p187), a prominent neo-liberal academic, refers to as *impulsive, profligate and irresponsible* individuals. Nor, argues Marsland, should it *be shy of making positive use of shame and stigma, where it is appropriate, to encourage people to shift into self-reliance*. This would help ensure that only the genuinely needy and destitute would seek assistance.

The assistance given should be temporary and conditional

Neo-liberals argue that unconditional welfare has an inevitable tendency to corrupt and should be avoided. Receipt of public support – whether housing, health care or income maintenance – should be dependent upon good character, and the performance of obligations and duties. Hence, recipients of unemployment benefits should be expected to engage in useful work or training in return for any assistance given. It may even be necessary to link access to other publicly funded welfare services, such as health care, to character, as is the case in some states in the United States (in the US, access to means-tested publicly funded health care for families who have no private health care insurance can be denied on grounds of character).

It should be delivered by voluntary or private organisations rather than state agencies

Although neo-liberals accept the validity of some limited form of public welfare provision, they tend to argue that the state's role should be restricted to funding and regulating the delivery of services, and not providing them. Large-scale state welfare agencies should be broken up, and private and voluntary organisations should deliver services currently provided by government. Their preference would be for these agencies to be locally based, so as to enable an intimate knowledge of the reputations and characters of potential recipients, and a more effective monitoring and control of those receiving assistance. There would be little, if any, role for social workers in this ideal-type neo-liberal public welfare system. For those such as Marsland (1996, p188), *the dangerous temptations of social work should be avoided altogether*, or at the very least there would need to be a radical overhaul of social work training and practice:

> There should be a decisive shift away from the current emphasis on rights to education in the practical skills required to help people to help themselves and to the inculcation of values appropriate in a free society ... The prevailing attitudes of social and welfare workers, in particular their simplistic and exaggerated conception of rights and their impertinently anti-democratic commitments to liberating their clients from oppression, are a major impediment to genuine welfare.

Thus, rather than social workers, there should be a reliance on the private and voluntary sectors. According to Marsland (1996, p179), the latter are more *committed to individualist rather than collective principles – and as such, better attuned to the ... fundamental mission of restoring those in need of help to self reliance*. Robert Whelan (2001), another neo-liberal academic, makes a similar set of recommendations, calling for a radical overhaul of social work practice. Like many other neo-liberals, he looks to the past for inspiration, arguing that social work should in future be based upon the individualist, self-help philosophy of the COS. What we require, he insists, *are the services of a friendly visitor trained in the COS approach, capable of assessing character, motivation and the relative significance of the behavioural and structural causes of welfare dependency in particular cases. Alas*, he laments, *no such cadre of helpers now exists*. The idea that social workers should seek to actively modify their service users' behaviour, teaching and coercing them to act as decent, law abiding citizens has, he insists, *evaporated entirely*:

> The reform of welfare will entail the reform of social work, and one option we might consider is taking it away from the state (certainly in so far as training is concerned) and returning it to the voluntary sector, where it began.

(Whelan, 2001, p96)

Conservative governments 1979–1997

The election of Margaret Thatcher's Conservative government in 1979 is often seen as a defining political moment. It is frequently thought to have signalled an end to the social democratic consensus and the beginning of a radical new neo-liberal era. Conservative administrations governed Britain until 1997, and during this period neo-liberal values permeated all areas of welfare policy, including social work. That is not to say, of course, that what emerged was a mirror image of the ideal type neo-liberal welfare regime outlined above. As we stated in Chapter 3, politicians may be deeply influenced by their ideological convictions, but in formulating their policies they cannot completely ignore electoral concerns or public opinion. Hence, Conservative ministers shied away from some of the more radical and politically unpopular proposals advocated by some within their ranks, such as the outright privatisation of the National Health Service.

Nonetheless, the changes were significant. In the economic sphere, we saw the introduction of a range of measures designed to promote business interests, such as income tax cuts, financial deregulation, the privatisation of publicly owned industries, the erosion of workplace rights and the curtailment of trade union power. Government subsidies to 'ailing' manufacturing industries were also cut, leading to unprecedented, sustained levels of high unemployment, particularly in manufacturing areas. Meanwhile, the social policy sphere experienced radical reform, which included significant reductions in the value of social security. Child, unemployment, disability and lone parent benefits were cut, as were housing subsidies and the value of the state pension. In addition, eligibility for most forms of social security – in particular unemployment and disability benefits – was tightened, the assumption being that many fit and able people were simply 'choosing' not to work. In justifying such cuts, Conservative ministers utilised language similar to that used by the architects of the Poor Law Amendment Act, claiming that the 'pain' being suffered was a 'price worth paying' in the fight against' welfare dependency'. Local authority social service budgets were also reduced, adding to the workload pressures of social workers, and restricting the support they could provide service users (Jones, 2005).

At the same time, Conservative governments sought to encourage individuals to make provision for their own welfare, offering financial incentives for them to turn to the private sector for their education, housing, pension, health and social care needs. Indeed, the social care sector found itself at the centre of attempts to introduce competition, markets and private enterprise in the delivery of public services, and it was radically transformed. We saw the introduction of what has become known as the 'purchaser/provider split', whereby local authorities would become facilitators and enablers of services rather than direct providers of care. Social workers would become 'care managers', who would buy in services from a variety of different providers in the voluntary and private sector. The intention was to reduce the role of the state in the direct provision of care and increase the role of the private sector in particular. This 'purchaser/provider split' has now become well established in social work practice. Many practitioners believe that this has changed the nature of the profession for the worse, *as the task of social work intervention is now increasingly to assess clients' needs, not help them solve their problems* (Jones and Novak, 1999, p161). Jones (2005, p100) interviewed social workers who experienced these changes, and time and again found them referring to their frustration about how this had bureaucratised social work, diluting the welfare-focused ethos of the profession:

> *I was regaled by talk of budgets and not only their appalling paucity to meet the needs of clients, but also the manner in which budget management and control had become the key concerns of the agency, stripping out its welfare ideals in the process.*

Undoubtedly, there were many 'winners' during this period of Conservative governance, but all the contemporary analyses undertaken into economic and social conditions in 1979–1997 point to widening inequality, poverty and social deprivation. The poorest and the most vulnerable had benefited least from the Conservatives' economic and social policy reforms. Indeed, during 1979–1994 the real incomes of the poorest 10 per cent of the population fell by 13 per cent. This was a period when average income rose by 40 per cent and the income of richest increased by 60 per cent. In real monetary terms, by 1997 the poorest 10 per cent in the UK were £520 pa worse off after 18 years of Conservative government, whereas the richest 10 per cent were £12,220 pa better off (Ferguson and Woodward, 2009). At the same time, poverty soared. In 1979, 13 per cent of the population (7.1 m people) were living in poverty, but by 1996/7 this had increased to more than one-quarter of the population. During the same period, child poverty increased from 14 to 34 per cent (1.9 m– 4.3 m). Such trends were unprecedented and inevitably led to accusations that the neo-liberal reforms pursued by the Conservatives were contributing to a divided, fractious Britain, where the well-off disproportionately benefited at the expense of the poor. The disregard Conservative ministers seemed to show for the casualties of their policies reinforced this perception. This was no more evident than in their refusal to accept that the growing levels of poverty identified by organisations such as the Child Poverty Action Group and the Joseph Rowntree Foundation were a problem. Indeed, as we have shown elsewhere, ministers denied the existence of any poverty in the UK. They claimed that everyone had access to the basic means of subsistence and hence nobody was 'poor' (Cunningham and Cunningham, 2008).

In summary, the welfare state inherited by New Labour in 1997 was radically different from that of 1979. Margaret Thatcher's first administration instigated a distinct ideological shift, one which was continued by successive Conservative administrations, including those led by John Major. As we will see later in the book, after 1979 many of the features of our ideal-type neo-liberal welfare model did shape future policy and practice, including, according to some commentators, that followed by Labour governments between 1997 and 2010.

Labour governments 1997–2010

During its 17 years in opposition, Labour had attacked the record of successive Conservative administrations, claiming that ideologically motivated neo-liberal policies had led to deep social divisions. When Labour was elected in 1997, many social democrats hoped to see Tony Blair's new government initiate a decisive break with neo-liberalism and a return to traditional social democratic agenda. However, prior to the general election, the Labour leadership had made it clear that its election would not herald a restoration of 'old' social democratic values and that it would seek to develop a 'new' 'Third Way'; a 'renewed' social democracy that would steer a more pragmatic course between the perceived extremes of 'left' and 'right'.

In practice, this approach led Labour governments to adopt a mixture of social democratic, structural interpretations for social problems and neo-liberal, behavioural ones. So, on the one hand, Labour acknowledged that it was the government's responsibility to help provide the environment and opportunities for individuals to develop and thrive, and to seek to promote social justice. On the other hand, as we will show in later chapters, Labour's social policies contained a strong moralistic undertone, at times embracing neo-liberal behavioural, pathological explanations for economic and social ills. The relative influence of structural versus behavioural explanations in shaping Labour's social policies is a matter of much debate. Some argue that Labour's policies did represent a 'renewed' social democracy that was more suited to the changed conditions of the late twentieth/early twenty-first century. They point, for instance, to the Labour's introduction of the minimum wage, its commitment to the NHS and its pledge to eliminate child poverty as evidence of a social democratic influence. Others, however, argue that New Labour was little more than 'Thatcherism in trousers'. They accuse Labour of embracing the neo-liberal legacy that it inherited and argue that Labour's economic and social policies, like those of previous Conservative governments, were largely shaped by neo-liberal rather than social democratic principles (Hall, 1998). Much of the rest of this book is devoted to an analysis of the direction of social policy and social work since 1997, so we do not intend to discuss in any great depth the Labour government's record on social policy and social work in this chapter. Our brief comments here on Labour's period in office are simply intended to draw your attention to the ongoing debate over the ideological trajectory of its economic and social policies.

Coalition government

Prior to the 2010 General Election, David Cameron had sought to distance himself and his party from the widely held perception that Conservatives were ideologically wedded to a neo-liberal strategy that showed a casual disregard for the poor (Cunningham and Cunningham, 2008). He accepted that previous Conservative governments were wrong to deny the impact of their policies on levels of poverty and inequality, and in other areas he sought to distance the Conservatives from the 'extreme' policies they had traditionally been associated with. Hence, early on in his leadership of the party, Cameron criticised what he referred to as the 'Old Right' who, he stated, believed that the only way of promoting responsibility and social and economic well-being was to cut the supply of state services:

> *The fact is, we cannot arbitrarily withdraw welfare benefits for the most*
> *needy of our fellow citizens. Yes, if we did that, no doubt in 20 years' time*

people would have become more self-reliant – but think of the misery of those 20 years. Some people will always need help and support – and we should not imagine that government simply withdrawing from the social field will automatically and instantly cause new, independent bodies to spring up in their place.

(Cameron, 2006)

As we now know, no single party won an outright majority in the 2010 General Election, and at the time of writing the UK is still governed by the Cameron-led, Conservative-dominated coalition government formed in its aftermath. Despite Cameron's pre-election criticisms of the 'Old Right', his coalition government has initiated a process of reducing and dismantling welfare rights at an unprecedented pace. In part, this process has been justified by claims that the cuts are a necessary component of the government's deficit-reduction strategy. However, the coalition's welfare reforms appear to have been accompanied by an ideological zeal that has left many commentators questioning the extent to which the Conservative Party has, in reality, moved away from its unquestioning embrace of neo-liberal principles. Indeed, it is not too difficult to detect a neo-liberal influence in the speeches Cameron made before the General Election. In these speeches, he frequently claimed that 'big government' had inhibited initiative, and that the welfare state had destroyed self-improvement and responsibility. In keeping with neo-liberal critiques of the welfare state, Cameron's 'solution' to the problem of the 'broken society' is to move away from 'big government' provided state welfare to what he refers to as the 'Big Society', where individuals and communities are responsible for securing their own economic and social well-being.

The 'Big Society'

David Cameron first floated his vision of the 'Big Society' in November 2009. Although many people remain unclear as to exactly what it entails, at the heart of the 'Big Society' lie two key neo-liberal aims.

1. A determination to tackle 'dependency' by creating what Cameron refers to as a 'culture of responsibility', whereby individuals and communities will come together to solve their own problems.
2. A desire to radically reform public welfare services, expanding the role of the private and voluntary sectors.

The 'Big Society' and the 'responsibility' agenda

On the specific issue of responsibility, Cameron argues that individuals, families and communities should stop looking to the state for guidance or assistance and should search 'within' for the cures to their problems:

We want to give citizens, communities and local government the power and information they need to come together, solve the problems they face and build the Britain they want. We want society – the families, networks, neighbourhoods and communities that form the fabric of so much of our everyday lives – to ... take more responsibility.

(Cabinet Office, 2010, p1)

In a short time the coalition has sought to encourage and indeed coerce individuals to take more responsibility for their own social and economic needs. On the 'coercion' side, the coalition's social security reforms are designed to make life on welfare 'less attractive', with a view to increasing the incentives for people to support themselves rather than relying upon the state. While they follow a similar trajectory to the previous Labour government's reforms, they do represent a significant acceleration of pre-existing policy trends, reducing the value of social security and tightening eligibility conditions still further.

RESEARCH SUMMARY

A 'Benefit Cap'

Among a range of other cuts to social security, the government has proposed an overall 'benefit cap' of £26,000 pa for families. In part, ministers have sought to justify this initiative with reference to the parlous state of the nation's finances and the need to make 'prudent' cuts. However, this has been accompanied by a robust ideological justification, with ministers publicly claiming that families have a responsibility to look after themselves. Jeremy Hunt, the coalition's Conservative Culture Minister, controversially argued that it was not the state's responsibility to fund the 'inappropriate' family-planning choices of 'shameless' individuals. The number of children that you have, *he insisted,* is a choice and what we're saying is that if people are living on benefits, then they make choices but they also have to have responsibility for those choices ... It's not going to be the role of the state to finance those choices *(cited in Gentleman, 2010a, p14). Welfare rights organisations have condemned the proposed 'benefit cap':*

Forcing children into destitution on the arbitrary basis of how many brothers and sisters they have is abhorrent. As families brace themselves to discover whether their jobs will survive the cuts it is awful that those with larger families should face this extra anxiety.
(Child Poverty Action Group, cited in Martin, 2010)

The homeless charity, Shelter, also expressed serious reservations about the potential of the 'cap' to impact upon homelessness among larger families, whose benefit income would no longer be sufficient to meet their housing needs. It estimated that much of the south-east of England would become unaffordable to families on benefits who have more than two children, and many would simply lose their homes (Helm and Boffey, 2011). It seems that Shelter's fears may not have been unfounded. Despite ministerial reassurances that the 'benefits cap' would not lead to destitution, it has subsequently emerged that the Department for Communities and Local Government (DfCLG) has estimated that, if implemented, it would make 40,000 families homeless. Moreover, the
Continued

> **RESEARCH SUMMARY** *continued*
>
> *A 'Benefit Cap' continued*
> *DfCLG calculated that the costs of supporting these homeless families would be consid-
> erably more than the amount saved by the benefit cap itself (Sparrow, 2011). Such
> findings serve to reinforce suspicions that ideology, rather than a pragmatic concern
> to reduce public spending, is driving the coalition's welfare reform programme. As a
> number of commentators have pointed out, these reforms have, after all, been imple-
> mented at a time when the opportunities for individuals to engage in what are consid-
> ered to be 'responsible' behaviours – for example, employment – are more slender than
> they have been for decades (Ellison, 2011).*

Alongside these 'coercive' social security initiatives, we have seen the introduction of
'inducements' designed to 'encourage' people to take more responsibility for themselves and their communities. Hence, the coalition is implementing a number of
measures which it claims will empower local communities, providing them with
opportunities to respond themselves to issues that affect them. For example, it is
envisaged that local organisations will be given a right to take over 'community
assets' that are threatened with closure, such as libraries, post offices and other
council services. Community groups will also be given the 'right to challenge' local
authority provision of services – including many social services – and run them as
community bodies, charities or even for-profit social enterprises. The mechanics of
this process are, at the time of writing, vague, but despite their superficial 'democratising' appeal the proposals are not without controversy. For example, the 'relevant
bodies' who will be allowed to challenge to take over local authority services have yet
to be defined, leaving open the possibility of 'backdoor privatisation' (House of Commons Library, 2011). Nor have the services that will be open to challenge yet been
identified, meaning that key local authority-provided social services may be continu-
ally open to 'challenge' and take-over, with potentially destabilising consequences to
the standards and quality of care and services. In addition, of course, while a particular 'community body' may be given control of a key service, there is no guarantee
that they will operate that service in the interests of the community as a whole.
Indeed, there may be a danger of creating a 'democratic deficit'. In the absence of
any effective democratic oversight of services (as currently exists with local authority
provision), the voices and interests of the most disadvantaged, marginalised and
poorly organised individuals and groups may be submerged by those of the more
articulate and organised. It is the latter who are more likely to 'bid' for and gain
control over services.

The 'Big Society' and the reform of welfare services

More generally, Cameron's 'Big Society' plan for public services has involved a dramatic rethink in the way welfare is delivered, with a much greater role for the
voluntary and private sectors in education, health, social security and social work.
In education, the 'free schools' initiative and the expansion of academies both seek

to reduce the state's role in the delivery of schooling in the UK, and extend the influence of the private and voluntary sectors. The government's health care reforms also controversially envisage a significantly expanded role for the private sector in the delivery of health care, and although public and professional concerns about the implications of this for patient care have perhaps moderated the speed at which this will occur, it seems likely that for-profit private corporations will become increasingly involved in health provision in the UK. The same trends can be found in social security provision, where the private and voluntary sectors are to be the main providers of the coalition government's welfare-to-work reforms. In each instance, the shift away from public sector provision has been justified by the claim that the private and voluntary sectors are both more 'efficient', and 'attuned' to the needs of users of services. The infusion of greater heterogeneity in the provision of welfare will, Cameron argues, increase choice, but also drive up standards, as providers are forced to improve the quality of their services in order to attract 'consumers' and indeed government funding.

RESEARCH SUMMARY

Is the private sector more efficient in delivering welfare than the state sector?
Despite the apparent plausibility of claims concerning the 'superiority' of the private and voluntary sectors in delivering welfare, evidence from the UK and elsewhere points to a more nuanced picture. The US's private health care system, for instance, is desperately inefficient, consuming more than 16 per cent of GDP in 2009 (compared with the UK's 9 per cent), while at the same time leaving tens of millions, including children, without any health insurance at all (World Bank, 2011). Closer to home, research has shown that UK Jobcentres have a more effective record at delivering welfare-to-work schemes than either the voluntary or private sectors. It is simply not true, noted the Department for Work and Pensions (2009) all-party Select Committee of MPs, that either the private or the third sector has a consistently better record in the provision of employment services than in-house staff. A similar picture emerges in relation to social care. Hence, in 2007/08, 79 per cent of council-run services were rated as 'good' or 'excellent', whereas only 66 per cent of private sector ones were (Commission for Social Care Inspection, 2009). At the time of writing, the collapse of the private Southern Cross social care corporation, which found itself simply unable to make a profit from social care without compromising service users' needs, also suggests that the private sector is not necessarily the panacea for shortcomings in welfare provision. Again, such findings have helped reinforce accusations that the coalition's attempts to expand voluntary and private provision are motivated primarily by ideological considerations, rather than an understanding of what works best.

As we have already hinted, social services and social work are not exempt from the coalition's reform agenda. Private and voluntary sector initiatives have both been advanced as methods of improving the quality of what are considered to be 'bureaucratically driven', 'inflexible' statutory social work services. For example, the coalition is expanding the previous Labour government's *Social Work Practice* initiative, which envisages the contracting out of social work services to social worker 'co-operatives', or private sector 'practices'. Currently, a number of 'pilot' projects are in the process of being evaluated, but it is the clear intention of the coalition to roll these out in future. Also evident is the government's clear desire for a significant level of private sector involvement in this process. Currently, the BASW and the Social Care Institute for Excellence support this initiative, but front-line social workers and unions have expressed concern that this will lead to the privatisation of social work, adversely impacting upon the welfare ethos of the profession, as well as the quality of care:

> *The Tory-led Government is enthusiastic about private social work practices because they fit into its 'Big Society' agenda. But we know that it is using mutualisation and social enterprise as a way to dress up wholesale privatisation plans. Without waiting for the evaluation of the initial 'pilot', the Government is rolling out private social work practices and investing considerable effort and money (including set-up grants) to persuade local authorities to go down this road.*

(UNISON, 2011, p1)

Unpaid 'voluntary' social work has also been suggested by the coalition as a possible future model for the profession. Indeed, prior to the General Election in 2010, the Conservative Party made it clear that in government one of its aims would be to promote unpaid 'voluntary social worker' schemes, staffed by, for example, *retired city bankers or ex-insurance brokers* (Gentleman, 2010a, p21). *Volunteer social work*, the Conservatives have argued, *should be encouraged and expanded* (Conservative Party, 2009, p20). Comments made since the General Election by the Children's Minister, Tim Loughton, suggest that this proposal is likely to influence the Coalition's approach to social work and social care in government.

ACTIVITY 5.2

It is estimated that there are around 227,000 volunteers currently working in a range of social care settings, performing useful and very necessary assistance to different service user groups. However, the coalition's proposals, briefly sketched out in numerous policy documents and speeches, envisage a much more strategic role for unpaid voluntary workers in providing services formerly, or simultaneously provided by social workers. In support of their initiative, ministers have pointed to the experiences of a small number of pilot schemes run by Community Service Volunteers (CSVs), where unpaid volunteers are given 18 hours' training before being embedded in child protection teams.

Of course, the use of voluntary workers to provide important social work services is not a particularly novel phenomenon. Indeed, as we saw in Chapter 2, voluntarism, philanthropy and charity played a key part in social work provision throughout the nineteenth century and the first half of the twentieth century. In this activity we want you to think about the possible impact of a significant expansion of this initiative.

- *List some of the potential 'advantages' and 'disadvantages' of moving towards a system whereby 'voluntary' workers are drawn into key social work roles, such as child protection. While doing so, you might want to bear in mind some of the issues we identified with 'voluntary' social work in Chapters 1 and 2.*

COMMENT

In setting out his vision for expanding the use of unpaid voluntary social workers, Tim Loughton, the Children's Minister, stated that, The introduction of volunteers to supplement the work of frontline child protection officers was an example of how the ... 'big society' might work in action and would save local authorities money *(cited in Kerrigan Lebloch and Beresford, 2010, p39). In this sense, the rationale he advanced was partly financial; he suggested that it was* an additional resource that, at a time when we are well stretched, it makes a lot of sense to explore. *Statutory social workers, he acknowledged,* had very little time to visit service users, *and* volunteers would provide an extra set of eyes and ears. *However, he also implied that unpaid volunteers could also compete on grounds of quality. They would, he insisted, be more in tune with the needs of service users, and their 'independence' from social services would allow them to build more trustworthy relationships:*

> The voluntary social workers will form a more empathetic relationship with the family. They will probably give them a ring every day, help them fill in their benefit forms ... They are much more trusted by the families, and they are an extra set of eyes and ears to report back to the social workers, who can only afford the snatched half an hour visit every week ... I don't see why it couldn't apply everywhere.
>
> *(cited in Gentleman, 2010, p21)*

The minister's claims seem to be supported by volunteers who have participated in such schemes. As one such volunteer stated, Initially, families are scared about why you are there, but after a few weeks the barrier comes down and you build a bond ... It helps that I'm not a professional and that I've got children myself *(Valios, 2010). Research funded by the CSV itself into its pilot projects also suggested that positive outcomes may result from the use of volunteers (Tunstill, 2007).*

Others, though, are less convinced about the government's motives in promoting the concept of unpaid voluntary social work, and are more cautious about its potential impact upon the quality of service provided. Some interpret it as an ideologically influenced attempt to undermine the profession and get social work done 'on the cheap'. Kerrigan Lebloch and Beresford (2010, p39) argue that the opening up of children's services to voluntary workers is *prompted not by the safety of children but by a strategy steered by cuts in services using unqualified and minimally trained volunteers to visit children with complex protection needs.* It is no coincidence, they insist, that these proposals are advanced by a coalition government that is ideologically committed to reducing the role of the state, and one that has imposed a severe package of retrenchment on public sector welfare agencies. Voluntary provision has an important role to play in social care, but the measure proposed by Loughton *risks becoming, at a time of ever-reducing welfare services, a substitute for the professional expertise that vulnerable, abused children are entitled to* (p39). The minister himself accepts that social workers are 'stretched', but rather than accepting the implications of this – the need for more professionally qualified, skilled social workers – his government's expenditure cuts have had precisely the opposite effect, reducing resources and adding to the pressures faced by social service departments. Critics argue that

75

'patching up' hard-pressed child protection teams with unpaid, unqualified volunteers carries with it a whole range of risks and pressures to children, and indeed the volunteers themselves.

'Big Society' or ideological smokescreen?

Inevitably, the rhetoric used to justify Cameron's 'Big Society' has been uniformly progressive, but there are concerns that the initiative represents little more than an ideological smokescreen, disguising what is a neo-liberal-influenced attack on the welfare state. It is, critics argue, a crude attempt to roll the country back to a mythical 'golden age' of individualism and self-improvement, where the state provided only a bare minimum of social protection and individuals were left to fend for themselves.

It is perhaps notable that even ostensible supporters and beneficiaries of the 'Big Society' have expressed caution as to the direction of policy. Voluntary organisations, many of whom theoretically stand to benefit from the promotion of philanthropy and voluntarism, have argued that their capacity to plug the gaps left by cuts in state provision have been hit hard by dramatic reduction in their own public funding. According to one estimate, £5.1 billion (40 per cent) of government funding for charities has been lost, leading to the redundancy of key professionals and the closure of many valuable voluntary social care initiatives (Toynbee, 2011). At the time of writing, the government has only devoted £470 million to support voluntary groups 'build' the 'Big Society', a sum that comes nowhere near to matching the public money charities have lost (Ellison, 2011). As the Association of Chief Executives of Voluntary Associations (CEVAs) has warned, the government's *over-rapid and poorly managed public spending cuts* may damage the sector *disproportionately and irrevocably*. The CEVA has also echoed concerns that the 'Big Society' agenda was being used to justify an ideological agenda. The vision, it argues, *should not be equated with reducing the size of the state, or lead to the state abdicating its responsibilities, particularly with regard to the most vulnerable* (Commission on Big Society, 2011, p5).

Church leaders have also questioned Cameron's 'Big Society' vision, with the Archbishop of Canterbury controversially describing it as a *painfully stale* concept. There was, he argued, *a widespread suspicion* that the coalition's emphasis upon the 'Big Society' *had been done for opportunistic or money-saving reasons*. He argued that this was not helped, *by a quiet resurgence of the seductive language of 'deserving' and 'undeserving' poor, nor by the steady pressure to increase what look like punitive responses to alleged abuses of the [welfare] system* (Williams, 2011). The perception that the 'Big Society' is merely an elaborate ruse, designed to justify ideologically influenced cuts, also seems to be shared by the general public. A survey for *The Times* (8 February 2011), for instance, found that 78 per cent of people agreed with the statement that the *Big Society is just an attempt by Government to put a positive spin on the damage public spending cuts are doing to local communities.*

CHAPTER SUMMARY

As we have shown in this chapter, neo-liberals oppose state intervention in the welfare sphere, believing it to be a morally corrupting, dependency-inducing influence. While neo-liberals do not doubt that the architects of the post-war welfare state, such as Sir William Beveridge, were well intentioned, they argue that the welfare services developed after 1945 have exacerbated the economic and social problems that they were designed to solve. Echoing the architects of the New Poor Law, they argue in favour of a restoration of the 'principles of 1834', and advocate strong dose of 'self-help'. State welfare services should be cut and individuals should be encouraged, and where necessary coerced, into supporting themselves through their own efforts and initiative. Governments can legitimately provide a very basic, means-tested safety net for the very vulnerable, but anything over and above this minimum should be provided by the voluntary and private sectors in a competitive 'welfare market'. As we have illustrated, in policy terms neo-liberalism has been at its most influential since 1979, and it is particularly associated with Conservative governments between 1979 and 1997. However, as noted above, there are those who argue that Labour's economic and social policies were infused with neo-liberal principles. Moreover, a clear neo-liberal thread can be detected in the coalition government's welfare reform strategy, as well as its 'Big Society' agenda.

As future welfare practitioners and social workers, you can hopefully now see why it is important for you to have a basic understanding of the key principles underpinning neo-liberalism. Firstly, neo-liberal ideas and values have led to a fundamental transformation of the welfare state, as well as social work practice. There is now a much greater emphasis upon marketisation, competition, consumerism and the voluntary and private provision of welfare, and this will inevitably impact upon your professional futures. Secondly, and just as crucially, it is important to bear in mind the impact of neo-liberal economic and social policies upon vulnerable service users. The 'legacy' of neo-liberalism in the 1980s and 1990s was a more divided, unequal, fractious society, which was characterised by unprecedented levels of poverty and associated social problems. This inevitably led to increased caseloads for social workers, at a time when funding for social work services was cut. Alongside this, we saw the restoration of behavioural interpretations for disadvantage, which apportioned blame for misfortune upon individuals and families themselves. These developments inevitably created a difficult environment for social workers to operate in. Social workers were portrayed as overly sentimental, politically motivated 'do-gooders', whose misguided 'help' was encouraging and reinforcing fecklessness and irresponsibility. Current policy trends seem to be pointing in the same direction. Just as social service departments are feeling the impact of the coalition government's austerity-driven public expenditure cuts, unemployment, inequality, poverty and the range of ills associated with these problems are set to increase. At the same time, as the Archbishop of Canterbury pointed out, we have seen a resurgence of the seductive language of the 'undeserving' poor, which holds individuals morally culpable for the marginalisation that they experience. Alongside the other reforms contemplated by the coalition that we have mentioned – for example, the privatisation and contracting out of local authority services, as well as the extension of 'voluntary' social workers – this looks likely to create an extremely challenging environment for social workers to operate in.

FURTHER READING

The following texts are written from a neo-liberal perspective, and provide a classic neo-liberal interpretation of the welfare state:

Bartholomew, J (2004) *The welfare state we're in*. London: Politicos.

Marsland, D (1996) *Welfare or welfare state? Contradictions and dilemmas in social policy*. New York: St Martin's Press.

The following texts offer a radical critique of the impact of neo-liberalism on social policy and social work practice:

Ferguson, I and Woodward, R (2009) *Radical social work in practice: Making a difference*. Bristol: Policy Press.

Ferguson, I (2008) *Reclaiming social work: Challenging neo-liberalism and promoting social justice*. London: Sage.

Chapter 6

Marxism, social policy and social work

Introduction

As we noted in Chapter 4, the emergence of neo-liberalism was not the only important ideological trend emerging from crisis of British social democracy in the late 1960s. A concurrent development was the resurgence of Marxism, an ideology based upon the work of the nineteenth-century political philosopher, Karl Marx. Although Marxism would have little or no influence in shaping the policy programmes of the established political parties in the UK, its influence within academic, activist and practitioner circles was and remains relatively significant.

Karl Marx

Karl Marx (1818–1883) was a German nineteenth-century revolutionary political philosopher who lived in England at a time when the emergence of industrial capitalism was creating widespread economic and social division. He was deeply uncomfortable with what he witnessed; people whose lives were blighted by utter poverty and despair, coexisting with those whose lives were characterised by opulent riches and affluence. Marx's life work was devoted to exposing the economic and political arrangements that he felt led to such gross and unjust inequalities, and in doing so he identified two main groups in capitalist society: the bourgeoisie (rich manufacturers) who owned the means of production (factories), and the proletariat (or workers) who were forced to sell their labour to the bourgeoisie in return for a wage. In their insatiable search for profits, the bourgeoisie exploited the proletariat remorselessly, forcing them to work long hours, in appallingly unhealthy conditions, for wages that were barely enough to meet their subsistence needs.

Marx referred to this exploitative economic system as *capitalism*. It was, he argued, bolstered by the state elite (including governments, senior civil servants, judges and military officers), whose policies and interventions were always, ultimately, designed to promote the interests of the rich and economically powerful. As Marx and Engels argued in their *Manifesto of the Communist Party*, published in 1848, *The executive of the modern state is but a committee for managing the common affairs of the whole of the Bourgeoisie* (Marx and Engels, 1969, p44). Even nineteenth-century welfare measures, which ostensibly seemed to help the poor, were, from a Marxist perspective, actually influenced by economic rather than altruistic concerns. Thus, legal restrictions on the employment of children were, from this viewpoint, motivated less by humanitarian sentiment or popular democratic pressure, and more by recognition that the brutalising inhuman conditions under which the nation's children were forced to toil threatened future profit levels. It was, as one Marxist has subsequently argued, a fear that children – the next generation of wage labourers – were being *literally worked to death*, which *underlay a series of attempts by the state to control the hours and conditions of [their] work* (Gough, 1979).

Marx believed that at some point in history, the proletariat would come to see the true nature of their exploitation, and combine in a state of true class consciousness to overthrow the system that had always oppressed them. In its place, there would be a fairer communist society. Private property would be abolished and no one social group would exploit another. *The proletarians,* he proclaimed, *have nothing to lose but their chains. They have a world to win.* He optimistically called for *Working men of all countries unite!* (Marx and Engels, 1969, p96).

Marxism

Clearly, the communist revolution that Marx hoped for and predicted had not arrived in Britain in the 1960s, and society had obviously changed since Marx's death in 1883. For some, though, this had done little to dent the importance or relevance of his ideas for interpreting contemporary events. As we saw in Chapter 4, the post-war welfare state may have reduced some of the excesses of social and economic inequality, but as in Marx's day, British society continued to be characterised by poverty amid plenty. The political climate of the 1960s was also conducive to a resurgence of Marx's ideas. It was a decade of civil rights protests and political turmoil, and Marx's revolutionary critique of capitalism appealed to a new generation of activists, academics, practitioners and students. These Marxists argued that capitalist societies continued to be characterised by exploitation, widespread poverty and gross inequalities in income and wealth. Welfare policies, they insisted, had never really been designed to eradicate these problems. On the contrary, the primary objectives of welfare, including social work, were to promote economic interests by increasing profit accumulation and controlling the labouring population. Marxists accused social democrats of being delusional for assuming that it was possible to reform a system that was based upon naked exploitation, and that depended upon the fear of poverty to drive people into low-paid, unrewarding exploitative labour. Like Marx before them, this new generation of Marxists argued that capitalism could not ultimately be reformed and that the proletariat's true interests lay in the overthrow of the system, and the creation of a more just, egalitarian society.

At the heart of this developing critique of welfare was a challenge to the notion that the state in capitalist societies was a neutral entity, open to bargain, persuasion and reform. In this sense, a new generation of Marxists sought to develop Marx's analysis of the state, and demolish what they saw as the myth that the state was merely a democratic servant of the people, with no inherent bias towards any one class or group. One of the most influential attempts to do this can be found in Ralph Miliband's (1973) *The state in capitalist society*, first published in 1969. Like Marx, he argued that the state was primarily and inevitably the guardian and protector of the interests of the bourgeoisie. In explaining why, Miliband highlighted a number of factors, including:

- the similar educational and social class backgrounds of the state elite and the bourgeoisie;
- the sheer economic power possessed by major, privately owned corporations;
- the structural constraints imposed upon all governments in capitalist societies.

We examine each of these factors in greater detail below:

The similar educational and social class backgrounds of the state elite and the bourgeoisie

Miliband sought to highlight the links between the state elite (for him, this consisted of senior politicians, senior civil servants, judges and military officers) and leading sections of capital (business). Many of the state elite were, he pointed out, from business backgrounds themselves, with a number (particularly politicians) maintaining close links to important sectors of the economy. He argued that this inevitably gave them a vested interest in the implementation of business-friendly policies. Even where the direct links between the state elite and business were less tangible, their similar educational, social and class backgrounds meant that they were conditioned to think, speak, behave and react the same way as each other. In the context of the UK, for example, the state elite and leading business figures had invariably attended the same small selection of elitist fee-paying independent public schools and studied at either Oxford or Cambridge universities. They knew each other, shared the same personal ties, connections, value base and world view. In short, the state elite were a product of the same mould as the bourgeoisie, and this led them to share their political and ideological outlooks, and to support policies conducive to the interest of capital. To quote Miliband (1977, p69), *a common social background and origin, education, kinship and friendship, a similar way of life, result in a cluster of common ideological and political positions and attitudes, common values and perspectives.*

The sheer economic power possessed by major corporations and privately owned industries

As we have shown, the social origins of the state elite are seen by some Marxists as a crucial factor in shaping the class bias of the state, but it is not the only factor. The sheer economic power of the bourgeoisie – their ownership and control of economic, technological and media interests – means it possesses immense coercive power, which it can use to encourage or force states to adopt policies conducive to its interests. It can do this through bribes or political donations, or via the funding of negative media campaigns, or through threats to remove investment from the country. While this may sound far-fetched, it is important to bear in mind that some of the world's corporations have higher turnovers of income than many nation states. Moreover, there are occasions in relatively recent British political history when governments have been coerced into modifying their political agenda in order to accommodate the needs of business. For example, when the Labour Party won the General Election in 1964, the head of the civil service informed the new Prime Minister, Harold Wilson, that it would be 'unwise' from a business point of view to implement Labour's manifesto commitments. As Wilson recalled in his autobiography, *a newly elected Government with a mandate from the people [was] being told ... by international speculators, that the policies on which we had fought the election could not be implemented* (Wilson, 1971, p65).

The structural constraints imposed on all governments in capitalist societies

Marxists also point to the in-built, structural constraints that force all governments in capitalist societies to introduce pro-business policies, irrespective of the social origins of the state elite, or their political allegiances. To quote Miliband (1977, p72), *There are structural constraints which no government, whatever its complexion, wishes and promises, can ignore or evade. A capitalist economy has its own rationality to which any government and state must sooner or later submit, and usually sooner*. In a sense, Miliband is right. Governments in capitalist countries such as Britain – whether left or right wing – are presiding over economies that are closely integrated into the world capitalist system, and the success or failure of these economies depends upon their ability to attract investment and compete. In such a capitalist context any reform is bound to be limited to measures which enhance, or certainly do not threaten, the economic efficiency and profitability of businesses. Thus, to give one hypothetical (and perhaps extreme) example, a UK government may wish to introduce a minimum wage of £200 per hour, but to do so in the context of a world capitalist economic system would be economic suicide. Such a policy would increase the costs of UK businesses dramatically, affecting their ability to compete with lower-waged countries, potentially leading to job losses and crippling the economy. In this sense, the system itself constrains governments to act in a way that promotes business interests.

Marxism and welfare

If, as Marxists assert, the state always acts in the interests of capital, why does it fund and provide welfare services that ostensibly help the poor, the marginalised and the vulnerable? This was a question that Marxist-influenced social policy academics sought to answer in the 1960s, when we saw the development of an explicitly Marxist critique of the welfare state. This critique sought to demystify social policies, aiming to shatter the notion that the welfare state was motivated by humanitarian sentiment. In doing so, Marxists drew attention to the 'legitimation' and 'accumulation' functions of welfare.

Legitimation functions of welfare

By 'legitimation', Marxists meant that the welfare state served an ideological role, creating the image of a caring capitalism that is interested in the welfare of its citizens. Marxists noted that welfare had historically been presented as the compassionate, civilised face of capitalism, and was genuinely seen by many as an example of society's preparedness to care for and support some of the most vulnerable members of society. In this sense, welfare provided legitimacy to existing exploitative economic and political arrangements, acting as an ideological smokescreen. It detracted attention from the exploitative nature of capitalism, and the fact that workers' interests lay in its overthrow.

Accumulation functions of welfare

Welfare was also said to perform a crucial 'accumulation' function in that it served to enhance profits. For example, education and health care systems helped maintain a relatively healthy and educated workforce, key prerequisites for modern capitalist societies. Likewise, social security systems ensured that redundant workers were fed, maintained and disciplined at the public's expense, providing employers with an acquiescent 'reserve army of labour' when necessary. Those who did stray from the 'straight and narrow' would be subjected to targeted interventions from social workers and other welfare professionals, with a view to 'reintegrating' them into society. Put simply, by providing employers with an appropriately educated, healthy and disciplined workforce, welfare states in capitalist societies actively promoted business interests.

Radical social work

The emergence of radical social work theory in the 1970s was one example of the growing influence of Marxism within academic, activist and practitioner circles. While other theoretical traditions could be found within radical social work, most of those who embraced it were socialists, attracted to the movement because of its commitment to revolutionary change. The publication of Bailey and Brake's seminal text, *Radical social work* (1975), is seen as a formative moment in the development of the movement. It represented a devastating critique of British social work, and at the same time it sought to map out a radical approach for future social work practice. A key premise of the radical social work movement was the notion that social democratic welfare strategies in capitalist societies were always doomed to failure. The capitalist economic system itself was the cause of inequality and oppression, and until this was abolished social justice and equality could never be achieved. The ruling class and its representatives within the state apparatus might be prepared to grant concessions to workers in the form of piecemeal welfare policies, particularly in periods of economic boom and high employment. However, these reforms were inadequate, tentative, and always at risk of reversal in less certain economic times. Moreover, they could never be sufficient to meet need. *The idea of the state as a neutral arbiter between different sections of society was,* it was argued, *wholly inadequate*, and there was a need to appreciate the extent to which social reform, and indeed social work itself, was shaped with a view to safeguarding *the interests and development of British capitalism* (Case Con Manifesto, 1975, p146).

Those influenced by radical social work called for a critical reappraisal of the nature and role of social work in capitalist societies. There was, they argued, a need to eliminate oppressive pathological casework approaches from social work practice and acknowledge the fact that *for most of the working-class material deprivation lies behind many of their problems* (Bailey and Brake, 1975, p9). Hence, the traditional casework method was dismissed as a *pseudo science – that blames individual inadequacies for poverty and so mystifies and diverts attention from the real causes – slums, homelessness and economic exploitation* (Case Con Manifesto, 1975). In addition, the myth of the 'caring' welfare state needed to be challenged, and the social control element of social work – the extent that it sought to manipulate and control the unwitting casualties of capitalism – had to be confronted. It was also important to acknowledge the limitations of social work; that is, the extent to which social workers themselves were *trapped in a social structure which severely delimits their power and hence their ability to initiate significant change* (Bailey and Brake, 1980, pp7–8).

Social work training was also targeted for specific criticism. According to Pearson (1975, pp34–6), social workers, were provided with a *prepacked work problem*, because their training failed to provide them with an awareness of the limitations of reform under capitalism. He argued that social work training was *punctuated by bad promises*, because it misleadingly offered a *spirit of hopefulness and betterment* and the vacuous promise of a *germ of advancement in capitalist society*. It put forward *a professional vision of a promised land of social welfare before the eyes of its recruits which is shattered in the world of work*. Training courses encouraged students to *act on the ideals of social work in a less than ideal world*, neglecting to impress on them the constraints on their actions imposed by the economic system itself. There was therefore a need, according to Leonard (1975, p49), for social workers to be aware of *the pathology of wider economic and political structures*. As long as capitalism existed, social workers could be little more than *social bandits, noble robbers*, or Robin Hood-like characters, blindly groping against social injustice. They were, Pearson argued (1975, p40), taught to *oppose injustice not by struggling for the defeat of injustice, but by getting round the edges of it* and their practical function was *at best to impose certain limits to traditional oppression in traditional society*.

Finally, there was a more optimistic strand to radical social work, which emphasised the social worker's role both in mitigating individual suffering caused by capitalism, and as a vanguard of revolutionary change. Regarding this latter point, social workers should, Leonard (1975, p57) argued, seek to play a crucial educational role, developing among themselves, other professionals and users of welfare services, *a critical consciousness of their oppression, and of their potential*. Clearly, they needed to help alleviate immediate suffering, but their long-term objective should be to actively fight for revolutionary change. Here is an extract from the Case Con Manifesto (1975, p147), which constituted a statement of political aims that many supporters of radical social work adhered to:

> *Case Con believes that the problems of our clients are rooted in the society in which we live, not in individual inadequacies. Until this society, based on private ownership, profit and the needs of a minority ruling class, is replaced by a workers' state, based on the interests of the vast majority of the population, the fundamental causes of social problems will remain. It is therefore our aim to join the struggle for the workers' state.*

One of the main criticisms radical social work faced was its emphasis upon the need for revolutionary change and its alleged failure to appreciate the importance of tackling injustice in the 'here and now'. It was, some argued, all fine and well for radicals to place their efforts into generating revolutionary ferment, but what about the social and economic well-being of service users in the meantime? As Pearlman, a contemporary critic of the movement, stated, *Man runs his short life span in six or seven decades. He should not have to wait – suffering, struggling, withering, as the case may be – while the wheels of social justice grind out social change* (cited in Pearson, 1975, p35). Linked to this criticism was the allegation that radical social work rarely moved beyond a critical mode, and that with the exception of proposals for revolutionary change, it offered little in the way of a practical programme for a progressive alternative. Radical social work was also accused of being gender and race blind, and of overly focusing on ruling-class oppression, at the expense of racist and sexist practices.

Langan and Lee, in their reappraisal of the impact of radical social work, accept that there is an element of justification to some of these criticisms, but their overall assessment of the impact and legacy of radical social work is overwhelmingly positive. The socialist 'workers' state' may not have been achieved, but radical social work's powerful critique of pathological casework techniques, as well as the primacy it gave to user involvement and structural explanations for the difficulties facing service users, constituted an enormously positive contribution to the future shape of social work train-ing and practice. According to Langan and Lee (1989, p2), the movement was a jolt to the complacency of a profession that was beginning to insulate itself from the essen-tially political nature of its tasks, and *many of the attitudes and values of the radical movement entered mainstream practice*. Nor should we think of Marxism or radical social work as being a distant phenomenon; a peculiar characteristic of the 1960s and 1970s. Recent years, for example, have seen the publication of a range of social policy and social work texts written from a radical, Marxist perspective, as well as the emer-gence of a practitioner movement – the Social Work Action Network (SWAN) – committed to pursuing many of the original radicals' aims.

This 'new' variant of radical social work shares many of the concerns that motivated the 'original' radicals, in particular their desire to transcend capitalism and move towards a more equal, socialist society. Like their predecessors, they emphasise the need for social workers to avoid and challenge pathological, neo-liberal interpretations for disadvan-tage, and to acknowledge the structural causes of the oppression that service users' face. They also articulate a strategy for a 'here and now' defence of the social work value base against what they see as the corrosive impact of neo-liberalism, which, they argue, has exacerbated pre-existing tendencies towards greater marginalisation and inequality. The 'new' radicals call upon social workers to 'reclaim' a political dimension to their practice, and to resist and oppose initiatives that undermine progressive work with service users. Indeed, Ferguson and Woodward (2009, p159), have encouraged social workers to perceive themselves *outlaws* engaging in *guerrilla warfare* against neo-liberal pressures to stigmatise service users and ration provision. While acknowl-edging the practical, organisational constraints that may make such *guerrilla warfare* difficult, they argue that social workers *need to be much more vocal, both about the way social policies are impacting on the lives of their clients and also about the value (as well as the limits) of their own role* (Ferguson, 2008, p136). Social workers also need to seek to build alliances and coalitions with the other radical, progressive groups, professions and movements that are challenging the neo-liberal trajectory of policy. Most of all, they should aim to promote *a modern engaged social work based around such core 'anti-capitalist' values as democracy, solidarity, accountability, participation, justice, equality, liberty and diversity* (Jones et al., 2004). According to Ferguson (2008, p136), it is only then that *social work can finally stop being a 'quiet profession' and can begin to play its proper role in the struggle for a more equal, more just society*.

ACTIVITY **6.2**

*In this activity we want you to reflect on some of the themes and debates that we have covered in this chapter. Firstly, download the SWAN's Manifesto for a new engaged practice (**http://www.socialworkfuture.org/**). Once you have done this, try answering the following questions.*

- *Can you detect a Marxist/radical social work influence in the* Manifesto?

- *What do you think of the* Manifesto *and how might its principles be translated into practice?*

CHAPTER SUMMARY

As we have seen in this and previous chapters, by late 1960s, there was a general feeling across the political spectrum that the social democratic welfare state had failed to deliver the 'New Jerusalem' promised by its architects. The evolution of Marxist interpretations of social policy and social work can be traced back to this period. Although Marxists agreed with many of the aims of social democrats – in particular, the creation of a more equal, socialist society built upon the principles of fairness and egalitarianism – they rejected social democratic strategies for achieving these objectives. As we saw in Chapter 4, social democrats believe that it is possible to reform capitalism from 'within' and for a benevolent, social democratic government to create a 'better world' through the enactment of progressive social reform. Marxists dismiss such claims, highlighting what they see as the powerful, entrenched bourgeois forces within the state apparatus which, they argue, will frustrate, check and dilute attempts to create a more equal society. At the same time, they argue that the structural constraints that capitalism imposes upon any government – the need to make profits and to compete with other capitalist countries – means that all governments, irrespective of their political orientation, are forced to introduce policies that are conducive to business interests. It is, Marxists insist, for these very reasons that ostensibly social democratic Labour governments have always failed to radically transform, or 'tame' capitalism. For Marxists, this also explains why welfare services have, ultimately, always had at their heart the promotion of the status quo rather than progressive economic and social change.

FURTHER READING

The following texts will be useful for those of you wishing to further explore Marxist interpretations of welfare:

Gough, I (1979) *The political economy of the welfare state*. London: Macmillan.

Ferguson, I, Lavalette, M and Mooney, G (2002) *Rethinking welfare: A critical perspective*. London: Sage.

The following two texts are seen as seminal in terms of the development of radical social work in the UK:

Bailey, R and Brake, M (1975) *Radical social work*. London: Edward Arnold.

Bailey, R and Brake, M (1980) *Radical social work and practice*. London: Edward Arnold.

These texts will be useful for those of you wishing to further explore more recent analyses written within a radical social work perspective:

Ferguson, I (2008) *Reclaiming social work: Challenging neo-liberalism and promoting social justice*. London: Sage.

Ferguson, I and Woodward, R (2009) *Radical social work in practice: Making a difference*. Bristol: Policy Press.

Lavalette, M (ed.) (2011) *Radical social work today: Social work at the crossroads*. Bristol: Policy Press.

PART TWO
SOCIAL POLICY, SOCIAL WORK AND SERVICE USERS

Chapter 7
Children, social policy and social work

This chapter will help you begin to meet the following National Occupational Standards.

Key Role 1: Prepare for, and work with individuals, families, carers, groups and communities to assess their needs and circumstances.

- Work with individuals, families, carers, groups and communities to enable them to assess and make informed decisions about their needs, circumstances, risks, preferred options and resources.

Key Role 2: Plan, carry out, review and evaluate social work practice, with individuals, families, carers, groups, communities and other professionals.

- Apply and justify social work methods and models used to achieve change and development, and improve life opportunities.

Key Role 3: Support individuals to represent their needs, views and circumstances.

- Advocate for, and with, individuals, families, carers, groups and communities.

Key Role 4: Manage risk to individuals, families, carers, groups communities, self and colleagues.

- Balance the rights and responsibilities of individuals, families, carers, groups and communities with associated risk.

Key Role 6: Demonstrate professional competence in social work practice.

- Use professional and organisational supervision and support to research, critically analyse, and review knowledge based practice.
- Identify and assess issues, dilemmas and conflicts that might affect your practice. Contribute to policy review and development.

The chapter will also introduce you to the following academic standards which are set out in the 2008 QAA social work benchmark statements:

4.2 Defining principles.

4.3 Defining principles.

4.6 Defining principles.

4.7 Defining principles.

5.1.1 Subject knowledge, understanding and skills.

5.1. Subject knowledge, understanding and skills.

5.1.3 Values and ethics.

5.1.4 Social work theory.

5.1.5 The nature of social work practice.

5.5.1 Manage problem solving activities.

5.5.3 Analysis and synthesis.

6.2 Teaching learning and assessment.

7.3 Knowledge and understanding.

Introduction

Children have been at the forefront of social policy and social work practice developments over the past decade. Within social work, the Victoria Climbié inquiry and more recently the Baby Peter Connelly case have placed a very public spotlight on social workers' attempts to safeguard children. However, in this chapter we argue that overly concentrating on 'safeguarding' and 'protection' can serve to divert attention away from the pressing need to address other factors that impinge upon children's life chances, such as poverty, poor educational opportunity and health inequalities. As future practitioners who may be working with children, it is crucial that you possess an awareness of this wider societal context that shapes children's lives. This chapter examines the UK's record on children's welfare, examining the wider social policy developments that shape the environments within which children live. We begin by discussing the emphasis that is placed upon issues relating to child protection in narratives on children's welfare. We then seek to introduce you to a broader conception of children's welfare, focusing upon wider structural determinants that impact upon their well-being.

Child protection or children's welfare?

Hardly a month goes by without some exposé of child abuse or neglect in the media. Clearly some cases achieve more prominence than others, but issues relating to the safeguarding and protection of children dominate media and political commentaries around children's welfare. Regarding the media, our own analysis of newspaper sources found that in the 12 months prior to 18 July 2011, UK national newspapers published almost 800 substantive articles on 'child abuse', 'child neglect' or 'child protection'. By contrast, during the same period, only around 100 substantive articles discussed 'child poverty', despite its long-standing recognition as a problem that blights the life chances of millions of UK children.

To an extent, the emphasis the media place upon 'child abuse' is understandable. As we have seen with the Victoria Climbié and Baby Peter Connelly cases, the tragic circumstances surrounding many child protection cases are newsworthy. These two child deaths were the subject of detailed public inquiries, generating a huge amount of media, political and public interest. Indeed, the names of the children concerned are now recognisable to even those with the most fleeting knowledge of social policy and social work. At the time of writing, the Baby Peter Connelly case alone had been the focus of over 2,500 substantive national newspaper articles. Naturally, the horrifying catalogue of neglect documented in these articles has the propensity to shock, and it is easy to see why child abuse as an issue resonates with the general public and politicians.

Nor, of course, should we underestimate the extent of child abuse and neglect, or their seriousness as problems. As Lord Laming's 2009 report showed, on 31 March 2008, 29,000 out of 11 million children in England had child protection plans in place and 37,000 were the subject of care orders. Laming also estimated that in 2007/08, 55 children were killed by their parents or somebody known to the child. Clearly, it is a tragedy when any child is put at risk, seriously injured, or dies unnecessarily as a result of neglect or intent to cause harm. However, the cumulative emphasis placed upon child protection by the media, social commentators and politicians helps to create and sustain the impression that extreme child abuse and neglect are a growing problem, and indeed the most important issue affecting children's welfare. There are two points to be made here.

Firstly, this impression is contradicted by evidence showing that significant improvements have been made in tackling the worst forms of child neglect. As Polly Toynbee pointed out in the wake of the Baby Peter Connelly case:

> ... the number of children killed has fallen steadily – down 50 percent in England and Wales since the 1970s ... Britain was fourth worst among Western nations in the 1970s. Now it is among the best: only four countries have fewer child murders per million. Compare America, where child murders have risen by 17 percent since the 1970s.

> (Toynbee, 2008, p35)

Secondly, the 'skewed' focus upon abuse and neglect means that other narratives, such as those which emphasise the damaging impact of poverty, poor educational opportunity, and health inequalities on children's welfare are 'crowded out'. The promotion of children's welfare is reduced to a concentration on 'abuse' and 'neglect', with little space given to the possibility that poor outcomes for most children are a result of structural problems that are largely beyond parental control. We are left with a one-sided account that ignores a whole range of other crucial variables that impact upon children's well-being. The continued existence of these endemic social problems does, some argue, represent a form of 'abuse' that is actually far more harmful to children than the physical dangers they face from parents, relatives or strangers. Lavalette and Ferguson (2009), for example, argue that:

> children in Britain continue to face all manner of societal abuse. The evidence shows that Britain, in comparison to other economically advanced countries, is failing its children. It also shows that the lives of poor and working class children are worse, more restrictive and more dangerous than their middle class peers on every front.

The media, the welfare state and child protection

In the section above, we hinted at the disproportionate emphasis the media place on child abuse, neglect and protection when they publish stories on children's welfare. However, it is not just the media's over-concentration on these issues that is potentially problematic. We also need to assess whether the nature and content of the material published impact upon how issues relating to children's welfare are perceived. Likewise, it is important to consider whether the way the media report child neglect cases may influence the way people think more generally about the legitimacy of the welfare state and its impact upon recipients of services.

In fact, the media's portrayal of child abuse and neglect is rarely balanced. As with the reporting of welfare news generally, there is a tendency to focus on the more lurid, scandalous elements of stories, in a way that undermines support for the principles underpinning welfare. The impression given is that of a welfare state that corrupts families, destroys personal responsibility and acts to the detriment rather than the benefit of children's interests. Analyses into the media's portrayal of welfare news have shown that this picture is not inadvertent or accidental; rather it part of an orchestrated attempt to manage welfare news in a way that corresponds with the media's own material interests and ideological allegiances.

The media and 'welfare'

Studies conducted into the media and welfare emphasise the extent to which media organisations tend to look for certain 'triggers' when choosing what issues to cover, focusing on aspects of stories that are most likely to boost sales, and/or which reinforce their own ideological positions. Newspaper editors, for instance, are well aware that lurid headlines sell newspapers and they carefully filter their welfare-related news accordingly. A link to crime, fraud and/or sex, and an ability to apportion blame will increase the likelihood of publication, as will the ability to identify 'villains' and to link issues to wider social ills (Brindle, 1999). As one journalist who specialises in welfare-related news stories has put it:

> A good story – contrary to popular social work belief – is not about some worthy policy development, practice initiative or social services personality. It is about raw emotion, disagreement between professionals and, best of all, culpability.

> (Fry, cited in Brindle, 1999, p43)

The reporting of social policy issues is also shaped by the ideological predications of particular news corporations. UK newspapers, least of all the tabloid variety, are not renowned for their sympathy for either welfare recipients or welfare professionals. Those in receipt of state welfare are invariably portrayed as selfish scroungers, fraudsters and feckless deviants, while those who administer services (including social workers) tend to be depicted as self-serving, 'bungling', politically correct bureaucrats. This portrayal of welfare recipients has a long historical pedigree and despite it invariably being based upon inaccuracies, partial truths and wildly inflated generalisations, it continues to resonate with the wider public (Golding and Middleton, 1981).

The media and child protection

In this context, it is easy to see the appeal of child abuse, neglect and protection stories to news editors. They invariably hit all the 'triggers' that constitute a 'good' welfare story, providing lurid, compelling, sensational copy that appeals to the more voyeuristic instincts of their readers. There are, for example, no shortages of 'villains' to blame, whether these are the 'evil' perpetrators of abuse, or the 'neglectful' social workers who are said to have failed in their duty to protect children. Reporters are also often able to tenuously link the issue to wider social malaise, and the claim is often made that particular cases of abuse or neglect are representative of much wider problem of declining morals, or the 'broken society'.

The media's coverage of child protection cases can also often be structured in a way that links into the anti-welfare bias of particular newspapers, adding to their appeal. The reporting of the high-profile Sharon Mathews case was fairly typical in this respect. Sharon's mother, Karen Mathews, had faked the kidnapping of her daughter, allegedly in order to profit from a reward when her daughter was found. The media reacted with predictable outrage when it discovered that Karen had numerous children while 'on welfare'. As has happened in previous cases, 'welfare' was seen to lie at the heart of Britain's 'child abuse problem'. Melanie Phillips (2008, p12), a columnist in the *Daily Mail,* claimed the case was *but the latest of a series of child abuse horrors which have left people aghast at Britain's culture of brutishness and its link with welfare dependency*. It was clear, according to Phillips, that *child benefit, and all the multifarious other welfare incentives to irresponsibility, are intrinsically linked to the emergence of households where, in truth, civilisation has given way to barbarism*. As the following extract on the Baby Peter Connelly case from *The Times* illustrates, such interpretations of child abuse are not uncommon even in the more 'serious-minded' sections of the media:

> *The unspeakable case of Baby P raises profound questions about the state of Britain today. The welfare state has created some communities with no morality ... The story of Baby P is one that will haunt Britain for years to come. But for some, its message is already all too clear: that this has become a country where the State's largesse can be a lifelong livelihood; where parents can have as many children with as many partners as they please without feeling obliged to care for any of them.*

(The Times, 2008, p37)

This portrayal of child protection cases has a significance that stretches well beyond social work practice. Although the 'incompetence' and 'political correctness' of social workers themselves are often the target of such articles, it is the welfare state itself that is in the 'eye of the storm'. In this sense, we can perhaps see the appeal of this interpretation of child abuse and neglect to neo-liberals, who are ideologically committed to the retrenchment of state welfare. It seems to provide corroboration to their claims that welfare is a morally corrupting influence, which seduces recipients into lives of deviancy and dysfunctionality. Indeed, what more shocking justification for retrenching welfare can there be than the claim that it contributes to child abuse and neglect?

The policy-making implications of this kind of an approach are clear. Cuts in social security to families are thus portrayed as being necessary and in the interests of society, families and children themselves. In relation to social work practice, progressive, community development and family support-based initiatives are dismissed as counter-productive distractions from the 'real' role of social work – the policing of 'abuse' and 'neglect'. At the same time, demands are made for a radical overhaul of social work training, and for a renewed focus to be placed upon the need for social workers to be equipped to detect and address the immoral behaviour of 'feckless' families and their 'feral' children.

As we discuss below, there is no empirical evidence linking welfare dependency with 'abuse'. Nonetheless, this interpretation is now rarely challenged in the mainstream media, or by large sections of the public, whose critical faculties have become desensitised by the dramatised presentation and shocking images associated with particular tragic cases. We would, though, caution you to view this interpretation of child abuse and neglect through a more critical lens. The assumptions that seem to underpin it, that the best way to promote children's welfare is to reduce the financial support available to needy families and to adopt a more disciplinary, moralistic form of social work, are clearly problematic.

Child neglect and welfare

Claims that child neglect and abuse are a consequence of 'lavish', over-generous welfare are simply not borne out by the evidence. As the Child Poverty Action Group argued in response to media suggestions of a link between the Baby Peter Connelly case and welfare dependency, *there is no evidential basis for suggestions that the welfare state has made such appalling cases more common*:

> *No domestic correlation exists between the number of benefit claimants and infanticide. Internationally, there is no evidence linking countries with the best welfare provision to higher rates of child abuse and infanticide. The legacy of the welfare state is the protection of millions of children from suffering caused by homelessness, hunger, sickness and disability. Without the welfare state child protection would be far worse.*

(Green, 1999, p37)

In fact, contrary to popular perceptions, the UK's benefit system is one of the least generous among all developed countries (see below). If there was a correlation between generous welfare support and child abuse, we would expect to find soaring rates of neglect in Scandinavian nations, where welfare really is set at relatively generous levels. This is not the case. Indeed, as we discuss later, research shows that Scandinavian countries are characterised by the highest levels of child well-being.

In the next section we want to broaden our analysis of child well-being, moving away from a focus on 'abuse' and 'neglect', towards a more rounded appreciation of the many different factors that can impact upon outcomes for children. As the United Nations Children's Fund (UNICEF) argue, any effective assessment of child well-being must involve a much broader analysis of factors other than 'safeguarding' and 'protection', and include other indicators such as poverty, educational opportunities and risk behaviours (UNICEF, 2007).

Child well-being in the UK

You would be forgiven for thinking that the UK has a strong record in terms of the provision it makes for children's welfare, given the multitude of measures and proce- dures that exist to safeguard and protect children from physical harm. Indeed, some commentators argue that our children are 'too protected' and 'mollycoddled' and that their development is seriously hampered by a combination of risk-averse social policy and the 'paranoid parenting' of overbearing, anxiety-ridden parents. These two mutually reinforcing traits are said to have created an environment which has fru- strated and stifled children's sense of adventure and independence (Furedi, 2002). Certainly, as we have already discussed, as a society we do place a disproportionate emphasis upon the need to protect children from harm, and this does have wider implications, not least for social policy and social work practice.

However, in this chapter we are seeking to move beyond a narrow conception of children's welfare which sees it as being primarily about 'safeguarding' and 'protec- tion'. If we adopt a much wider definition of child well-being – such as that utilised by UNICEF – we find that the UK's record is far from adequate. Indeed, comparative welfare studies have consistently shown it to be one of the worst in the developed world. UNICEF's 2007 report, *An overview of child well-being in rich countries,* posi- tioned the UK at the bottom of the organisation's league table of child well-being in developed OECD nations. The UNICEF study was based upon an analysis of a number of social and economic indicators in each country, including:

- lack of material well-being, or child poverty;
- health and safety of children;
- children's educational well-being and opportunities;
- children's risk behaviours.

We examine the UK's record on each of these four indicators below.

Lack of material well-being, or child poverty

According to UNICEF, a lack of material well-being is one of the key factors detrimen- tally affecting children's lives. Poverty, more than any other variable, presents a *decided and demonstrable disadvantage* to children, because it is so closely linked to other social problems:

> *Poverty ... affects many aspects of child well-being in many well-documented ways: particularly when prolonged, poverty has been shown to be likely to have an effect on children's health, cognitive development, achievement at school, aspirations, self-perceptions, relationships, risk behaviours and employment prospects.*

> (UNICEF, 2007, p39)

International surveys have consistently shown the UK to have one of the developed world's worst child-poverty records. UNICEF's (2000) *A league table of child poverty in rich nations*, placed the UK 20th out of 23 in its child-poverty rankings, with only Italy,

Mexico and the United States having worse records. A follow-up UNICEF (2005) survey of 26 'rich' nations found that the UK had the 20th worst record. In all, 27 per cent of children were living in households with below 60 per cent of median income (the definition of poverty chosen), compared with 7.5 per cent in Norway, 8 per cent in Finland and 9.2 per cent in Sweden. Despite some very slight improvements in the UK's child-poverty rate, its record remains one of the worst in the European Union (EU). One 2010 survey commissioned by the European Commission ranked the UK 21st out of 26 EU nations (TARKI Social Research Institute, 2010).

There does, in fact, seem to be a consensus in the UK that poverty has a profound harmful effect on the immediate and future life chances of children. For example, the previous Labour government's commitment to eradicating child poverty by 2020 was based upon an acknowledgement of its harmful impact. Labour ministers described child poverty as one of the most corrosive issues facing the country. It seems that neo-liberal ministers in the current coalition government, such as the Conservative, Michael Gove (2009), share these concerns:

> *Child poverty today remains a terrible blight. It is a reproach to all of us that so many children should be growing up in homes deprived not just of the resources which allow them to play a full and equal part in our society but of the basic security they need to live free of fear.*

Of course, while there is something of a political consensus over consequences of child poverty and its implications, there is little agreement as to its causes, or the solutions that should be adopted to reduce its incidence and tackle its symptoms. We will examine these differences later.

Health and safety of children

The UK's record on securing the health and safety of its children – assessed by a comparison of indicators related to deaths from accidents and injuries (including murder and violence), infant mortality rates and low birth weights – is more mixed. Interestingly, its record on deaths from accidents and injuries is very good. UNICEF ranks it second best out of 25 OECD nations it has surveyed. Indeed, the UK is only one of four countries, the others being Sweden, the Netherlands and Italy, that have *reduced the incidence of deaths from accidents and injuries to the remarkably low level of fewer than 10 per 100,000* (UNICEF, 2007, p15). These findings corroborate the point we made earlier about the UK's improved record on reducing child deaths from neglect or abuse.

However, the UK performs poorly on a whole range of other child health indicators. For instance, it possesses some of the worst records in the developed world on birth weights and infant mortality. In the UK, around 7.5 per cent of babies weigh less than 2,500g at birth, whereas the equivalent rates for Sweden, Norway, Finland and Iceland are below 5 per cent. As UNICEF note, low birth weight has been linked not only to increased risk to life and ill health in the early stages of life, but also to longer-term cognitive and physical development. The UK's infant mortality rate also lags behind that of many other developed nations. UNICEF ranks its performance at 20th out of 25 OECD nations. Its rate of just over 5 per 1,000 live births is twice that of Iceland's (just over 2 per 1,000) and almost twice as high as other Scandinavian countries such as Sweden and Finland (both with rates of around 3 per 1,000). As UNICEF (2007, p13) point out, the infant mortality rate is one of the most commonly used and widely accepted indicators of child health. It reflects a basic provision of the Convention on the Rights of the Child, which calls on all countries *to ensure the child's enjoyment of the highest attainable standard of health, including by diminishing infant and child mortality*. The UK's relatively high levels of infant mortality are, therefore, deeply concerning.

RESEARCH SUMMARY

The links between infant mortality and material well-being

In England and Wales alone, 3,281 children died before reaching their first birthdays in 2008 (Office for National Statistics, 2010a). All the evidence suggests that these deaths do not occur 'randomly' and that there is a direct correlation between infant mortality and material disadvantage. For instance, infant mortality rates across the UK are not uniform – they vary geographically and by social class. Regarding geographical variations, the rates are significantly higher in deprived areas than in non-deprived areas. Babies born in the most deprived areas in England and Wales are six times more likely to die in infancy than those born in other areas. The difference is even higher in some districts. In relatively deprived Bradford in West Yorkshire, the infant mortality rate is seven times higher (9.1 per 1,000 births) than the relatively affluent Yorkshire town of Selby, which is less than 40 miles away (1.3 per 1,000 births) (Bradford District Infant Mortality Commission, 2006, p21). We also find that the infant mortality rate for babies with fathers in lower-paid 'routine' occupations is around twice that for those in higher paid managerial occupations (Office for National Statistics, 2010a).

All the evidence, therefore, points to infant mortality and low income or poverty being strongly linked. Indeed, the Department of Health (2007) has acknowledged this. Its Good practice guide for reducing infant mortality emphasises the need to tackle child poverty and to provide adequate financial support for families. This approach is supported by research that has been undertaken into infant mortality rates in particularly deprived areas, which suggests that tackling poverty – by improving incomes – is the most effective mechanism of cutting infant deaths. One such study undertaken in Bradford concluded that equalising incomes across the district would have led to 78 per cent fewer infant deaths, saving the lives of around 55 children annually (Bradford District Infant Mortality Commission, 2006). Just to put this into context, this is roughly equivalent to the total number of children who are killed each year by their parents and relatives across the whole of England and Wales. These data, linking infant mortality with poverty, seem to corroborate UNICEF's claim that there is a direct link between low levels of material well-being and more general poor outcomes for children.

Educational opportunity and well-being

Educational opportunity is another key indicator of child well-being. Once again the UK's record on this is not good. In fact, UNICEF's (2007) league table of educational well-being ranks the UK's performance as 20th out of 25 developed nations. A key contributory factor in this low ranking is the UK's relatively high level of educational inequality. In fact, research has consistently shown that the UK's education system is characterised by significant social class variations in attainment. Poor children tend to perform less well academically and gain fewer educational qualifications than their more affluent peers. Indeed, the evidence suggests that poverty impacts upon children's cognitive abilities well before school age, and clear differences between the poorest fifth of children and others are evident when children are as young as three (Goodman and Gregg, 2010). Inequalities in educational attainment in the UK become more pronounced once children attain school age, continuing to deteriorate as they progress through their school careers. At age 11, 25 per cent of children from the poorest fifth of families fail to achieve the government's expected levels at Key Stage 2, compared to only 3 per cent of children from the most affluent fifth. Poverty continues to blight the opportunities of children at secondary schools. Only approximately 21 per cent of the poorest fifth of children receive five A*-C GCSEs, compared with 75 per cent of the richest fifth of children, an alarming 54 percentage point difference (Goodman and Gregg, 2010).

The UK also performs poorly on many other indicators of educational well-being, including the percentage of 15–19s remaining in education. For example, only around 76 per cent of 15–19 year olds in the UK are involved in full- or part-time education, considerably fewer than their peers in most other OECD countries. In Belgium, 95 per cent of children are, and numbers approaching 90 per cent can be found in Germany, France, Sweden, Finland and Norway. The percentage of UK 15–19 year olds who were not in education, employment and training (NEET) is also worryingly high. In all, almost 10 per cent are NEET, compared with less than 5 per cent in Norway, Denmark, Sweden, Germany and the Netherlands. As UNICEF (2007) state, these children were *clearly at greater risk of exclusion or marginalisation.* Again, the data we have presented here seem to confirm UNICEF's claim that poverty shapes wider aspects of children's well-being.

Children's risk behaviours

UNICEF (2007, p27) describe children's 'risk behaviours', such as substance misuse, experience of violence outside the home, and early pregnancy as *an important and elusive dimension of child well-being.* Once again, the UK's record on such indicators lags behind that of many other developed countries. In fact, according to UNICEF, the UK has the worst record on *risk behaviours* out of all the nations it has surveyed. Early pregnancy is seen as one of the key areas of risk and the UK's teenage conception rate is considerably worse than most other developed countries. Its rate of around 27 per 1,000 live births, is significantly higher than other countries, such as the Netherlands, Denmark, Sweden and Finland, all of which have rates of less than 10 per 1,000 live births.

RESEARCH SUMMARY

Material disadvantage and teenage pregnancy

The links between material disadvantage and teenage pregnancy are now well established. As with infant mortality rates, there is a close link between the incidence of teenage pregnancy and area deprivation. The Labour government's Social Exclusion Unit estimated that teenage pregnancy rates in the poorest areas in England were more than six times those found in the most affluent areas. Data on the social backgrounds of teenagers who become pregnant seem to confirm this link. One estimate suggests that the risk of becoming a teenage mother is almost ten times higher for a girl born into unskilled manual family than a professional one (Cater and Coleman, 2006).

International comparative data on teenage pregnancy provide further corroboration of the links between poverty and teenage pregnancy. As Wilkinson and Pickett (2010) have shown, the highest teenage pregnancy rates are found in those nations with the highest levels of poverty. Hence, the UK and the US have particularly poor records. By contrast, countries with the lowest levels of teenage pregnancy, such as Sweden and the Netherlands, are those that are characterised by much lower levels of inequality and poverty.

ACTIVITY 7.1

In this group activity, we want you to discuss among yourselves the following questions.

- *How surprised are you at the UK's record on children's well-being?*

- *Do you think a consideration of such issues is of relevance to you as students wishing to work in a welfare or social work-related field?*

- *Linking back to our discussion of ideologies in Chapters 3 to 6, briefly try to sketch out how you might think a neo-liberal explanation for the UK's poor record on child well-being might look like. How might this differ from a social democratic interpretation?*

COMMENT

Many of our students are often surprised when confronted with this child well-being data. To an extent, this is understandable. The UK is, after all, the world's fourth richest nation and hence it should be in a position to ensure that its children's social and economic needs are well catered for. However, children born in the UK are more likely than those in most other developed countries to die in infancy and to suffer from low birth rates. They do seem to engage in more risk behaviours and are also far more likely to be brought up in families that are materially poor.

An understanding of this broader context of child well-being is crucial to you as future social workers and welfare practitioners. On a practical level, on graduating many of you will be seeking to discourage vulnerable children from engaging in risk behaviours that you know will detrimentally affect their life chances and opportunities. You may also be working with disaffected young people who are finding it difficult to engage with

Continued

COMMENT *continued*

education, training or employment. In addition, many of you will undoubtedly encounter children who are living in materially disadvantaged families. As individuals who have chosen to pursue a social work or welfare related career, you must be curious as to why it is that children in the UK are more likely to be affected by these problems than those in most other developed countries. In short, you should be interested in these issues because they are directly relevant to your chosen career path.

We would, however, go further and argue that as future practitioners you have a duty to consider the wider environment within which the children you may be working with live their lives. Welfare and social work with children are concerned, primarily, with improving outcomes for children, and hence it would be negligent to ignore the many different variables that can affect their life chances and opportunities. Embracing this broader conception of child well-being can, of course, have important implications for practice. It may, for instance, lead to a questioning of the overarching emphasis that seems to be placed upon abuse and protection in debates on children's welfare, to the exclusion of other equally important factors.

Competing explanations for children's poor outcomes: Neo-liberalism versus social democracy

In the discussion below we examine two contrasting interpretations that have been advanced to account for the UK's relatively poor record on child well-being. The first is essentially a neo-liberal approach, which sees it as a consequence of welfare-induced dysfunctional patterns of behaviour within certain families. The second interpretation, which has more in common with social democratic approaches, seeks to draw attention to the impact of wider structural inequality on children's opportunities and life chances.

A neo-liberal approach to child well-being

Commenting on the UK's poor standing in UNICEF's league table of child well-being, David Cameron (2007), the current Prime Minister and leader of the Conservative Party, described the findings as *a clear call to action*. Cameron's analysis mirrored that of other conservative commentators, drawing strongly on traditional neo-liberal interpretations of social ills. The UK's poor record was, he argued, a consequence of an over-generous, bloated, administratively lax welfare system, which had:

- sapped individual responsibility and encouraged the emergence of an inter-generational dependency culture;
- encouraged the growth of 'dysfunctional', non-traditional family units and destroyed the traditional two-parent family.

We examine each of these claims in greater detail below.

The erosion of individual responsibility and the growth of welfare dependency

For many families, Cameron (2007) argues, *welfare has become a way of life – a generational pattern of dependence and unemployment which is a complete denial of the responsibility of adulthood.* Cameron believes that families are being seduced into a life 'on welfare'. Rather than supporting and nurturing themselves and their children independently through their own initiative, effort and hard work, parents are increasingly expecting the state to perform these functions, with devastating effects on children's well-being. Consequently, millions of children are growing up in households with relatively low incomes, where access to a benefit income is seen as a 'way of life'. Welfare is thus having a morally corrosive impact, encouraging parents to neglect their responsibilities for socialising children appropriately, meaning that they fail to discipline them, or instil in them a sense of right or wrong.

For neo-liberals such as Cameron, the psychological impact of this experience is just as damaging as its impact upon material living standards. Children in such families lack effective role models, and hence inherit their parents' dysfunctional, fatalistic outlooks on life. They disengage from education and emerge into adolescence without any sense of responsibility or work ethic, lacking aspiration or hope. This, more than anything, helps explains the UK's poor record on child well-being. Welfare has created a 'culture of dependency', which is passed down from one generation to the next, increasing the likelihood of children engaging behaviour that is deleterious to their well-being.

This approach has much in common with Charles Murray's influential neo-liberal explanation for the emergence of a so-called 'underclass' in Britain. According to Murray (1999, p26), the welfare state has created a scenario whereby *Britain has a growing population of working-aged, healthy people who live in a different world from other Britons, who are raising their children to live in it, and whose values are now contaminating the life of entire neighbourhoods* (p26). Murray's work inevitably attracts a great degree of controversy, but it has been politically influential. In policy terms, it helped shape the welfare reform strategies of successive Conservative governments in the 1980s and 1990s, which were geared towards cutting welfare and tightening eligibility. Murray's ideas also have much in common with the coalition's approach to welfare reform.

RESEARCH SUMMARY

Frank Field and 'The foundation years'
On entering government David Cameron commissioned Frank Field, a Labour MP and long-standing commentator on poverty-related issues, to undertake an inquiry into child poverty. Field is a former director of the Child Poverty Action Group and was previously a vociferous opponent of neo-liberal interpretations for poverty. In particular, he had been a fierce critic of Murray's 'underclass thesis', which he accused of ignoring the structural determinants of social and economic problems (see Field, 1989). However, in recent years, his position has changed. Field is now an enthusiastic proponent of behavioural
Continued

Frank Field and 'The foundation years' *continued*
explanations for disadvantage and social exclusion. This sea-change in Field's thinking is reflected in the report he produced for the coalition, The foundation years: Preventing poor children becoming poor adults *(2010), in which he rejected redistributive solutions for tackling child poverty:*

I no longer believed that the strategy of concentrating on income transfers could achieve the goal of abolishing child poverty … Something more fundamental than the scarcity of money is adversely dominating the lives of these children. Since 1969 I have witnessed a growing indifference from some parents to meeting the most basic needs of children, and particularly younger children, those who are least able to fend for themselves.

(p16)

Throughout the report, Field highlights the 'futility' of strategies for tackling child poverty that are geared towards boosting the incomes of the poor. It is, he argues, family background, parental education, good parenting … that together matter more to children than money, in determining whether their potential is realised in adult life (p5). He insists that any 'modern' approach to child poverty must take into account those children whose parents remain disengaged from their responsibilities (p15). The report chimed well with the Conservative-led coalition's desire to shift the focus away from structural determinants of child poverty towards interpretations that concentrate on 'problematic', 'irresponsible behaviour', and the 'perverse incentives' generated by the welfare state. Commenting on the report, Maria Miller, a Minister in the Department for Education (2010), stated that Labour's attempts to tackle child poverty by improving incomes had resulted in 5 million people trapped in welfare dependency, a benefits system which actually disincentivises work, and a complete failure to address the reasons behind so many children growing up in poverty. The report, she insisted, provided ample justification for the coalition's plans to engage in the most comprehensive and radical reform to the welfare system since its inception.

The growth of 'dysfunctional' family units and the 'destruction' of the two-parent family

The welfare state also stands accused by neo-liberals of destroying family life, once again to the detriment of children's interests. 'Profligate' welfare is said to have encouraged an explosion of family breakdown and lone parenthood, which in turn has led to greater levels of neglect and poorer outcomes for children. Underpinning this approach is the view that the traditional, heterosexual two-parent family is by far the most effective means of rearing and socialising children. In the words of David Cameron (2010), *children are more likely to do well when both parents are there for them, together providing the love and the discipline.* Indeed, he goes further, arguing that it is *the poverty of the parent-child experience* generated, in particular, by 'non-traditional' families *that leads to poor child outcomes rather than poverty of a material kind.*

The notion that lone parenthood is necessarily linked to poor levels of child well-being is an often repeated claim among right-wing commentators and politicians. James Bartholomew (2006, p275), for example, argues that children of lone-parent families are more likely to be depressed, emotionally and educationally stunted, to have under-age sex, to smoke, consume drugs and alcohol, to engage in criminal or violent disruptive behaviour, and to be vulnerable to physical and sexual abuse:

> *The epidemic of ruptured and never-formed families has ... caused misery for the children ... The lives of such children have been ruined and they, in turn, have damaged the safety and quality of life of others.*

> (p281)

As we saw in Chapter 2, this is not a novel argument. Similar claims about teenagers and other young women 'working the system' and being 'enticed' into lone parenthood by the prospect of lavish, morally corrupting welfare provision were made in the nineteenth century. The solutions proposed then – to end public support for lone mothers and 'let nature take its course' – are not too far removed to those advocated by many neo-liberals today. For example, Charles Murray's (1999, p127) demand for the elimination of benefits for unmarried women altogether, and for the state to *stop intervening and let economic penalties occur*, contains more than a faint whiff of the Malthusian principles we discussed in Chapter 2.

From this perspective, increasing the attractiveness of welfare payments will exacerbate the problems it is intended to solve and welfare-induced deviant patterns of behaviour will continue to be passed down to succeeding generations. The solution lies in a radical reform of the welfare state, involving cuts in support and a reinforcement of the notion of personal responsibility. Once again, we see links here between past and present debates about the role, function and impact of welfare provision. Indeed, the similarity between the statements made by neo-liberals today bear a striking resemblance to those made by the architects of the Poor Law Amendment Act in the 1830s.

Implications for social work

The acceptance of this neo-liberal interpretation for low levels of child well-being in the UK would clearly have implications for social work training and practice. The sociological and social policy content of social work courses would be rejected, in favour of a more moralistic syllabus, designed to teach student social workers the skills they need to imbue 'deviant' families with a strong sense of personal responsibility (Whelan, 2001). Hence, in advocating a model for the future, neo-liberals look backwards; to the late nineteenth and early twentieth-century work of the Charity Organisation Society (COS). Welfare, and more specifically social work, should be geared towards modifying behaviour, closely monitoring 'at risk' groups and 'educating' them in the habits of self-reliance and effective parenting. Indeed, some neo-liberals, such as David Marsland, have gone further, suggesting that social workers should be provided with powers to recommend irreversible sterilisation for 'at risk' groups such as alcoholics, drug addicts and the mentally disabled, who he feels are unfit to raise children effectively. He claims that this is the only effective way to prevent the abuse and neglect of children whose parents are incapable of looking after them:

> We have to prevent such people from abusing or gravely neglecting children ... Permanent sterilisation ... is the only way to reduce and control the killing, torture and neglect of our children. Decisions would be taken by and within the child protection system, involving social workers, the police and crucially and ultimately the courts.

(Marsland, 2010)

ACTIVITY 7.2

In April 2010, a US-based organisation, Project Prevention, was launched in the UK by Barbara Harris. It describes itself as an agency committed to raising public awareness to the problem of addicts/alcoholics exposing their unborn child to drugs during pregnancy. *Like Marsland, it is a vociferous advocate of sterilisation of drug users. Its tactics have involved outreach workers scouring inner cities for drug users and offering them £200 incentives to become 'voluntarily' sterilised. Its sister organisation in the US goes further, offering additional financial incentives to drug users who successfully 'refer a friend' for sterilisation.*

Like Marsland, Harris has encouraged social workers to embrace her organisation's approach, and to this end Project Prevention has distributed leaflets to social service departments in an attempt to educate social workers about the 'benefits' of its work. Sterilisation will, it argues, reduce the burden of this social problem on taxpayers, trim down social worker caseloads, and alleviate from our clients the burden of having children that will potentially be taken away *(Project Prevention, 2010).*

Not surprisingly, the organisation's work has generated a good degree of controversy, both in the US and the UK. In one incident, the police were called after its volunteers were found randomly harassing mothers leaving a health centre in Glasgow. Barbara Harris has sought to defend her organisation's strategy:

> We don't allow dogs to breed ... We spay them. We neuter them. We try to keep them from having unwanted puppies, and yet these women are literally having litters of children ... Women have told me about leaving their babies in a shoe-box in a crack den, selling their children to dealers for sex, even leaving babies in the trash – things so bad I can't even tell you ... I didn't know who I was more angry with – the mothers for having these children or the system for allowing it to happen ... If you pay a woman not to abuse a child, it's the best £200 you can spend ... These women have so many children that even if they do get clean they have more children than they can care for.

> (Swaine, 2010; Appleyard, 2010, p36)

Continued

In this task, we want you to engage in a group discussion about the strategy and aims of schemes such as those organised by Project Prevention. In particular, we would like you to critically analyse its work, and think of a number of reasons why such strategies may be inappropriate and counter-productive. You might want to consider the following questions.

- As future social work practitioners and welfare workers, how comfortable do you feel with the strategy adopted by Project Prevention? How might its strategy conflict with the social work value base?

- Does the 'voluntary' nature of the Project Prevention's strategy make it morally acceptable?

- Is there a danger that Project Prevention's work might lead for calls for sterilisation to be extended to other 'undesirable' groups of people?

COMMENT

Firstly, although the scheme is 'voluntary', there is the obvious question of whether drug users are in a sound state of mind when asked to make such a radical and (for the most part) irreversible step in their lives. So even if one accepts the validity of the highly contestable principle of 'sterilisation by consent', there is still a serious ethical issue over whether consent in what are often desperate, fraught circumstances can ever be seen as 'voluntary'. As Julian Shearer, the British Medical Association's (BMA's) Ethical Manager asks, Would the addiction render consent invalid? Is the payment a coercive means of getting people to agree to a sterilisation they would otherwise not contemplate? (Doward, 2010, p3). Critics fear that drug users coming into contact with Project Prevention run the very real risk of making fundamental, life-changing decisions that they would subsequently regret, to the detriment of their long-term psychological and emotional well-being.

Secondly, an implicit assumption underpinning Project Prevention's policy of sterilisation seems to be that current drug users are 'incurable' and cannot be trusted to be responsible parents in the future. What this ignores is that many drug-using parents often reduce their misuse, or often completely cease misusing drugs. Many inevitably go on to have children, providing them with caring and stable environments. Indeed, according to Martin Barnes, Chief Executive of DrugScope, for many parenthood has proved to be the catalyst for change, and been the powerful motivation to seek help with their addiction and other problems in their lives (Doward, 2010, p3).

Thirdly, Project Prevention's strategy is based upon the flawed assumption that all drug users are not responsible parents. While parenting can undoubtedly be affected by substance misuse, many children of drug-using parents do live happy, well-adjusted lives. One estimate suggests that around 200,000–300,000 children have parents with a serious drug problem, and around one half of these live with their parents, with the active support of social services (Forrester and Harwin, 2007). Hence, an approach based upon sterilising drug users not only ignores the fact that addiction is not incompatible with adequate parenting; it also carries with it the danger that attention and resources will be diverted away from the very necessary programmes of support needed by parents with

Continued

substance misuse problems, exacerbating the difficulties such families face. As the chief executive of the drugs and alcohol charity Addaction argues, It doesn't deal with addicts who are already parents, it doesn't help people recover and it doesn't offer any positive solution *(Davies, 2010, p11).*

Finally, if we accept the principle of sterilisation in the case of drug users, what rationale have we got for opposing calls from those such as Marsland for it to be extended to other so-called 'undesirable' groups? As Martin Barnes argues, Where should the line be drawn – women who drink? Women who smoke? Women with mental health problems? Women who themselves have been the victim of abuse? *(Doward, 2010, p3). Perhaps even women in living in poverty should also be sterilised? Bizarre though it may sound, this is the intention of another Project Prevention initiative, which is aimed at sterilising women in earthquake-hit Haiti, for no other reason than they are living in abject poverty. The women in Haiti, Harris states, are having children they can't even feed, so why are they getting pregnant? As an 'incentive' for them to sacrifice their fertility, her organisation intends to offer vulnerable, poverty-stricken women food vouchers (Kleeman, 2010, p14).*

Despite Project Prevention's claim that it is altruistically motivated, the ethos underpinning its strategy has much in common with that of the eugenics movement, which was influential in many countries during the inter-war years. As we have shown elsewhere, eugenicists used pseudo-scientific claims to support their assertion that certain groups or races were 'genetically inferior' to those within the 'mainstream'. The dubious 'evidence' they accumulated was subsequently used to justify a range of injustices, from compulsory sterilisation programmes for 'undesirables' in some countries, to Hitler's programmes of mass murder of millions in the 1930s and 1940s (Cunningham and Cunningham, 2008). At the time of writing, Project Prevention has, reluctantly, temporarily ceased paying for sterilisation procedures in the UK, due to the opposition of the BMA. However, its work in other countries continues unabated, and the organisation has made it clear that it is seeking to influence a shift in the BMA's stance here in the UK.

A social democratic approach to child well-being

We examined the key principles underpinning social democracy in Chapter 4. As we stated there, social democrats tend to embrace structural explanations for economic and social ills. Hence, in explaining the UK's poor record on child well-being, social democrats emphasise causal factors that they believe are largely beyond the family's control, such as unemployment, low family income, poor housing conditions and poverty. Like UNICEF, they believe that poverty, in particular, is one of the key factors detrimentally affecting children's well-being. This is the variable that needs to be most urgently addressed, through, for instance, the provision of improved benefits and greater opportunities to families. In advocating a model for the future, social democrats, not surprisingly, look towards Scandinavian countries, such as Sweden, Denmark, Norway and Finland. These nations have for many years accepted responsibility for securing their citizens' welfare and their records on child well-being are among the best in the world. In fact, the term 'social democratic' model is frequently utilised to describe the welfare regimes in these countries, out of recognition that their development has been shaped by social democratic principles (Esping Andersen, 1990). The summary below, which provides a brief comparison of various benefits available to citizens in the UK and Sweden, illustrates the generosity of levels of services and provision found in nations characterised by 'social democratic' welfare regimes.

RESEARCH SUMMARY

A comparison of welfare between Sweden and the UK

- *In 2009, there was a maximum monthly charge for child care of around £109 per month in Sweden, irrespective of the income of the family.*

  - *By contrast, there is no maximum monthly charge in the UK, and the average cost for a child under two in England was £88 per week in 2009.*

- *Swedish parents are entitled to 480 days' parental leave, per child, anytime between children being born and reaching nine years of age. While undertaking their leave, they receive 80 per cent of their previous income (up to a limit of around £369 per week). This can be divided between fathers and mothers, and is intended to enable parents to bond with their children and enhance their social, physical and emotional well-being. Parents also receive an additional 'bonus' of around £1,200 if both utilise the same amount of parental leave, a policy designed to promote gender quality.*

  - *In contrast to this, UK parents are entitled to apply for three months' unpaid parental leave, per child, anytime between the child being born and it reaching six years of age. Employers can turn requests down if they feel it is detrimental to their business interests.*

- *Unemployment insurance benefits in Sweden are earnings-related and paid at around 80 per cent of previous earnings (up to a limit of around £422 per week in 2009). The intention is to ensure that family incomes are not drastically reduced as a result of unemployment, to the detriment of either adults or children.*

  - *In the UK, unemployment benefit is paid at a flat rate and in 2010 this was £66.45. No attempts are made to ensure family living standards are maintained during periods of unemployment. Indeed, the opposite is the case and benefits are kept deliberately low in order to maintain work incentives.*

- *Higher (university) education in Sweden is free. Students do not pay tuition fees, and there are a range of grants and loans available to support their maintenance costs.*

  - *In the UK, students are required to pay tuition fees. At the time of writing, the indications are that these will rise to an average of £8,500 per year in 2011/12.*

- *State pensions in Sweden are earnings-related and are designed to provide a retirement income of around 80 per cent of previous earnings. Again, the intention is to maintain the previous living standards of recipients, a key feature of the Swedish welfare state.*

  - *The UK's state pension is a flat-rate benefit, which provides single pensioners with a weekly income of just £97.65 in 2010.*

Many of our students express surprise at the generosity of the level of welfare provision in Sweden. The high rates of taxation needed to fund such services should, they tell us, have a stifling effect on the Swedish economy. The standard rate of income tax in Sweden is just over 50 per cent, compared with the UK's 20 per cent, so surely this will impact adversely on entrepreneurial activity, putting the Swedish economy at a competitive disadvantage? In addition, the generous levels of support that are a characteristic feature of Sweden should theoretically encourage idleness and the other dysfunctional behavioural traits that in the UK are said to be linked to benefit 'dependency'. In relation to children specifically, if the neo-liberal interpretations of the UK's poor record on child well-being are correct – and it *is* a result of a lavish, morally corrupting welfare state – then we would expect Sweden to possess an even worse record.

In fact, none of these assumptions turns out to be true. Regarding Sweden's economic performance, the influential World Economic Forum (2010) ranks the Swedish economy fourth out of 133 nations in its Global Competitive Index. The UK's position was 13th. In addition, Sweden, like the other Scandinavian countries, emerged from the recent global recession much earlier than the UK, and at the time of writing its economic growth rates are higher than the UK's. Levels of unemployment are (and have historically been) broadly similar, serving to dispel the myth that generous welfare necessarily encourages 'voluntary' unemployment.

Nor have the generous levels of support provided to families – both couples and lone parents – contributed to 'poor parenting', or a 'culture of irresponsibility'. On the contrary, 'responsibility' is actively encouraged by mechanisms of support that enable citizens to balance their work and family responsibilities. For example, good quality, cheap child care and flexible parental leave arrangements enable parents – including lone parents – to remain engaged with the labour market and to support themselves independently. This is reflected in comparative labour market data, which shows that the employment rate of lone parents in Sweden is 81.9 per cent, compared with only 56.2 per cent in the UK (OECD, 2007).

One feature that the UK does have in common with Sweden is a high level of family breakdown and lone parenthood. Indeed, the percentage of children living in lone-parent families in Sweden is virtually identical to the UK's – around 17 per cent of 11, 15 and 17 year olds do so (UNICEF, 2007). However, Sweden is not characterised by the poor levels of child well-being that UK Conservative politicians, such as David Cameron, claim are associated with 'family breakdown'. As we have already seen, Sweden's record on child well-being is among the best in the world. What this suggests is that neo-liberal claims that there is a direct and definite correlation between lone parenthood, family breakdown and poor outcomes for children are incorrect. The experiences of Sweden (and other Scandinavian countries) imply there is not necessarily a link between family structure and poor outcomes for children. When support mechanisms are put in place to enable all families to balance work and family life responsibilities (such as affordable child care, flexible parental leave schemes and income transfers), family structure becomes a far less relevant factor in determining children's material and social well-being.

Relevance to the UK?

Social democrats have long argued that we have much to learn from the way Scandinavian countries organise their welfare provision (Mishra, 1984). The welfare policies adopted by Scandinavian nations are seen to provide a viable, working 'alternative' to the failed, socially divisive neo-liberal policy prescriptions that have been implemented in the UK. In relation to children specifically, Scandinavian countries' excellent records on child well-being are seen to be a direct result of their distinctly social democratic approach to welfare. More than anything else, it is this that explains their high ranking in international league tables on child welfare.

By contrast, the UK's relatively poor record on problems such as infant mortality, teenage pregnancy and the high number of youngsters who are NEET, can be traced to its equally poor record on material well-being. In short, the UK suffers from a high incidence of these problems because it also has relatively high adult and child poverty rates. These claims are supported by international evidence which shows that societies that are characterised by greater income equality, less poverty and well-funded, generous welfare states possess the world's best child welfare records (Wilkinson and Pickett, 2010). From this perspective solutions should focus upon improving the opportunities and incomes of families living in deprived areas. Rather than cutting already low levels of benefits, a strategy that will exacerbate the difficulties such families face, welfare policies should be targeted at providing them with the incomes and support they need to lift them out of poverty. Neo-liberal claims that the welfare state is culpable of enticing individuals and families into a state of feckless dependency are therefore dismissed. Governments should follow the Scandinavian, social democratic model and provide citizens with greater opportunities to balance work and family life responsibilities. More, rather than less, state intervention is thus required.

Implications for social work

Social workers would also have an important role to play in any social democratic strategy designed to tackle the underlying causes of poverty-linked problems. The nature of social work practice with children would, though, have to change. In particular, more resources would be needed to ensure that children's social workers are liberated from the intensive 'protection' and 'safeguarding' work that currently dominates their caseloads. Because they are currently understaffed and overwhelmed with work, social workers naturally focus on what is, in reality, the most pressing and immediate issue – protecting the most vulnerable children from harm. However, this is a resource-led, crisis-response approach, which is shaped by a policy environment that has consistently denied the profession the resources necessary to undertake truly effective, preventative social work with children and families. Social democrats, therefore, would argue in favour of a greater injection of resources into children's social work in order to 'free up' practitioners to engage in crucial, preventative welfare-related work that their current workloads preclude them from undertaking.

Surveys suggest that significant numbers of practitioners would support such a pro-gramme. In fact many social workers have expressed frustration at the way resource constraints make it extremely difficult for them to engage in community-based, pre-ventative welfare work with children and families. They feel that they are forced to crisis-manage overstretched child protection cases, and are unable to engage in the progressive welfare work that they know will prevent less urgent cases from escalating into more serious ones. The following comments, made by one children's social work-er in a *Community Care* survey, were representative of those made by many others who replied to the journal's request for information:

> *The increase in my caseload has meant that I am merely troubleshooting and lurching from crisis to crisis without being able to do any of the preventative work to stop things getting to crisis point.*

(Smith, 2010, p9)

Similar issues were raised by children's social workers who responded to the Social Work Taskforce's *Social Workers' Workload Survey*. The ability of practitioners to engage in preventative work was, many stated, *being challenged by the need to deploy nearly all their resources into child protection and high level statutory work* (Baginsky *et al.*, 2010, p95).

> *It was difficult, if not impossible, for most of those interviewed to see how the social work role as currently constituted could be redefined from one which predominantly concentrated on making sure children were not harmed to one which was mainly concerned with promoting the welfare of vulnerable children.*

(Baginsky et al., 2010, p94)

For social democrats, such comments point to the need for a better resourced, more liberating, welfare-focused form of practice with children. Rather than concentrating almost all their efforts upon protection work and 'controlling' 'at risk' groups, the efforts of social workers should instead be geared towards, for instance, ensuring that families have sufficient income and opportunities to meet their needs and require-ments. At a national level, they and their professional associations would be expected to campaign for improved, more comprehensive welfare provision for deprived families. At a practice level, one of their roles would be to ensure that families receive their full entitlement to benefits and support, and to direct them to agencies and organisations that can help provide for any needs not provided by an inadequate welfare system. They might also become involved in encouraging community-led action, helping families in deprived areas to organise their own campaigns for improved welfare provision.

More generally, the welfare state should follow the model of Scandinavian countries and be infused with principles that place a primacy on citizens' welfare needs. This might lead social workers to become involved in a whole range of tasks that are currently performed by unqualified administrators in the UK, few of whom have been trained to consider the holistic, long-term needs of service users. In Sweden, for instance, social assistance benefits are administered by social workers, and this changes the whole ethos of the way they are delivered. Unlike the UK, where provision is highly stigmatised and recipients tend to be treated with suspicion, in Sweden a welfare-first principle predominates. As Jones *et al.* (2006, p430) argue, the more generous and crucially less stigmatising, 'welfare'-orientated nature of Swedish social assistance means the poor are more 'resilient' in Sweden – they are *not made to feel so useless, or so guilty for their plight.* Other studies have shown how particular groups of service users, including children and young people, benefit from this broader conception of social work, which places the welfare service users and their families at the heart of any intervention.

CHAPTER SUMMARY

We began this chapter by drawing attention to the overwhelming emphasis placed upon issues relating to child abuse and neglect in media and political commentaries on children's welfare. As we pointed out, this has led to a scenario whereby children's social work has become all but synonymous with child protection, to the exclusion of other factors that impact upon children's well-being. We have sought to counter this perception and hope that our discussion has encouraged you to embrace a much broader conception of children's welfare than that which you commonly encounter. As we have shown, while it is clearly important for you as students to be aware of issues relating to child protection, your education and training should also encompass an analysis of other factors that affect children's welfare.

Finally, we also hope that our discussion prompts you to think critically about some of the 'common sense' assumptions that tend to govern thinking on welfare in the UK, many of which are based upon inaccuracies, mistruths and popular myths rather than established fact. In this respect, our discussion of welfare in Sweden has perhaps led you to challenge some of your own preconceptions about the welfare state, and introduced you to an alternative welfare model which contributes to very different outcomes to those generated by the UK's welfare state.

FURTHER READING

For a useful introduction to issues relating to the media and welfare see:

Franklin, B (1999) *Social policy, media and misrepresentation*. Florence, KY: Routledge.

If you are interested in comparative data on children's welfare and well-being, the following UNICEF publications are informative, well written and accessible:

UNICEF (2005) *Child poverty in rich countries*. Florence: UNICEF. **www.unicef-irc.org/publications/pdf/repcard6e.pdf**

UNICEF (2007) *An overview of child well-being in rich countries*. Florence: UNICEF. **www.unicef-irc.org/publications/pdf/rc7_eng.pdf**

For an influential introduction to different 'models' of welfare pursued by different countries see:

Esping Anderson, G (1990) *The three worlds of welfare capitalism*. London: Polity Press.

For a useful analysis of how social policy and social work is organised in other countries see:

Lawrence, S, Lyons, K, Simpson, G and Huegler, N (2009) *Introducing international social work*. Exeter: Learning Matters.

More generally, we would recommend you consult the websites of organisations such as the Child Poverty Action Group (**www.cpag.org.uk**) and the Joseph Rowntree Foundation (**www.jrf.org.uk**), both of which contain a wealth of information on children's well-being.

Chapter 8
Youth, social policy, social work and the 'crisis of youth'

Introduction

Young people have always been the subject of social policy and social work interventions. One of the reasons for this is that 'youth' is seen as a formative, but potentially troublesome 'transitional' period between childhood and adulthood; it is perceived as a life stage which offers great opportunities, but one that is also fraught with potential risks. This view of young people was reflected in the previous Labour government's Green Paper, *Youth matters*, which set out its strategy for ensuring that all young people achieved their potential. *Life for teenagers*, the Secretary of State indicated, *is full of opportunities, and most take full advantage of them* (DfES, 2005, p1). However, the Green Paper's concern was that, despite the opportunities that were now available, a sizeable minority were still experiencing marginalisation and exclusion. In this chapter we will look at competing explanations for youth exclusion and marginalisation, contrasting neo-liberal 'behavioural' interpretations with social democratic 'structural' ones. We also discuss the trajectory of recent youth-related social policy, assessing the relative influence of each of these ideological perspectives. We end the discussion by outlining an alternative, Marxist, interpretation for youth exclusion. The chapter begins, though, with an examination of societal perceptions of youth exclusion, and an activity that is designed to elicit your perceptions of 'young people'.

Perceptions of youth

Research suggests that there does seem to be a general agreement about the characteristics and behaviour patterns that are associated with 'youth' and 'young people'. Indeed, it is quite likely that you, yourself, will associate 'youth' and 'young people' with certain features and behavioural characteristics.

ACTIVITY 8.1

This activity is designed for use in groups. Here, we want to assess your perceptions of 'young people' in order to encourage you to think about how these might impact upon your future practice. This is important because many of you will be working with and providing services to young people, and it is crucial that you are aware of how your own preconceived perceptions might impact upon your practice.

- *We want each of you to write down on a piece of paper half a dozen words or phrases that come to mind when you hear the terms 'youth' or 'young people'. It is important that you try to be as honest as possible, and in order to facilitate this we would suggest that you complete this exercise anonymously, without writing your name on the piece of paper.*

Once you have completed this, gather all the separate pieces of paper, shuffle them together, and nominate one person to read out the responses.

COMMENT

Over the years, we have tried this exercise with different cohorts of our own students. Their responses are invariably the same, which suggests to us that the concepts of 'youth' and 'young people' do conjure up certain images in most people's minds. The words and phrases that our students have associated with 'youth' and 'young people' tend to contain an interesting mix of what could loosely be categorised as 'positive' and 'negative' elements. On an ostensibly positive note, they seem to associate 'youth' with 'adventure', 'fun', 'energy', 'excitement', 'freedom' and 'partying'. Young people, our students tell us, are 'lively', 'fast-living' and 'fun-loving'; they are 'active', 'full of life', live 'carefree lifestyles' and have 'few ties'. We describe these words and phrases as having 'ostensibly positive' connotations, because on closer inspection it is also possible to detect a 'less positive' undertone of 'hedonism' and 'risk' within them. For example, for many people the 'freedom', 'energy', 'sense of adventure' and 'carefree' nature of 'youth' is deeply problematic, contributing to a series of risk-taking behaviours that are associated with far more negative undertones and outcomes. Hence, our students also tell us that young people are 'trouble makers', 'thugs', 'out of control', 'selfish', 'immature', 'wild', 'loud', 'temperamental', 'disrespectful', 'moody', 'risk taking', 'lazy', 'impulsive' and 'arrogant'. They also associate young people with 'alcohol', 'drugs', 'sex', 'rebellion' and 'anti-social behaviour'. There is also a tendency to characterise young people into loosely related pejorative groupings, and they are often referred to as 'hoodies', 'chavs', 'yobs' or 'hooligans'.

We suspect that some of your group's comments will not have been too dissimilar to those we describe above. This is hardly surprising, because young people do tend to be perceived in a negative light, and they are increasingly associated with anti-social behaviour, crime and community breakdown. Opinion poll surveys tell us that there is a widespread feeling that youth crime and anti-social behaviour are escalating, and that young people are responsible for a large proportion of crimes that are committed. In one such 2006 survey, 62 per cent of respondents stated that they felt that the number of young offenders had increased in the previous two years, while only 4 per cent stated that the numbers had fallen. Respondents to the same survey said that they believed that young people were responsible for almost one-half of all crime committed in the UK (Ipsos MORI, 2006). A more recent survey of public opinion concluded that *the term 'anti-social behaviour' has, to many, become synonymous with young people generally* (Ipsos MORI, 2010a).

To what extent, though, do people's 'feelings' about young people's declining morals accord with the evidence? In fact, such perceptions are contradicted by research. In 1998, for example, more than a quarter of participants in the British Crime Survey felt that young people were responsible for 'most' crime, yet fewer than one-quarter of offenders committing indictable offences in 1998 were aged between 10 and 17 (Halsey and White, 2008). Recent crime data also show a clear and persistent decline in young people's first-time offending and reoffending. Hence, in 2007–08 there was a 27 per cent fall in first-time offending by young people, while between 2000 and 2008 youth reoffending fell by 24.8 per cent (Youth Justice Board, 2010). Qualitative research into young people's behaviour also provides evidence to challenge popular conceptions over the levels and trends of crime/anti-social behaviour. As Halsey and White's (2008) review of the evidence has shown, self-reported rates of crime among young people have remained relatively static since 1992.

Negative perceptions of young people are also contradicted by research which suggests that most young people are more rather than less positively 'engaged' in society than ever before. The evidence points to a high degree of conformity between young people's aspirations and societal norms, values and expectations. A recent inquiry into young people's aims and goals in life found that more than nine out of ten agreed that *working hard at school/aiming to do the best you can will help their future success in life*, and a similar proportion thought that having good qualifications/ exam results would help their future success (Ipsos MORI, 2010b, p4). Indeed, the educational attainment rates of young people – at GSCE, advanced and degree level – are now higher than ever, a development which suggests that predictions about growing levels of 'irresponsibility' among young people may be inaccurate. Other indicators of youth 'engagement', such as youth volunteering, also suggest positive rather than negative trends. For instance, levels of youth volunteering are at unprecedentedly high levels. Approximately seven out of ten young people participate in volunteering each year, making important and positive contributions the communities in which they live (Pye *et al.*, 2009). As Smith (2008, p17) argues, such developments suggest that there is actually *much to celebrate* about the state of 'youth' today.

Why, then, do people's perceptions of young people continue to be shaped by the view that their outlooks and behaviour are increasingly problematic? As we have argued elsewhere, successive media-inspired moral panics around 'youth' have frequently served to reinforce inaccurate, negative stereotypical attitudes about young people (Cunningham and Cunningham, 2008). As Cohen (2006) argues, *Working-class yobs are the most enduring of suitable enemies* of the press. They are, to be blunt, an 'easy target' and when newspaper editors decide to publish sensational, salacious stories about 'feral', anti-social young miscreants they know that they are able to tap into long-standing fears and prejudices about youth. Widespread, sweeping generalisations are made on the basis of the most limited evidence, yet the persistence and regularity of the message means that it resonates. As one recent government report acknowledged, young people are rarely portrayed in a positive light by the media and this inevitably impacts upon the way they are perceived:

> *Young people are ... faced with the challenge of growing up in a culture that has widespread negative perceptions of youth. Adults and the media commonly associate young people with problems such as anti-social behaviour – 71 per cent of media stories about young people are negative, a third of articles about young people are about crime ... Sometimes, these views have been an unintended consequence of Government policies to tackle some serious problems affecting the lives of some teenagers. Rather than presenting a positive vision for youth development, national priorities and local services have been organised and targeted around avoiding and addressing problems, such as crime, substance misuse, or teenage pregnancy.*

> *While it is right to continue to focus on addressing these issues … it [is] also important to be aware of the influence this has on popular perceptions.*

(HM Treasury and Department for Children, Schools and Families, 2007)

The point made here about public perceptions of young people being influenced by the disproportionate emphasis placed upon the negative aspects of youth by both the media and government is important. Indeed, coming as it does from an official government document, it constitutes something of an admission that social policies have served to reinforce the inaccurate, negative imagery of young people propagated by large sections of the media. The quotation suggests that this has been an unintended consequence of government policy, though many academics would take issue with this. They argue that successive Home Office ministers have pandered to such sentiments, utilising concerns about the 'problematisation of youth' to divert attention away from the structural causes of (and costly solutions to) the problems many young people face. Rather than challenging inaccurate stereotypes, ministers stand accused of embracing them, utilising heightened anxieties about 'youth' as justification for implementing coercive social policies. Certainly, as the influential report published by the Independent Commission on Youth Crime and Anti-Social Behaviour (2010, pp17, 23) argued, senior politicians have not been averse to indulging in sensationalist rhetoric that can only serve to strengthen pathological conceptions of 'youth'. *For many years*, this Independent Commission concluded, *politicians appear to have been caught in a war of words on the basis that public opinion would favour whichever party sounded 'tougher'*. It accused politicians of engaging in an *exceptionally fierce, punitive arms race*, with each party seeking desperately to sound 'meaner' than its opponents on youth crime, *despite sound evidence that it has been falling for the past 16 years*.

A mythical 'golden age' of youth?

Hardly a day goes by without some commentator or politician discussing the decline in the public morals of today's youth, contrasting our current 'worrying' predicament with a previous 'golden age' of harmony and respect. According to Pearson (1983), this view of British history as one founded on stability and decency is deeply ingrained on the self-understanding of the British people, and is based upon a number of key assumptions.

- Firstly, it is assumed that public and political concerns over the problematic behaviour of young people are relatively recent in origin. Civility, adherence to the law and an unquestioning respect for authority were, it is claimed, once characteristic features of the British way of life, but these have now given way to a 'deluge' of anti-social behaviour.
- Secondly, it is felt that the customs, laws and regulations that traditionally ensured that young people conformed to appropriate moral and legal boundaries have somehow been diluted or lost, and that this is the principal cause of the

exclusion and marginalisation many young people face. There is, it is assumed, a deep malaise at the heart of Britain, one which has led to an erosion of the traditional 'checks' that regulated young people's behaviour.

- Thirdly, it is assumed that it is possible to create conditions that are conducive to the restoration of 'civility' and the rehabilitation of 'youth'.

Many of these assumptions have faced criticism for offering an overly simplified, 'romanticised' view of young people in both the past and the present. However, there can be little doubt that they are largely shared by the general public and policy-makers alike. As we have already seen, many people today agree with the claim that the behaviour of young people has progressively deteriorated. The question of whether young people in Britain are engaging in more anti-social behaviour is now rarely asked – the focus instead is on why this is so. The notion that young people are increasingly uncontrollable and badly behaved is invariably taken as given. All the evidence, we are told, seems to point to a lost 'golden age' of youth.

ACTIVITY 8.2

Although we tend to think of the problematisation of youth as being a relatively recent phenomenon, historical research shows this not to be the case. As Pearson (1983) illustrates, successive generations have always identified young people as a threatening 'social problem group' in need of close surveillance and control. In addition, individualised explanations for the difficulties young people face, which locate their causes with a breakdown in young peoples' respect for authority and in an absence of parental control, have been a regular feature of commentaries around 'youth' for centuries.

In this fairly straightforward task we want you to try to date the quotations below. In order to help you with the task, we have provided you with dates. All you have to do is match the quotation to the correct date! You can find the answers to this task located at the end of the chapter:

c4000 BC	*4th century BC*	*1274 AD*
1900	*1960*	*1977*

1. We live in a decaying age. Young people *no longer respect their* parents. *They are rude and impatient. They frequently inhabit taverns and have no self-control.*
2. The young people of today think of nothing but themselves. They have no reverence for parents or old age. They are impatient of all restraint ... As for the girls, they are forward, immodest and unladylike in speech, behaviour and dress.
3. What is happening to our young people? They disrespect their elders, they disobey their parents. They ignore the law. They riot in the streets, inflamed with wild notions. Their morals are decaying. What is to become of them?
4. What are we to do with the hooligan? ... Every day in some police court are narrated acts of brutality of which the sufferers are unoffending men and women ... There is no looking calmly, however, on the frequently recurring outbursts of ruffianism, the

Continued

ACTIVITY 8.2 continued

systematic lawlessness of groups of lads and young men who are the terror of the neighbourhoods in which they dwell ... The most obvious and popular remedy for this organised lawlessness is that the guilty should be flogged freely.

5. On one point we must all agree. The spirit of bravado or whatever it is called, has led to a wave of senselessly destructive hooliganism that shows no signs whatever of dying down ... kindly and inspiring efforts to reform the little thugs have, beyond question, been .... ineffective ... Unfortunately, there is no question but that, as matters stand, they laugh, often openly at attempts to control them.

6. No group in the community has a more rapidly rising crime rate than young people, especially those in their teens. Burglaries and crimes of violence in particular tend more and more to be committed by younger and younger people.

COMMENT

We are sure that like our own students who have undertaken this task, many of you will have found it difficult to identify the correct dates for these quotations. If so, this tells us something about the accuracy of claims surrounding a supposed 'golden age' of youth. As Pearson (1983) has shown, British society has been shaped by a remarkable degree of continuity in terms of its anxieties and fears surrounding 'youth'. While the labels attached to young people may have changed – ranging from the nineteenth-century 'artful dodgers', 'street arabs' and 'hooligans', to their twentieth-century equivalents, the teddy boys, mods, rockers, skinheads and punks – the message has remained broadly the same. Each, in its own time, has been accused of varying degrees of insubordination, depravity and anti-social behaviour, just like their twenty-first-century forebears, the 'chavs' and the 'hoodies'. British history is littered with a liberal scattering of moral panics about youth, and hence it is important to put today's concerns about young people in context. In short, we would caution you against uncritically accepting the notion that we are facing an unprecedented 'crisis of youth', whereby young people are becoming increasingly unruly and disaffected.

Youth exclusion and the 'crisis of youth'

Despite evidence to the contrary, over the last 25 years or so, politicians, journalists and various social commentators have undoubtedly come to the conclusion that 'youth' is 'in crisis'. Such concerns cross the political spectrum and tend to centre on debates about 'youth exclusion'. Although explanations for and solutions to youth exclusion differ, it is possible to identify two broad strands of thought in mainstream debates, one which embraces a neo-liberal perspective, the other a social democratic perspective. We examine each of these in turn below, ending the discussion with an alternative Marxist interpretation of youth exclusion.

Neo-liberalism and youth exclusion

Neo-liberal interpretations of the 'crisis of youth' often have a strong moral undertone, with young people, or their families, increasingly being held personally responsible for the difficulties they face. The problems experienced by young people are seen to be largely a result of their own, or their parents' making, sometimes reinforced by an over-generous, perverse welfare system. Welfare, it is argued, has seduced parents and young people into a life of irresponsibility and dependence, and this, together with 'soft', liberal criminal justice policies, is said to have encouraged a host of dysfunctional, deviant patterns of behaviour. From this perspective, the solution to the 'crisis of youth' is quite straightforward. This is to introduce stringent criminal justice policies that will deter delinquent behaviour, while at the same time reinforcing parental responsibility and reducing the welfare available to young people.

Neo-liberal interpretations of youth exclusion are perhaps best epitomised in the work of the American sociologist Charles Murray (1999). In 1989, he claimed to have identified a burgeoning youth 'underclass' in the UK, which was characterised by growing levels of illegitimacy, labour market 'dropout' and criminal activity. 'Welfare' was said to lie at the heart of each of these social problems. Illegitimacy, for example, was said to have risen because misguided social policies had eroded the punishing, but necessary, social and economic penalties that used to be associated with it. Put simply, the provision of benefits meant that the *economic feasibility of raising a baby without the support of a father has changed fundamentally since the end of the Second World War* (p48). Youth unemployment was also said to result from the generosity of welfare provision. Murray insisted that labour market dropout, or 'idleness' among young people, had been encouraged by an irresponsible culture of welfare, which allowed *young men to grow up without being socialised into the world of work* (p41). Murray also maintained that 'liberal' welfare policies had contributed to a proliferation of youth offending and anti-social behaviour. Echoing the architects of the 1834 Poor Law Amendment Act, he argued that welfare-induced idleness provided greater opportunities for young people to engage in criminal activity. In addition, the criminal justice system had been 'captured' by well meaning, but fundamentally flawed rehabilitative values, which meant that crime *has become dramatically safer in Britain throughout the post-war period, and most blatantly safer since 1960* (p45).

Perhaps not surprisingly, Murray's ideas were embraced by ministers in Margaret Thatcher's Conservative government. His explanations for 'youth exclusion' were very much 'in tune' with this government's own ideological outlook, and his claims, which were actually based upon very little substantive evidence, provided justification for the government's plans to reduce welfare. The links between Murray's ideas and the social policies of successive Conservative administrations can be seen in the numerous social security and housing benefit cuts that have affected young people since the 1980s. The assumptions underpinning Murray's 'underclass thesis' have subsequently provided inspiration for a number of UK-based neo-liberal social policy commentators, who have adopted an identical position (Marsland, 1996; Bartholemew, 2006). Like Murray, they argue that the solution to youth social exclusion lies in coercive, targeted interventions designed to deter and control the inappropriate, 'deviant' patterns of behaviour that lie at its heart. The focus of attention (and intervention) is on a relatively small group of recalcitrant young people and their families, ignoring underpinning economic and social structures that constrain their lives.

Media and political commentaries on the 'crisis of youth' have tended to be shaped by similar neo-liberal principles, which point to its allegedly pathological, behavioural causes. What is needed, from this perspective, is less 'welfare' and 'care' and more 'control'. Indeed, it is 'soft', 'caring' social-democratic-inspired social policies and social work interventions that are said to be responsible for the 'crisis of youth'.

ACTIVITY 8.3

The following comments, taken from an article in the Express newspaper, are fairly typical of the media's representation of young people. After reading the extract, try answering the questions we have posed.

Instead of protecting the public the state acts as the simpering ally of juvenile thugs and bullies. Hand-wringing social workers, enfeebled youth officers, nervous probation staff, dripping-wet judges and cowardly politicians all collude in a destructive culture that allows vicious young criminals to swagger through our streets with impunity … The justice system has become so soft because of a malign cocktail of sentimentality and Marxism. Since the Sixties, our civic institutions have been increasingly gripped by a politically correct ideology which holds that young offenders are really the victims of social disadvantage. Therefore, according to this dogma, what they need is constant support rather than punishment. … It [is] true that a large proportion of delinquents come from broken homes, partly because the vast welfare state provides so many perverse incentives towards family breakdown and mass idleness.

(McKinstry, 2011, p12)

- *Why are social workers and other welfare practitioners portrayed in this way?*

- *How can the above quote be criticised? You may wish to think about some of the young people that you have come across on placement.*

COMMENT

As we discussed in Chapter 7, the media's portrayal of welfare-related issues is rarely balanced. There is a tendency for it to focus on the more lurid, scandalous elements of stories, in a way that undermines support for the principles underpinning welfare (Brindle, 1999). This is particularly the case with youth-focused stories (Cohen, 2006). The impression given is that of a welfare state that corrupts 'youth', destroys personal responsibility and acts to the detriment rather than the benefit of young people's interests. Hence, young people are frequently portrayed as violent, selfish scroungers, fraudsters and feckless deviants who have been seduced by a lax, over-generous welfare state into a life of irresponsibility and idleness. Welfare practitioners who provide services to young people hardly fare any better. As is the case with the above article, they are invariably

Continued

depicted as 'left-wing', politically motivated, misguided do-gooders, whose interventions generate more harm than good. Clearly, this is an overly simplistic misrepresentation of young people, and an inaccurate portrayal of welfare work with young people, but the regularity and pervasive nature of the media's message resonates with the public. As we have already seen, this interpretation of the 'crisis of youth' has gained a good deal of currency, and opinion poll surveys tell us that it is a view shared by large sections of the general public.

Neo-liberal influence on youth policy?

There can be little doubt that in recent years there has been a discernible shift in both policy and practice to an approach which focuses upon young people's irresponsibility or behaviour rather than their potential social and economic needs. A negative 'deficit' model has predominated, focused on what young people are said to 'lack', whether this be aspiration, motivation, appropriate values or moral decency. By contrast, analyses that point to the structural barriers that inhibit the effective participation of young people in society appear to have been missing from official policy documents. Some, such as Levitas (2005), argue that Labour's social exclusion strategy was typified by this 'deficit model' approach. She suggests that the ostensibly progressive rhetoric underpinning Labour's approach to social exclusion was little more than a smokescreen, disguising its underlying neo-liberal influences. Structural interpretations for youth exclusion were, she insists, largely marginalised by an agenda that focused attention upon relatively small groups of young people who were deemed to pose a threat to the social order. Hence, Labour's Social Exclusion Unit (SEU) reports focused on issues such as truancy, youth homelessness, teenage pregnancy and young people who were NEET, prioritising concerns about behaviour rather than material hardship. Where references to structural inequality were made – as in its *Teenage pregnancy* report – these were effectively obscured by the behavioural recommendations of the reports and the pathological rhetoric subsequently utilised by ministers.

Teenage pregnancy: The SEU report
The SEU's Teenage pregnancy report was published in a fanfare of publicity in June 1999. The SEU found that levels of teenage births had actually fallen since the early 1970s, and no evidence was found to suggest that there was a link between welfare and teenage pregnancy. In theory, the report therefore provided evidence to contradict the commonly made claim that it was the 'honey pot' of welfare that seduced young girls into pregnancy. However, these findings were not reflected in the tone of the report itself, or in the political and media reaction to it. Indeed, the report adopted an apocalyptic tone, concluding that The facts are stark... Action on a range of fronts is now
Continued

Teenage pregnancy: The SEU report *continued*

long overdue. The tenor of Tony Blair's introduction to the report was similarly alarmist, suggesting that Britain had a shameful record, and that too many teenage mothers simply fail to understand the price society will pay (SEU, 1999, pi).

The possible 'solutions' examined by the report, like the statements subsequently made by ministers, focused upon strategies intended to modify behaviour, despite the acknowledged correlation between teenage pregnancy and structural inequality and poverty (see Chapter 7). Thus, the report discussed the potential of US-style temporary sterilisation programmes for childless young women, as well as the desirability of forcing teenage mothers to live in supervised accommodation centres. This latter proposal – to compel teenage mothers to live in supported or supervised settings in order to reduce the 'inducements' to teenage pregnancy – had been advanced by ministers in John Major's Conservative government some three years previously (Redwood, 1995). At the time, senior Labour figures expressed dismay at the suggestion, claiming that The Tories want to return to the 19th century and put mothers and their babies in the workhouse *(John Prescott, cited in Doughty, 1999, p15). However, as the following comments made by Tony Blair (1999, p17) show, Labour's stance once in government had clearly changed:*

> I don't believe leaving a 16-year-old girl with a baby in her own flat, often halfway up a tower block, benefits her, the baby or the rest of us. It gives her too much ... It could send out a signal to young teenagers that having a baby is a fast track to their own flat and the symbols of adulthood ... We are going to change the rules so that under-18 teenage mothers will no longer be given lone tenancy of a council house. Instead, we want them to be housed in semi-supervised accommodation.

The 'behavioural undercurrent' running through the SEU's report, and the government's response to it, was inevitably picked up by elements of the right-wing press, which enthusiastically emphasised the sensationalist elements of the report. Why we should stop giving lone teenage mothers council homes, *read one* Daily Mail *(14 June 1999) headline, while a column in the* Mirror *(16 June 1999) encouraged the government to* Single out the selfish breeders *and to come down hard on the* shameful club of gymslip mums. *The right-wing* Mail, *encouraged by the moralistic undertones of the government's response to the report, praised Blair for* not shying away from a confrontation with outraged liberal opinion *(cited in Toynbee, 1999, p18).*

Our own research has shown that within one week of the report's publication, national newspapers contained more than 50 substantive articles on the topic, the bulk of which were shaped by behavioural, pathological interpretations of teenage pregnancy. The issue was amplified, distorted and simplified, and what the SEU report itself had admitted to be a declining issue in numerical terms was suddenly cast to the forefront of the public's attention. The impression given was that teenage pregnancy had never been higher and was increasing, rather than actually falling. Young people, once again, were

Continued

Teenage pregnancy: The SEU report *continued*
placed in the eye of the storm and their reckless, immoral, welfare-induced behaviour was said to be responsible for a whole range of societal ills. Politicians were encouraged to act to stem this 'tide of irresponsibility', to slash and stigmatise welfare so as to reduce the 'positive incentives' to teenage pregnancy. This therefore appeared to be a good example of the trend that we outlined earlier, for government policy to reinforce negative perceptions of young people.

As we have already stated, some of the more pertinent facts included in the report – a reduction in teenage pregnancy, an acknowledgement of the links between poverty and teenage conceptions and a dismissal of the claim that 'welfare' was the principal cause of teenage pregnancy – were largely lost in the media and political commentaries that followed its publication. Like the position adopted by previous Conservative governments, Labour's approach to this issue seemed to have the effect of pathologising teenage mothers and child rearing.

It is not only in the field of teenage pregnancy that social policy in relation to 'youth' appears to have been influenced by neo-liberal discourses. More generally, the youth policy agenda has shifted away from a concern for 'welfare', towards an approach designed to meet the perceived need to address 'deviant', 'irresponsible' behaviour by imposing a range of control measures on 'problematic' young people and/or their families. In the field of social security, this has included Labour's New Deal for Young People (NDYP), which compels 18–24 year olds who have been unemployed for six months or more to engage in some form of work-related activity, education or voluntary work. This scheme will be replaced by the coalition's 'Work Programme' for young people, but the ethos and assumptions underpinning the two initiatives are largely the same. The rhetoric surrounding both schemes contains a mix of progressive and coercive elements, but the basic premise is that youth unemployment is primarily a motivational, 'supply-side' problem, rather than being caused by a lack of opportunity to work. Young people need to be 'incentivised' through compulsion and the threat of benefit sanctions to take up the opportunities that are 'readily available'.

ACTIVITY 8.4

The NDYP
Nothing sounds more reasonable than the notion that 'lazy' young people on benefits should be forced, under threat of benefit sanction, to take up the education, work and training opportunities that are available to them. According to the then Labour government, this is precisely what its NDYP would ensure. In future, 18–24 year olds who had
Continued

been unemployed for six months or more would be expected to engage with one of the following options:

- *a subsidised job;*
- *education or training up to a level 2 qualification (GCSE level);*
- *voluntary work;*
- *an environmental task force.*

When the NDYP was introduced, ministers made it clear that there would be no 'fifth option' of a life on welfare, and sanctions of up to six months' withdrawal of benefits could be imposed upon those failing to engage with the scheme. The NDYP would be implemented nationally, without variation, and all young people would be subjected to the same regulations, irrespective of local labour market conditions, or their own diverse needs. Ideologically, the inspiration for the NDYP, like most recent labour market 'activation' schemes, has come from the US, where what are known as 'workfare' programmes have forced people to fulfill work-related duties and obligations in return for their welfare (hence, the term 'workfare').

In theory, the four options had equal parity, but in practice there was a hierarchy, with the subsidised job option being seen by both New Deal advisors and clients as being the one that was most likely to lead to a positive outcome. However, due to shortages in placements, only 15.3 per cent of participants had been able to choose this preferred option by 2007, with the remainder spread among the other three options (Field and White, 2007). The environmental task force was widely seen as the least attractive, and it had the worst record on moving people into employment.

As future social workers and welfare practitioners, you may well be working with groups of excluded and marginalised young people. Bearing in mind, the types of young people you will be working with, try answering the following questions.

- *Can you think of any problems that sanctions regimes, such as that contained in the NDYP, might pose?*
- *Is there a danger that the complex and particular needs of some young service users will be compromised by this kind of universal, one-size-fits-all approach?*

COMMENT

Research funded by the government itself suggests that social workers have good reason to be concerned about the operation of schemes such as the NDYP, for it tends to be the most vulnerable, marginalised young people who are sanctioned for non-compliance. Moreover, the evidence suggests that many of those sanctioned are not 'lazy' and 'feckless', but victims of a standardised, universal 'one-size-fits-all' approach to youth exclusion which ignores the complex, diverse needs of many young people. The following extract is taken from a Department for Work and Pensions-funded study which assessed the impact of the NDYP's sanctioning regime:

Continued

Many of the 26 week sanctioned clients in our sample had significant problems which could prevent them getting work. Using information provided by NDPAs [New Deal personal advisors] and the clients themselves, these problems fall into the following categories:

- Literacy problems
- Learning difficulties
- Confidence, nerves, psychological problems
- Alcohol and drug addictions
- Criminal records
- Lacking in social skills
- Tendency to violence
- Living in 'vulnerable' housing (for example, temporary accommodation)
- Health problems

(Saunders et al., 2001, pp9–10)

This and other research has found that many of the vulnerable young people who are sanctioned for non-compliance have not knowingly failed to comply with the regulations, but are simply victims of misunderstanding, poor communication or a failure of those administering the scheme to acknowledge their complex needs (Saunders et al., 2001; TUC, 2002). Research has also found that vulnerable youngsters considered 'difficult' to place – such as those with learning difficulties and those with psychological problems – have invariably been placed on the environmental task force option. This has frequently consisted of little more than picking up litter and cleaning graffiti. Not surprisingly, the demeaning, de-motivating nature of this kind of work means that drop-out rates have been higher for this option than the others. One Trades Union Congress (2002) survey found that the sanctioning rate for the environmental taskforce option was 44 per cent, compared with only 7 per cent for the subsidised job pathway. What many of these young people really needed was a long-term package of intensive support, to help them overcome the particular problems and obstacles they faced, but instead they were effectively 'parked' on what many perceived to be little more than a punitive 'community service' programme.

Hopefully, you can now see some of the difficulties that can be associated with schemes such as the NDYP, which ostensibly sound 'reasonable' and 'fair'. Unlike in some other countries (such as Sweden), where equivalent programmes are administered by social workers, the UK's NDYP is administered by relatively low-paid, poorly trained staff, who do not have the time, or the qualifications to take into account the holistic needs of participants. In addition, of course, the historic culture of mistrust that pervades welfare in the UK (see the history chapter) encourages benefit-office staff to adopt generalised, stereotypical assumptions about welfare recipients, which means they are less likely to appreciate the complex reasons which might underpin the non-compliance of vulnerable young people. Even more worryingly, evidence has emerged that the higher rates of sanctions experienced by the most vulnerable young people on schemes like the NDYP may not be entirely inadvertent. For example, an investigation by the *Guardian* newspaper found that benefits staff are tacitly encouraged to target vulnerable young people in order to meet their office's targets for reducing welfare caseloads. It found that since the election of the coalition government Jobcentre staff had each been set weekly targets for sanctioning claimants, and this led them to target those deemed easy to knock off benefits.

ACTIVITY 8.5

The comments below, made by a Jobcentre Plus employee, describe the sanctioning regime that he and his colleagues were told to enforce. After reading his comments discuss the implications of this approach for young, vulnerable service users that you may be working with.

> Suddenly you're not helping somebody into sustainable employment, which is what you're employed to do. You're looking for ways to trick your customers into 'not looking for work'. You come up with many ways. I've seen dyslexic customers given written job searches, and when they don't produce them – what a surprise – they're sanctioned. The only target that anyone seems to care about is stopping people's money ... Saving the public purse is the catchphrase that is used in our office ... It is drummed home all the time. Feel good about stopping someone's money, you've just saved your own pocket. It's a joke ... We were told suddenly that [finding someone to sanction] once a week wasn't good enough, we were far behind other offices, and we went to a meeting where they compared us with other offices, and said we now have to do three a week to catch up. Most staff go into work and they're thinking about it from moment one – who am I going to stop this week? ... The young often fall into it, because they haven't been there long enough, they are generally a major target. The uneducated are another major target. I've seen people with ... seriously low educational standards and it's easy to exploit them.

> *(Domokos, 2011, p1)*

Perhaps not surprisingly, much of the research evidence suggests that schemes like the NDYP can actually be counter-productive in helping young people develop their skills and find work. This was the conclusion of a recent government-funded review of the international evidence of 'workfare' programmes, which found *little evidence that workfare increases the likelihood of finding work. It can even reduce employment chances by limiting the time available for job search and by failing to provide the skills and experience valued by employers* (cited in House of Commons Library, 2009). It also concluded that such schemes are particularly unsuitable for the most vulnerable young people who are experiencing multiple barriers in their search for employment.

Critics argue that rather than 'punishing' young people, by forcing them to participate on such schemes, governments should follow the approach adopted by some other countries and seek to provide good-quality, long-term education, flexible training and employment programmes that genuinely enhance their skills, knowledge and employability. Such programmes may be costly in the short term, but will reap long-term social and economic benefits. On the one hand, young people will be able to find sustainable employment and realise their potential, while on the other, society as a whole will benefit through the creation of a better educated, trained and motivated workforce. We have only focused here on the issues of teenage pregnancy and youth unemployment. However, the same, individualistic, moral undertones can be found in other areas of policy, most notably in recent criminal justice policies designed to combat youth offending, including Anti-Social Behaviour Orders, Curfew Orders, and Youth Inclusion Panels. A number of commentators have drawn attention to the extent to which this 'coercive turn' in social policy has changed the nature of welfare and social work with young people, with the emphasis now placed upon 'controlling' rather than 'caring' for young service users. As Smith (2008, p97) argues, there has been a *reorientation of thinking about intervention*, which has been based less upon meeting the present welfare needs of young people and more upon assessing and preventing future problematic behaviour. Consequently, we have seen the introduction of a plethora of *prescriptive forms of community based intervention incorporating large doses of behaviour management, surveillance and control ... and tightly enforced sanctions for non-compliance*. Even where social workers themselves are not directly involved in administering such programmes, they increasingly have to deal with the casualties who (often inadvertently) have contravened the tight regulations.

Social democracy and youth exclusion

The social democratic perspective rejects many of the assumptions that underpin neo-liberal interpretations of youth exclusion. It sees the 'crisis of youth' as a manifestation of the growing, chronic levels of marginalisation experienced by certain sections of young people. Here, far less emphasis is placed upon the problems caused by young people and more on the problems experienced by them, such as family poverty, poor educational opportunities, inadequate housing provision and an increasingly punitive criminal justice system. Each of these factors shapes the lives of young people, constraining their opportunities for 'inclusion' and inhibiting their ability to achieve their full potential. Social democrats, therefore, point to a need to acknowledge the disadvantaged structural environments that many young people come from and are currently living in, which detrimentally impact upon their ability to secure 'inclusion'. They caution against the adoption of simplistic explanations which fail to take into account the real difficulties that many young people have faced which may have contributed to the problems they experience.

With this approach, therefore, explanations focus on the far-reaching economic and social changes that have occurred which have made 'youth' a particularly precarious life stage. As Furlong and Cartmel (2007, p8) argue, *changes occurring over the last three decades or so have led to a heightened sense of risk and individualization of experiences of young people*. These changes include an increasingly deregulated, casualised, insecure labour market, which has made it more difficult for young people to obtain good, sustainable, well paid work. As Jones (2002, p8) points out:

> *The employment of young people has been marginalised. Many of the jobs typically held by school leavers have disappeared, and opportunities for 16-year-old school leavers have reduced. Traditional craft apprenticeships for young men and clerical/secretarial jobs for young women have been [re]placed by sales occupations, often part-time and low paid.*

At the same time, cuts in social housing provision and the promotion of home ownership have led to a boom in the price of houses, forcing many young people into longer periods of difficult, involuntary semi-dependency upon their parents. The impact of these developments has, it is argued, been exacerbated by neo-liberal-inspired welfare reforms – in housing and social security – that marginalise or exclude young people from accessing social rights that most other citizens take for granted. For example, most 16–18 year olds are now prohibited from claiming social security and housing benefits, and as we have seen, there has been a more general marked 'coercive' turn in social policy directed at young people. From this perspective, solutions to youth exclusion should focus upon the urgent need for governments to address or reverse these changes, tackling the structural problems that blight the lives of many young people. They should *recognise the cumulative nature of some of the difficulties they encounter, whether these are the multiplier effects of different aspects of social exclusion ... or the impact of unequal and discriminatory treatment* (Smith, 2008, p3).

While social democrats acknowledge that young people as a whole are disproportionately susceptible to exclusion, certain groups of young people who are thought to be especially vulnerable are singled out as being in particular need. Young people, they point out, are not a homogeneous entity, and some face a series of disadvantages and obstacles which increase the likelihood of them being exposed to a range of social problems and difficulties as they make the transition to adulthood. For example, disabled young people are more likely to experience exclusion than their non-disabled peers. Thus, almost one-quarter of young people who had a special educational need or a disability while at school are not in education, employment or training by the age of 19 (DfES, 2005). Young people from minority ethnic backgrounds are also more likely to suffer from marginalisation in comparison with other young people. Hence, in September 2009, the unemployment rate among black and black British young 16–24 year olds was 48 per cent, compared with an average youth unemployment rate of 18.4 per cent (Institute for Public Policy Research, 2010). In both cases, discrimination rather than moral culpability is likely to have been a significant factor in contributing to exclusion. Care leavers are another group who are susceptible to higher levels of exclusion than other young people, including educational disadvantage, unemployment, homelessness and other housing problems. Given the difficulties that these young care leavers have faced, and indeed continue to experience, social democrats argue that it would be absurd to hold them responsible for the situations in which they find themselves. Their exclusion cannot be seen in isolation to the other aspects of their lives over which they have very little control. Frequent and abrupt changes in living arrangements, regular interruptions to education, variable standards of care, as well as potential histories of neglect and abuse are bound to have an impact on their life chances and opportunities.

Herein, social democrats argue, lies one of the fundamental flaws of the neo-liberal approach to youth exclusion. The real world is far more complicated than neo-liberals imagine, and far more nuanced explanations need to be embraced in order to understand the dynamics that contribute to young people's marginalisation. Many require high-quality, well-resourced, tailored support that recognises the particular difficulties they face in, for example, accessing education and employment opportunities and decent-quality housing provision. Instead, they tend to be treated as a 'problematic' homogeneous 'mass', by a poorly resourced, inflexible, increasingly coercive welfare system that is simply incapable of meeting their complex needs. Solutions, from a social democratic perspective, should not be based around negative, pathological assumptions, which locate the blame for exclusion with vulnerable young people themselves. On the contrary, there should be an open acknowledgement of the obstacles and barriers that many groups of young people face in securing inclusion. Interventions at an individual level may be necessary in order to enhance, for instance, skills and improve the low levels of confidence of young people. Just as importantly, though, societal change will be necessary. Good-quality welfare support would also be considered fundamental to any social democratic approach to tackling youth exclusion.

Social workers would also have a crucial role to play in any 'social democratic' solution to the problems faced by young people. In their practice, social workers come across young people who are experiencing difficulty and marginalisation and are consequently ideally placed to help mitigate the difficulties they face. They do, though, need to ensure that their interventions are informed by an understanding of the structural constraints that shape young people's lives and not influenced by negative, value-laden perceptions of their 'culpability'. This is not an easy task. Like other members of society, social workers and welfare professionals are constantly bombarded with narratives and images which locate the blame for young people's marginalisation on the shoulders of young people themselves. In addition, as Smith (2008) argues, in many (though by no means all) scenarios it is young people's perceived problematic behaviour that will have prompted the intervention in the first place, perhaps reinforcing the notion that young people themselves are to 'blame' for their situation. This makes it all the more important that welfare professionals are able to challenge common-sense assumptions and acknowledge the fact that the difficulties faced by many young people frequently stem from the disadvantage, discrimination and marginalisation that they have faced or are experiencing. As Smith (2008, p12) states, *The fact that wider society harbours a considerable degree of apprehension and uncertainty about its younger members should not, of itself, lead us to believe that this is based upon a fair or accurate portrayal of the underlying reality of their lives.*

Marxism and youth exclusion

We end this chapter with a discussion of Marxist interpretations of youth exclusion. As we pointed out in Chapter 6, Marxism has enjoyed something of a renaissance recently, and it is worth considering how Marxist approaches to youth exclusion might differ from the two we have already outlined. In fact, Marxists tend to share some of the concerns expressed by social democrats. They too accuse neo-liberals of ignoring the structural constraints that detrimentally impact upon young people's opportunities. However, Marxists see youth exclusion, and the state's punitive response to it, as an inevitable feature of the capitalist economic system itself. More-over, they accuse social democrats of being naive for assuming that it is possible to reform capitalism into a more humane, progressive system. Capitalism, they argue, is a system which is based upon naked exploitation. It depends upon the fear of poverty to drive people into low-paid, unrewarding exploitative labour, and until capitalism is abolished the marginalisation and exclusion young people experience cannot be fully addressed.

Marxist interpretations of youth start from the premise that the state views young people solely in terms of their future potential as workers, or 'proletarians in the making', who needed to be moulded into acquiescent, mature adult workers. Wyn and White (1997) point out that 'youth' is the *threshold to adulthood*, and as such the capitalist state takes a close interest in those experiencing this life stage, seeking to monitor young people's behaviour and shape it in a way which is conducive to the future interests of capital. The state's interventions are therefore designed to socialise young people into becoming future loyal, law-abiding, compliant citizen-workers, and it is in this context that punitive coercive interventions in youth policy must be inter-preted. Behaviours that are deemed to contravene bourgeois values, or which are seen as being deemed 'inappropriate' to the effective functioning of capitalism – such as economic inactivity, teenage pregnancy and youth misbehaviour – are accordingly subjected to swift, targeted interventions from the state. However, it is not fear of young people themselves that prompts intervention; indeed, for Marxists, *the popular image of young people presenting a 'threat' to law and order represents young people as more powerful than they actually are* (Wyn and White, 1997, p12). Rather, it is the prospect of a future disaffected, potentially rebellious adult population that compels the state to pay extremely close attention to this particular life stage.

Marxists argue that this desire to instil conformity and an acceptance of the status quo into young people has been a constant influence on youth-related social policy since capitalism's inception. This process is said to have intensified in recent years. According to Jones and Novak (1999), the emergence of youth unemployment as an endemic feature of capitalist societies has led to an intensification of efforts to ensure labour discipline. The potential of youth unemployment to undermine traditional work ethic norms, and lead young adults to question the validity of capitalism, is too great to be ignored. Punitive social security reforms and dubious 'training' schemes, such as the Conservatives' Youth Training Scheme and Labour's NDYP, have been the principal means the state has used to force young people into accept-ing their fate and resigning themselves to the prospect of insecure, unrewarding low-waged work. At the same time, harsh criminal-justice policies ensure that young people are 'kept in check' and actively discouraged from engaging in active resistance and protest against their marginalisation. In recent years, the trajectory of such policy in the UK has, Jones and Novak (pp64–6) argue, been *unrelenting and peculiarly vicious,* having a marked negative effect on the living standards, opportunities and civil rights of young people:

> *The assault on young people has involved the imposition of new work
> disciplines, lower expectations in terms of both social security benefits and
> job security, pay and conditions, and a sexual, social and moral agenda that
> the neo-liberal project has pursued in the face of both uncertain evidence and
> immense hardship to some of the most vulnerable of the young.*

This attack on young people's eligibility to support is seen as an attempt to reduce future welfare expectations of citizens in capitalist societies. As, Jones and Novak argue, *The depression of young people's expectations – and especially the expectations of young working class people – has been a hallmark, even a target, of government policy since 1979* (p64). Marxists argue that instilling in young people a sense of acceptance of their fate will lead them to be more resigned to their future roles:

> *As future generations of adults, parents and workers their experience is
> crucial in determining what in the future will or will not be considered as
> acceptable, or at least unchallengeable.*

(p66)

The point, for Marxists, is that this coercive direction of youth-related policy is an inevitable and indeed necessary requirement in capitalist societies, whose labour markets are increasingly reliant upon the supply of cheap, amenable, disciplined workforces. From this perspective, a more humane, progressive approach cannot ultimately be implemented and sustained. The structural constraints of the capitalist system – that is, its need to generate a compliant workforce that is willing, or unable to be unwilling, to engage in exploitative, low-waged work – means that all governments, whatever their political complexion, are compelled to introduce policies that guarantee the requirements of business are met. This is the context within which Marxists interpret policies such as Labour's NDYP, its teenage pregnancy strategy and its youth justice agenda. They reject the rhetoric that accompanied the introduction of such policies, claiming that they represented little more than an attempt to force young people to conform with bourgeois values and to engage with an increasingly insecure, low paid, exploitative labour market.

What role then is there for social workers in youth-related policy? A Marxist approach to social work with young people would begin with an acknowledgement that social work practice cannot in itself solve the endemic exclusion they experience. Social workers working with young people can have as their aim the creation of a more fair, just society, but they cannot themselves achieve the fundamental changes that are needed to significantly improve the lives of marginalised young people. As Bailey and Brake (1980, pp7–8) argue, the potential to do this is constrained by the fact that social workers, like their young service users, are *trapped in a social structure which severely delimits their power and hence their ability to initiate significant change.*

This is, however, not to say that there is no role for social workers. Indeed, the early pioneers of Marxist approaches to social work made it clear that their intention was not to underestimate the potential of social work in the 'here and now'. *Our purpose*, Bailey and Brake insisted, *is not to discourage radical students from taking up social work, nor to depress those workers already struggling in contradictions which have not been created by them* (p9). As 'social bandits', or 'noble robbers', social workers have a crucial ideological and practical role to play in mitigating the injustices capitalism imposes upon young people's welfare, while at the same time fighting against the system itself. On the one hand then, they can operate as a 'buffer', alleviating some of the more destructive elements of capitalism by doing their best to ensure that young people's services are delivered in a non-judgemental way that acknowledges the structural constraints that have caused or contributed to their difficulties. On the other hand, they can seek to undermine capitalism from 'within', operating as 'grit' in the capitalist machine, wherever possible offering recalcitrance, resistance, obstruction (Ferguson and Woodward, 2009, p78), and seeking to encourage an awareness among young people and others of the need to transcend capitalism. This latter ideological/political role is one that is emphasised by Marxists such as Skott-Myhre (2005, p142), who point to *the potential of revolutionary collaboration between youth and adults.* He argues that 'youth' has always historically been at the vanguard of protest and revolution, and suggests that social workers have a role to play in cultivating this revolutionary potential. Clearly, there are many professional and organisational constraints which make it difficult for social workers to develop such a liberatory form of practice with young people. As Ferguson and Woodward (2009, p79 and 132) accept, *In the current controlled and controlling climate, such practice can be seen as radical, even subversive.* It can, they acknowledge, *be difficult, and, from an employment point of view, potentially hazardous to practise radical social work in isolation* (p132). Wherever possible, though, practitioners should seek to rise above these constraints, and build alliances with colleagues and like-minded welfare workers in related professions, in order to create a truly emancipatory form of practice with young people.

CHAPTER SUMMARY

This chapter began by challenging some of the more 'common-sense' perceptions surrounding 'youth' and 'young people'. As we saw, the notion that we are witnessing an unprecedented 'deluge' of youth irresponsibility and misbehaviour is not borne out by either historical or contemporary evidence. Indeed, as we stated, there is much to celebrate about the conduct and achievements of young people today. However, 'youth' is a life stage that is characterised by a higher likelihood of exclusion and marginalisation and certain groups of young people do experience particular difficulties. As we showed, different theoretical explanations have been advanced to account for this exclusion, but neo-liberal, pathological interpretations do appear to have been most influential in shaping UK youth exclusion policy.

FURTHER READING

The following, now classic text by Geoffrey Pearson provides an excellent analysis of the history of concerns about 'hooligan' behaviour among young people:

Pearson, G (1983) *Hooligan: A history of respectable fears.* London: Macmillan.

For those of you interested in moral panics around youth, Stanley Cohen's original classic text would be an excellent starting point:

Cohen, S (2006) *Folk devils and moral panics.* 3rd edition. London: Routledge.

The following text provides an excellent, thorough introduction to issues relating to social work with young people:

Smith, R (2008) *Social work with young people*. London: Wiley.

Answers to Activity 8.2

Quote 1 = c4000 BC. This quote was found in an Egyptian tomb (cited in Byron, 2009).
Quote 2 = 1274, Peter the Hermit (cited in Byron, 2009).
Quote 3 = 4th century BC, Plato (cited in Byron, 2009).
Quote 4 = 1900, *The Times* (30 October).
Quote 5 = 1960, *The Times* (13 June).
Quote 6 = 1977, *The Times* (20 April).

Chapter 9

Adults, social policy and social work: The personalisation agenda

This chapter will help you begin to meet the following National Occupational Standards:

Key Role 1: Prepare for, and work with individuals, families, carers, groups and communities to assess their needs and circumstances.

- Work with individuals, families, carers, groups and communities to enable them to assess and make informed decisions about their needs, circumstances, risks, preferred options and resources.

Key Role 2: Plan, carry out, review and evaluate social work practice, with individuals, families, carers, groups, communities and other professionals.

- Apply and justify social work methods and models used to achieve change and development, and improve life opportunities.

Key Role 3: Support individuals to represent their needs, views and circumstances.

- Assist individuals, families, carers, groups and communities to assess independent advocacy.
- Advocate for, and with, individuals, families, carers, groups and communities.

Key Role 4: Manage risk to individuals, families, carers, groups communities, self and colleagues.

- Balance the rights and responsibilities of individuals, families, carers, groups and communities with associated risk.

Key Role 5: Manage and be accountable with supervision and support, for your own social work practice within your organisation.

- Contribute to monitoring the effectiveness of services in meeting need.

Key Role 6: Demonstrate professional competence in social work practice.

- Review and update your own knowledge of legal, policy and procedural frameworks.
- Use professional and organisational supervision and support to research, critically analyse, and review knowledge based practice.
- Identify and assess issues, dilemmas and conflicts that might affect your practice. Contribute to policy review and development.

The chapter will also introduce you to the following academic standards which are set out in the 2008 QAA social work benchmark statements.

4.2 Defining principles.

4.3 Defining principles.

4.6 Defining principles.

4.7 Defining principles.

5.1.1 Subject knowledge, understanding and skills.

5.1.2 Subject knowledge, understanding and skills.

5.1.3 Values and ethics.

5.1.4 Social work theory.

Introduction

In their practice, social workers engage with a number of different groups of adult service users. By 'adults' we are referring to service users who are over the age of 18 and under the age of 65 (we examine policy in relation to older adults in Chapter 10). As with other service user groups, the work carried out by social workers with adults is shaped and constrained by wider ideological and policy trends. Recent policy developments, in many cases influenced by the views of user movements themselves, have focused upon the need to empower certain groups of adult service users, by giving them more control over their services. The emphasis that is placed upon the need for the development of more personalised systems of support is perhaps the most consistent theme to be found in recent policy documents relating to adult social care. Indeed, personalisation is universally portrayed as the new panacea, or the 'holy grail' of adult social care and its arrival on the social policy agenda has been welcomed by academics and politicians of all political shades. However, we will also show how this ostensibly progressive development should not be interpreted entirely uncritically.

Personalisation

Personalisation formed a key part of the previous Labour government's strategy for adult social care (Glasby and Littlechild, 2009) and by 2007/08 some 86,110 adult service users and 30,425 carers were in receipt of personalised services in the form of direct payments (Commons Hansard, 17 November 2010, c973–8). The Labour government's enthusiasm for extending personalised services is shared by the current Conservative-dominated coalition. The coalition's recent strategy document, *A vision for adult social care*, reiterates the positive messages contained in Labour's earlier policy documents:

> *People not service providers or systems, should hold the choice and control about their care. The time is now right to make personal budgets the norm for everyone who receives ongoing care and support – ideally as a direct cash payment, to give maximum flexibility and choice.*

> (Department of Health, 2010, p15)

As was the case with previous Labour governments, coalition ministers claim that their motivations are entirely altruistic, and are geared towards delivering *greater choice, control and independence, and ultimately better quality of life*. Personalisation, in short, is seen to provide the long sought-after, radical solution to the problems that have previously beset adult social care, and will progressively transform the way it is delivered.

Later in the chapter, we place some of the assumptions that underpin the 'personalisation agenda' under a more critical lens. One of the issues we examine is the extent to which political support for 'personalisation' is genuinely based upon benevolent, progressive principles. This is an important question, because as Spandler (2004) argues, the policy implications associated with personalisation can hold an appeal to those of both progressive and reactionary tendencies. For example, direct payments (a key mechanism of delivering personalisation) may, on the one hand, be interpreted as a progressive attempt to provide service users with a greater level of self-determination, improving and strengthening collectively funded provision. In this sense, one can see the attraction of personalisation to social democrats. On the other hand, direct payments could be seen as part of a less altruistic strategy to abrogate responsibility for 'difficult' service users and to transfer responsibility for securing welfare from the state to the individual. Herein lies the appeal of personalisation to neo-liberals who are committed to the retrenchment of state welfare. We will assess the complex confluence of ideological interests that shape current personalisation strategies in greater detail later. First, though, we examine some of the concerns that have provided impetus to the current shift towards personalisation.

Has statutory provision been unresponsive to the needs of adult service users?

As we explained in Chapter 4, the development of the social democratic welfare state after 1945 led to an unparalleled improvement in levels of economic and social well-being. In 1948 a universal National Health Service was established, which for the first time provided free health care to all on the basis of need. In addition, better social security and housing provision helped alleviate some of the chronic levels of poverty and destitution that were a feature of life before the welfare state. However, as we also saw in Chapter 4, the post-war welfare state was far from perfect and there have always been calls from within the social policy community for improvements to be made to the level and quality of provision. This has been particularly so in relation to adult social care provision. Research evidence has consistently highlighted significant levels of marginalisation and exclusion among adult service users. In addition, inquiries have pointed to a systematic failure of welfare services to meet the needs of certain groups of adult service users. Indeed, some investigations have shown services to be oppressive, demeaning and entirely unresponsive to the preferences of those whose needs they are designed to meet.

Adults with mental health and learning disabilities

The poor standard of care offered to adults with mental health and learning disabilities in the relatively recent past has been long acknowledged. The post-war years, for example, were littered with scandals, where professionals who were entrusted with caring responsibilities for vulnerable adults were found guilty of committing appalling levels of neglect. In the late 1960s and early 1970s consecutive inquiries in Ely, Farleigh and Whittingham hospitals uncovered a dreadful catalogue of abuse. There was, in short, an utter breakdown in care in these institutions, and it was clear from the major inquiries that were undertaken at the time that some welfare professionals placed their own selfish interests above the needs and wishes of their patients.

These scandals were illustrative of one of the darker periods in the history British postwar welfare, and partly as a consequence, we saw a shift towards community care and the acknowledgement of the need for welfare to be more responsive to the needs and preferences of adult service users. There was, therefore, a general recognition that welfare should not simply be 'imposed' by professionals upon vulnerable service users. There can be little doubt that as a result of this, standards of care for adults with mental health and learning difficulties have now improved. For instance, many of the old Victorian long-stay hospitals have closed and those who would have previously been resident in these institutions now receive social care and support in the community. Indeed, only approximately 3,000 people with learning disabilities continue to live as NHS inpatients (Healthcare Commission, 2006).

However, various inquiries and investigations have drawn attention to the continued failure to provide for the needs of many mental health and learning-disabled adult service users. In 2006, for instance, a joint inquiry undertaken by the Commission for Social Care Inspection (CSCI) and the Healthcare Commission (2006, p5) into the supported living arrangements for learning-disabled adults in Cornwall's NHS Trust found evidence of abusive practices that were reminiscent of those uncovered in the 1960 and 1970s.

ACTIVITY 9.1

In order to complete this activity you will need to access the report of the inquiry undertaken by the CSCI and Healthcare Commission that we refer to above. The full title of this is: Joint investigation into the provision of services for people with learning disabilities at Cornwall Partnership's NHS Trust. *We have provided the current web address for the report in the References, but in the event of this changing you should be able to locate it by simply typing the title into an internet search engine.*

This inquiry was conducted four years after the publication of Valuing People *(Department of Health, 2001b), the Labour government's key strategy document which set out the principles that it felt should underpin services for learning disabled adults. These included an emphasis upon:*

Continued

- *community support;*
- *rights;*
- *independence;*
- *choice;*
- *inclusion.*

- *What do the CSCI/Healthcare Commission's findings tell us about the integration of these principles into practice?*
- *Do the inquiry's findings and conclusions help you understand the growing demands made by adult service users for their voices to be heard in the organisation and delivery of welfare provision?*

COMMENT

Cornwall's NHS Trust's service users were being provided with support in the 'community', but the quality of that support was in many ways no better than that provided in the old Victorian 'asylums'. Adult service users in the Trust's 'supported housing', for example, were found to have no choice over where they resided, over who provided their care, or over the nature or quality of that care. 'Residents' were overly sedated, locked in their rooms and denied access to basic facilities like food and running water. There was, the inquiry found, evidence of physical restraint being used illegally and of excessive use of ... medication to control unacceptable behaviour in the Trust's assessment, treatment and supported living services. Incidents uncovered by the CSCI/Healthcare Commission included:

hitting, pushing, shoving, dragging, kicking, secluding, belittling, mocking and goading people who used the trust's services, withholding food, giving cold showers, overzealous or premature use of restraint, poor attitude towards people who used services, poor atmosphere, roughness, care not being provided, a lack of dignity and respect, and no privacy (p31).

Much of the abuse stemmed from the poor treatment meted out by certain members of staff. However, the inquiry also pointed to culpability of the hospital trust itself, in particular its failure to ensure its staff treated service users with dignity, respect and compassion. The following extract is taken from the Health Commission's report:

The trust's own investigations ... have shown that some people using its services have had to endure years of abusive practices and some have suffered real injury as a result ... Our investigation found that institutional abuse was widespread, preventing people from exercising their rights to independence, choice and inclusion. One person spent 16 hours a day tied to their bed or wheelchair, for what staff wrongly believed was for that person's own protection. One man told investigators that he had never chosen any of the places he had lived as an adult.

Continued

Learning-disabled people who utilised the trust's services were 'looked after', *instead of being supported to develop their skills. This, the report concluded, limited their ability to make informed choices and communicate their needs, rendering them largely powerless to control their environments or their lives (pp7–8). There was, therefore, a fundamental failure to understand or acknowledge the wishes of individual service users. Managers and staff at the Trust simply assumed that* 'they knew best'; *they determined the shape and quality of provision and no attempts had been made to empower service users or enable their voices to be heard.* The Trust's services, *the report concluded*, did not reflect the principles of rights, independence, choice and inclusion, set out in the Valuing People strategy *(p6)*.

In the light of such findings, one can understand the growing demands that have emerged for user empowerment to be at the heart of adult social care provision. Clearly, the abuses found at Cornwall's NHS Trust are not representative of provision generally, but as a recent BBC *Panorama* investigation into abuse at the privately run Winterbourne View assessment and treatment centre illustrated, such scandals continue to occur. This undercover documentary showed staff harassing, punching and kicking learning-disabled patients in their care. In one scene, a member of staff was seen goading a service user to jump out of a second floor window, while in another, a support worker was seen impersonating a Nazi camp commander, slapping a service user across the face with leather gloves (Brindle, 2011).

The mere fact that such pockets of neglect have continued to be exposed has, understandably, led to demands that the needs and views of service users must be far more central to future policy and practice. It is, critics argue, a failure to acknowledge the voices or wishes of service users that leads to neglect and poor quality provision. Consequently universal assumptions about what is 'good' for adult service users need to be rejected in favour of a more empowering, user-led model of policy and practice. Such concerns have been reflected in recent policy documents, which suggest that 'impersonal', inflexible welfare provision can, in some instances, serve to reinforce the disadvantages service users already face. As Labour's key strategy document *Putting people first* argued, *While acknowledging the Community Care legislation of the 1990s was well intentioned, it has led to a system which can be over complex and too often fails to respond to people's needs and expectations* (HM Government, 2007, p1). Labour's Green Paper, *Independence, well-being and choice*, made much the same point, this time identifying 'traditional' social work practices as a potential cause of marginalisation:

> *For too long social work has been perceived as a gatekeeper or rationer of services and has been accused ... of fostering dependence rather than independence. We want to create a different environment, which reinforces the core social work values of supporting individuals to take control of their own lives, and to make the choices which matter to them.*

> (Department of Health, 2005, p10)

Universalism versus particularism? The challenge to universalism

As we have already explained, allegations that the welfare state is unresponsive and unsympathetic to the needs and wishes of those that use its services are not, in fact, particularly novel. This critique of welfare helped draw attention to the flaws associated with impersonal, 'institutionalised' care in the 1960s and 1970s and influenced the policy trend towards community care and services. However, concerns about 'top-down', professionally led rather than service user-led welfare services became increasingly influential in the 1980s and 1990s. The 'universal' nature of the UK's welfare services, it was argued, had led to the development of a 'one-size-fits-all' model, which meant that the particular needs of different groups of service users, such as adults with disabilities, mental health issues and learning difficulties, had been largely ignored. While the worst excesses of 'institutionalised' services may, to an extent, have been tackled, service users were still often the unwilling recipients of services that were imposed upon them. This critique of the post-war welfare state sought to expose the extent to which the main institutions of collectivist welfare – health, social care, social work, social security, housing and education – had all failed to provide adequately for the diverse, conflicting and varied needs of different individuals and social groups. Fiona Williams (1992) was among those who were critical of the 'false universalism' of the post-war welfare state. It was, she argued, *built on a white, male, able bodied, heterosexual [nuclear family] norm*, and consequently those who failed to correspond to this 'norm' received inferior services, if any at all. The underpinning assumption, that uniform, standardised services were the most effective means of meeting the needs of all users of welfare services, was, it was suggested, fundamentally flawed. This model of welfare provision may have been introduced with the best of intentions, but, according to those such as Williams, it ignored the fact that users of welfare services often had differing and varied needs that 'mass', 'standardised', state-organised provision was failing to meet (Williams, 1989).

At the same time, the power and control wielded by 'expert' welfare professionals was subjected to critical examination. The post-war welfare state had, critics argued, always been characterised by a 'top-down' patronising mode of delivery, whereby users of welfare services had been expected to unquestioningly accept the prescriptions and services provided by welfare 'experts', such as nurses, doctors and social workers. Welfare professionals, including social workers, had *assessed and acted upon* service users, rather than engaging with them and giving them the control or power to tailor the services they received to their own individual needs. In short, it was argued that insufficient attention had been paid to the views and needs of certain service user groups, many of whom had been treated as 'passive' recipients of universal services rather than people with their own individual particular needs. Service users had, in many cases, been reduced to a *benign form of state clienthood* (Harris, 2004).

Arthur – *Arthur is a 45-year-old service user with moderate learning disabilities, who lives in a local authority-funded sheltered housing project. In common with accepted practice at the time, Arthur attended a 'special' school as a child. His parents would have preferred him to be educated in a mainstream school, alongside non-disabled children, but in accordance with national policy Arthur's local authority felt it was better to educate disabled children separately. It was generally felt that disabled children would find it difficult to cope in a mainstream school environment, and that the 'demands' of catering for disabled children in mainstream schools would be too onerous.*

Arthur was liked by his teachers at his 'special' school and was seen as one of the more academically able children in his cohort, but like the vast majority of his peers he left school with no formal academic qualifications. As was the case with many of the children in Arthur's class, it was assumed that on leaving school he would find employment in a government-funded 'sheltered workshop' for disabled adults, and would have no need for formal educational qualifications. Arthur worked in a sheltered workshop for a number of years after leaving school, but this closed ten years ago as result of cuts in government funding. Since then, Arthur has applied for numerous paid jobs elsewhere, without any success. His social worker has sought to arrange voluntary work experience for him, and along with a couple of other learning disabled adults, he currently helps out occasionally at a local charity shop.

- *How might Arthur's life chances have been impeded by the 'universal' assumptions made by welfare professionals about the 'best' way to provide welfare services to people with disabilities?*

Arthur's experiences of the welfare system serve to illustrate some of the problems associated with 'universal', 'professional-driven' forms of welfare. Such forms of provision can be based upon wide, often inaccurate generalisations about what is 'good' for service users. Individuals become categorised according to their collective, service-user-defined identities and they are subjected to universal, one-size-fits-all interventions, which take little account of their own particular needs, abilities and capabilities. In the case of children such as Arthur, the decision to segregate them into special schools will often have been taken without any assessment of their intellectual abilities, or without any appreciation of the consequences of denying them the opportunity of a 'mainstream' education. Likewise, the assumption that Arthur would be employed in a 'sheltered workshop' on leaving school will have been shaped by the belief that 'mainstream' employment was not right for Arthur. Welfare professionals who made decisions 'on behalf' of Arthur and his family may well have been motivated by the best of intentions, but the assumptions upon which they made those decisions have, over time, proven to be fundamentally flawed. The premise upon which they were based – that is, that it was unrealistic to think that disabled people should realistically expect to fully participate in society – is now widely acknowledged to be false and indeed oppressive. It is partly for this reason that welfare interventions that have been based upon wide, universal, generalised assumptions about what is 'appropriate' for service users were increasingly questioned in the 1980s and 1990s, and demands made for the implementation of a more empowering, user-led model of welfare.

Postmodernism and welfare

It is important to note that such critiques of the 'universal' post-war welfare state were articulated mainly by those on the social democratic left of the academic and political community who in no way wished to undermine support for the principles underpinning publicly funded state welfare. Many of these were attracted by 'postmodernism', an increasingly influential strand of sociological thought that seemed to provide a platform for the development of a more critical, emancipatory social policy and social work practice (Hillyard and Watson, 1996; Carter, 1998). They argued that while 'mass', 'universal' services may have been appropriate mechanisms for satisfying very basic, 'absolute' needs in the austerity-driven post-war decades of what they refer to as the 'modernist' era, there was now a need for a more nuanced approach. 'Mass', 'universal' welfare policy stood accused of failing to acknowledge the voices, desires and needs of many groups of service users. This, it was argued, could only be overcome though the injection of greater heterogeneity, diversity, flexibility and specialisation in the way welfare was delivered. Thus, a new political strategy, based upon a celebration of fragmentation and particularism was said to offer the basis for the development of a more progressive welfare model more befitting to the new 'postmodern' world. Voices that had hitherto been ignored should, as a matter of principle, be acknowledged, commitments to 'old-style' universalism should be abandoned, and more specialised, targeted services should be developed to take into account the different and diverse needs of 'newly enfranchised' groups of service users.

As already stated, the intention of most of those who were attracted to 'postmodernism' was to strengthen the foundations of collectivist, statutory provision by making welfare and social care more responsive to the needs of service users. This, it was felt, would be of benefit to service users, ensuring an end to soulless, 'professionals-know-best' provision, but it would also help reinforce the legitimacy of the welfare state, making it more difficult for those on the political 'right' to pursue their ideologically motivated strategies of retrenchment and cuts. As we will see, it also reflected growing demands from adult service users themselves for more control of the welfare they received.

However, the growing influence of postmodernism within social policy was not without its critics. Peter Taylor Gooby (1994, p403), for example, accused its advocates of being blinded by the rhetoric of welfare pluralism, consumerism, decentralisation and choice, ignoring the fact that this same rhetoric was concurrently being used by neo-liberal Conservative governments to disguise policies which had actually reinforced inequalities and made the position of many vulnerable social groups much worse. The retrenchment of state welfare in the 1980s and the movement from universalism to more targeted, means-tested forms of welfare provision had been justified by Conservative ministers through the rhetoric of 'choice' and 'flexibility', but the changes had heralded a shift towards a harsher, selective, and stigmatising form of welfare delivery. Hence, while accepting that the welfare state was 'imperfect', those such as Taylor Gooby (1994, p403) cautioned against 'crude', generalised attacks on the principle of universalism. Such assaults, alongside an uncritical acceptance of the concept of 'choice', could, he argued, serve to *cloak developments of considerable importance*:

> *Trends towards increased inequality in living standards, the privatisation of state welfare services and the stricter regulation of the lives of some of the poorest groups may fail to attract the appropriate attention if the key themes of policy are seen as difference, diversity and choice.*

In summary, 'postmodern' approaches to welfare were accused by their critics of failing to have an inadequate grasp of the power relations that often underpinned the rhetoric of 'choice' and 'flexibility'. The use of such language, it was argued, constituted little more than an 'ideological smokescreen', obscuring the regressive political interests that were driving the policies of successive Conservative administrations. 'Postmodernism' was, critics insisted, in danger of providing the 'right' with ammunition and support to amount an ideologically motivated assault on the very principles of the welfare state.

Service users' demands for greater autonomy

The articulation of this 'postmodern' critique within the social policy academic community coincided with growing dissatisfaction from within service user groups themselves with the services they received, many of whom consistently campaigned for the right to control their own welfare resources. Disabled people were one such group. Disabled activists had, for a number of years, been at the forefront of campaigns challenging the right of professionals to determine the shape of welfare provision, demanding that they be seen not as passive recipients, but as active participants in the design and delivery of the services they received (Morris, 1993). The expertise of these professionals and their ability to determine 'what was best' for disabled people was therefore increasingly questioned, and as part of this process disability activists championed the concept of independent living. They claimed that the money previously spent by the NHS and local authorities 'on behalf' of disabled people had previously had the effect of segregating and marginalising them. Welfare professionals, Morris (1997, p59) argued, *chose to spend large sums of money on segregated provision – which meant that disabled people had to live restricted and impoverished lives that the professionals concerned would never have chosen for themselves*:

> *For example, instead of spending money to help someone attend college, go to the cinema or pursue other leisure activities, visit friends and family and so on, money was spent on building Day Centres where people are still bused every day to do the kind of things that other people think are good for them.*

It would, disabled activists argued, be far better if disabled people themselves were given control over their own resources, allowing them to stay in their own homes and purchase the services they wanted. Organisations such as the Union of Physically Impaired Against Segregation, the British Council of Disabled People and the Disability Alliance were at the forefront of demands for greater choice and control (Leece and Bornat, 2006). Claims that disabled people were being 'duped' into inadvertently supporting a right wing, ideologically motivated attack on collectivist welfare were rejected:

> *To support a system in which the individual who needs the help has the power to determine how that help is delivered is not to support an individualist right-wing agenda. Rather, it is about promoting collective responsibility for protecting individual rights.*

(Morris, 1997, p59)

Partly as a result of the pressure applied by disabled people, in the late 1980s the Conservative government established the Independent Living Fund (ILF), which provided some disabled service users with small cash payments they could use to pay for their own care. What was initially intended to be a small-scale scheme, designed to compensate only a few hundred disabled individuals who had lost income due to wider social security changes, was quickly forced to expand to meet demand for more 'personalised' care. The scope of the ILF was still limited and circumscribed, and its funding was nowhere near adequate to meet need, but as Glasby and Littlechild (2002) point out, it did set an important precedent in the way it gave service users control over a portion of their care budget. They describe it as *a 'Pandora's box' ... which, once opened would be very difficult to close again* (p17).

The 1996 Community Care (Direct Payments) Act

The 1996 Community Care (Direct Payments) Act, passed by John Major's Conservative government, came into force in April 1997, and it placed the personalisation agenda firmly at the heart of government policy. The Act gave local authorities discretionary powers, enabling them to provide direct payments to adult disabled services users under the age of 65. John Bowis, the minister who steered the Bill though the parliamentary process, described it as representing a *significant step down the road of responding to people's wishes and enabling them to lead as normal a life as possible*. Henceforth, adult disabled people under the age of 65 would be given the opportunity to control social care resources that had previously been spent on their behalf by social service departments. They would be given the power to manage directly the services they received, deciding, for instance, from whom to buy services and who to employ to assist them. The crux of the government's case was that inflexible statutory social services had failed to respond to the varied and particular needs of adult disabled service users.

> *Time and again, I have heard from people who have a disability, but also hold down a job or voluntary work and whose working lives are obstructed by the rigidity of a council service rota; or people who do not like to complain, but would really like a different range of menus from the meal service; or people who have responsible jobs, but are treated by the care workers as if they were rather tiresome and untidy children. They have no real independence, no real choice and no real dignity. The Bill will change that.*

(Bowis, cited in Lords Hansard, 6 March 1996, c372)

The Act would, the government argued, help revolutionise the organisation of adult social care, transforming the way in which service were delivered to and experienced by adult service users. Old 'top-down' approaches, whereby service users were the passive, sometimes unwilling recipients of second-class, bureaucratically driven services, would be consigned to the past. Welfare bureaucrats and professionals would no longer be in sole charge of the resources that determine the services that people are able to access. Resources, control, choice and power would be transferred to the 'service-user consumer', who was better placed to determine their own welfare needs and preferences. Although initially restricted to disabled adults under the age of 65, the government made it clear that it would consider extending the principle of direct payments to other categories of adult service users. The ultimate aim was for all adult service users to be given the power to purchase their own services and to tailor them to their fit around their own particular needs. Put simply, they, rather than welfare professionals, would have the power to decide what suits them best.

Altruism or ideology?

The rhetoric used by ministers to justify this strategy for adult social care drew heavily from the empowering principles that have shaped the campaigns of service user groups for greater autonomy. As we have seen, ministers claimed that they were simply delivering what service users had long demanded, and the process was the result of a bottom-up struggle to force the state to relinquish control of welfare resources, and to develop a more progressive model of organising welfare. Benevolence, altruism and social justice were said to lie at the heart of the strategy. Personalisation, it was argued, held out the promise of a more democratised, self-determined model of welfare, one which would put the individual service user at the heart of provision. The message was clear. The move towards personalisation was motivated by progressive principles, and the outcome could not be anything but positive in terms of its impact upon the standard of services and quality of life afforded to adult service users.

Others remained less convinced of the government's claim that it was motivated by benevolent intentions. Conservative ministers had, for instance, previously been distinctly lukewarm towards the principle of direct payments, fearing that they would undermine accountability for public spending and, more importantly, lead to increased expenditure. Stung by the unexpected high demand for Independent Living Fund payments, ministers had previously feared that the costs of direct payments would become uncontrollable. Indeed, as late as 1993 John Major's Conservative government had reduced the scope for direct payments by closing the Independent Living Fund to newcomers and by establishing a new fund, the eligibility criterion for which was markedly more restrictive than the original scheme. The government's eventual 'conversion' to the principle of direct payments less than a year later was, some argue, motivated less by social justice concerns, and more by a gradual realisation that 'personalisation' could actually be cheaper and more cost-effective than locally authority provided services. As Pearson (2000) points out, the government's announcement that it was to legislate in favour of direct payments came less than a week after the publication of research suggesting they were between 30–40 per cent cheaper than service-based provision.

Direct payments also fitted in with John Major's Conservative government's wider neo-liberal ideological framework, which was focused upon privatising state provision, reducing the power of state welfare workers, and promoting a marketised model of welfare. Some such as Clare Ungerson (1997) (like Taylor Gooby earlier), feared that progressive social democratic language was being used to justify what was essentially a neo-liberal, cuts-led agenda. In embracing the powerful, persuasive, empowering rhetoric of service-user movements, neo-liberals were said by sceptics to have performed something of a *coup d'état*, 'co-opting' unsuspecting user movements into supporting their ideologically motivated strategy of welfare retrenchment. At the same time, the utilisation of the language of personalisation by Conservative ministers was said to have performed a powerful ideological function, allowing them to portray any criticisms of their policies for marketising social care as an extreme defence of 'old', 'oppressive' professionally driven services. Sceptics of the trajectory of policy, such as Ungerson, expressed their frustration at being cast as defenders of the 'unacceptable' status quo:

> *To query the empowerment of consumers of care is to appear to be against the interests of the vulnerable and the oppressed, and against the routes which might develop their currently very limited rights to full participation in society. The evidence is overwhelming that disabled people in the past have been demeaned, discriminated against, abused and ignored by those people funded by the state who were and are supposed to respond to their needs.*

(Ungerson, 1997, p46)

Perhaps not surprisingly, disabled adult service users were less concerned about the ideological origins of the 1996 Community Care (Direct Payments) Act and more interested in the fact that it enshrined the principle of direct payments in law. They widely welcomed the legislation, seeing it as the beginning of an acknowledgement of their historical struggle for self-determination and control of welfare resources. Some were critical of its limited scope, particularly the fact that only disabled people under 65 were initially eligible to benefit from its provisions, but overall the reaction was positive. *The new system of direct payments – with all its imperfections*, Morris (1997, p60) argued, was *an important stage in the achievements of a civil rights movement*. The Act was also welcomed by the Labour opposition, though it too was critical of the government's decision to restrict eligibility to disabled adults under the age of 65. This restriction was removed by Tony Blair's Labour government in 2000, and in 2003 local authorities were mandated to offer direct payments to all eligible people living in their areas. Both these developments were welcomed by service-user groups. There now appears to be little political disagreement over the principles of personalisation and all three major political parties in the UK are committed to progressing this agenda. As we have already seen, the current coalition government intends to press ahead with personalisation, seeing it as a means of shifting power *from the state to the citizen, from Whitehall to the town hall and from provider to citizen* (Department of Health, 2010, p21).

The benefits of personalisation

Analyses of the personalisation agenda have highlighted a number of beneficial outcomes and service users themselves have commented positively upon the greater autonomy afforded by direct payments. Surveys suggest that direct payments have contributed to higher levels of self-esteem among adult service users, increased control over their lives, as well as improved vocational and recreational opportunities. Research also suggests that significant cost-efficiency gains are associated with direct payments when compared with conventional services, with individual service users better able to micro-manage the care they receive (Stainton et al., 2009). The 'benefits' that are said to have been generated by personalisation are summarised below.

Better-quality services

Because the service user is the architect of provision, personalisation can lead to the development of more responsive, tailor-made services that are more finely tuned to match the particular needs of service users. Service users themselves are able to determine the type and shape of care they receive. They are also able to choose the staff/carers they feel are best qualified to deliver the support they require for their needs. In this sense, personalisation is said to provide much greater opportunities to develop closer, more continuous, trustworthy relationships with support workers, further enhancing the quality of provision (Spandler and Vick, 2005).

CASE STUDY

Arthur – *In this case study, we want to return to Arthur, the learning-disabled service user we introduced you to earlier. When he is not volunteering at the charity shop, Arthur regularly attends a day care centre along with a number of other learning disabled adults. This is funded by the local authority as part of Arthur's package of care. The centre lays on some leisure activities and Arthur quite enjoys the company of other service users at the centre, though he is often bored and rarely stimulated by the activities it offers. Staff at the centre have noticed he is becoming increasingly withdrawn, but they are too busy to pursue the reasons why this is the case. Unbeknown to them, Arthur's two real passions are watching football and gardening. Arthur's interest in football was stimulated by a visit of his local football team, Preston North End, to the day care centre a couple of years before, and he would dearly love to be able to afford to go and watch them every week. Arthur's interest in gardening was developed while at school, where he and other pupils were encouraged to tend the school's grounds and vegetable plots. However, none of the supported housing he has lived in since leaving school has had gardens. Arthur recently saw an advert for allotments in his local newspaper, but knows he could not afford the annual fees, let alone the tools that he would need to tend the allotment. His growing frustration stems from his inability to afford to pursue these hobbies.*

- *How might personalised care offer up new opportunities and possibilities for Arthur?*

COMMENT

Some of the money currently spent Arthur's behalf by the local authority could, if given to him directly, be used in a more personalised way, tailored to fit around his particular interests and needs. Arthur could still attend the day care centre occasionally, but a portion of his social care budget could, for instance, be utilised to pay for rent and tools he needs to tend his own allotment, and to purchase tickets to see his local football team. He, rather than social services, would be in charge of his budget, and he (perhaps with advocacy support) could tailor a flexible package of provision that would fit around his particular interests and needs at particular times. He might, for example, wish to enrol on a short gardening course to improve his horticultural skills. Alternatively, he might decide that he wishes to travel to watch his favourite football team play away from home occasionally. He could even choose to employ personal assistants who share his passions for gardening and football. The point is, Arthur would not be 'tied' to an inflexible package of care that was planned months, or even years in advance, which bore little or no relation to his current interests. In this sense, Arthur will benefit from the flexibility open to him to alter and adapt his programme of care as his interests and circumstances change. One can imagine the psychological benefits that could be derived from such empowerment and control, as well as its potential for enhancing Arthur's social and economic well-being.

Improved mental and psychological well-being

In fact, adult service users who utilise personalised services frequently report improvements to their psychological well-being. In part, this may be a result of improved service delivery. For example, in controlling how their own resources are spent, service users (like Arthur above) may be able to benefit from a whole range of health, education, training and leisure opportunities that would previously have been unavailable to them, and this will clearly contribute to enhanced levels of morale and mental health. However, such improvements are also thought to result from the greater feelings of empowerment and control engendered by personalisation. Many service users comment positively on the growing levels of self-respect and dignity derived from managing their own care packages and being in control of their lives.

More economically efficient services

As already noted, there is evidence to suggest that personalised services are more cost-efficient than 'traditional', local authority-organised services (for recent evidence see Stainton *et al.*, 2009). Service users, for instance, have a direct vested interest in ensuring that 'their' resources are spent efficiently and that the money allocated to them is utilised as effectively as possible. On a practical level, for example, they are able to employ neighbours, friends and in some cases relatives. Unlike local authorities or private-sector service providers, which often charge by the hour irrespective of the time spent providing support, such individuals are more likely to be prepared and capable of being flexible with their working arrangements, leading to a reduction in overall costs, as well as more effective care.

In the light of these positive findings, it is hardly surprising that the personalisation agenda can count upon such widespread support among service users, commentators and politicians. It seems to offer the potential of revolutionising state-funded social care provision, putting the individual in the driving seat, while at the same time driving up standards and reducing the costs of provision. As Peter Beresford (2008a, p11) acknowledges, it could lead to *a new era of social care where the consumer becomes king, able to pull down a much broader and more imaginative menu of support, either directly for themselves or for those close to them – all with state aid*. Beresford is a prominent advocate of user empowerment and he clearly sees the potential of personalisation to transform adult social care for the better. However, like many others who have long advocated in favour of a much greater level of user involvement, he has cautioned against an uncritical celebration of the personalisation agenda.

A critical analysis of the personalisation agenda

Concerns about the direction of the personalisation agenda can be divided into two categories – 'practical' and 'ideological'. Practical criticisms focus upon issues such as the adequacy of resources devoted to personalisation, or the perceived inability of some service users to benefit from it. Such criticisms seek to highlight potential limitations of the agenda as it is currently being applied, but they do not necessarily represent a challenge to the general trajectory of policy. On the other hand, ideologically based criticisms seek to highlight what some believe are more fundamental flaws in the personalisation agenda. Echoing those such as Taylor Gooby and Ungerson, they argue that politicians have utilised the progressive language of personalisation to justify neo-liberal-inspired strategies to reduce state welfare provision and transfer responsibility for securing welfare to individual service users. We discuss both these critiques in greater depth below.

Practical concerns

The (in)ability of some service users to benefit from personalised services

Clearly, for the reasons we outlined above, many adult service users will enthusiastically embrace the opportunities personalisation provides for them to control their own social care resources. However, some academics, as well as service user groups, have expressed concerns about the willingness or ability of many adult service users to exercise the 'choice' offered by personalisation. Not all adult service users, they argue, conform to the 'ideal' personalisation 'profile' presented by advocates of personalisation, and many may not wish to manage their own budgets, or they may simply be unable to do so. Rather than seeing personalisation as a 'liberating' experience, these service users may view the stresses associated with managing their own care with anxiety and trepidation. Hence, current plans to roll out personalised services are, some argue, in danger of marginalising the needs of those service users who value and rely upon 'traditional' services. The views of articulate, active, and 'able' services users are, it is suggested, in danger of drowning out the voices of those, for example, with complex needs who are reluctant or unable to embrace the 'new opportunities' on offer. As Burton and Kagan (2006) state, *The complex health needs of many ... and the need for knowledgeable and skilled specialists is not emphasised* in current policy discourses:

> *A kind of inadvertent trick takes place where the least impaired people are used in the imagery to stand for all the others (which reflects the higher profile of self-advocates), yet the life circumstances of many ... are ignored.*

ACTIVITY 9.2

- *Why might some adult service users be reluctant to embrace the 'opportunities' afforded by personalisation?*

- *What kind of support might those adults with complex social care needs require in order to benefit from personalisation?*

- *Does the requirement that personalisation be 'cost-neutral' restrict its potential to benefit such service users?*

COMMENT

The questions raised in the above Activity are important, yet they are sometimes ignored in national debates which tend to focus upon the potentially progressive outcomes associated with personalisation. In fact, studies have shown that some service users are uneasy with the new 'opportunities' afforded by personalisation, viewing them with foreboding rather than enthusiasm. A major government-funded review of the impact of personalisation on service users provided some evidence to support this conclusion. It found that the introduction of individual budgets for adults with learning disabilities had led to significantly lower levels of self-reported health and increased levels of anxiety and stress (Individual Budgets Evaluation Network, 2008, p70):

> They experienced the administration as stressful. 'What if I overspend?' 'I don't want to owe people money.' 'What if I don't fill the form in right?' 'What if there is no money left?' 'What if they cut my budget?' 'I can't recruit anyone!' Several interviewees ... feared that relationships with directly employed carers could break down, leaving users and/or carers to dismiss the paid carer, face threats of legal action, and possibly be left for a period without a paid carer. This was contrasted with situations in which a relationship with an agency carer broke down, where the agency could send a replacement carer straight away. Direct employment of carers ... was anticipated to carry more responsibility and risk for the use.
>
> (pp72–3)

In part, these fears may be unwarranted, and the reluctance to embrace personalisation may, understandably, stem from years of dependency-inducing reliance upon the direction of welfare professionals. Arguably, with encouragement and good-quality support,

Continued

this reluctance could be overcome and even the most anxious and hesitant of service users may, in time, come to realise the potential of personalisation. Certainly, research has drawn attention to the positive impact personalised services have wrought on the self-confidence and well-being of many adult learning-disabled people (Spandler and Vick, 2005; Taylor, 2008). However, such anxieties are, for the moment, very real, particularly among adult service users with complex needs (Lawton, 2009). While good-quality advocacy and support might well eventually enable even those with the most severe disabilities to benefit from personalised care, such support is not itself cheap, and the government's insistence that personalisation be 'cost neutral' creates obvious difficulties for those service users with complex needs that require a high level of support to enable them to take advantages of personalised care. The question of a lack of adequate resources has, in fact, been highlighted by social workers as one of the most serious impediments to the success of personalisation. In one recent survey, 82 per cent of social workers questioned said that a lack of resources poses a threat to personalisation (Dunning, 2010b).

The funding of personalisation

As we have already explained, one of the attractions of 'personalisation' to politicians lies in the potential it offers to reduce the costs of social care provision. Indeed, there is a general consensus that it was this, more than any altruistic concern to 'empower' service users, which convinced John Major's Conservative government to press ahead with direct payments in the mid-1990s. However, the notion that personalisation inevitably leads to reduced costs has been challenged:

> *Fawlty Towers got us used to saying: 'Don't mention the war'. But when it comes to personalisation, the difficulty is we aren't really meant to mention the money. Individual budgets were sold on being cheaper ... they aren't. It is impossible to see how true self-directed support, accessible to all, within a broader customised system of personalised social care will ever become a reality without some fundamental rethinking about who pays and how much money will be needed.*

(Beresford, 2008b)

Beresford, along with many other advocates of user empowerment, are concerned at the emphasis that has been placed upon cost containment and efficiency savings in debates on personalisation. Governments may have conceded to the principle of user-empowerment for adult social care, but, critics argue, funding is still subjected to the same local authority needs-based, means-tested, resource-driven constraints that have always determined the financing of services. In short, no real additional funding is available and personalisation has, in practice, involved a process of service users choosing to spend their existing resources differently. However, if personalisation is to be a truly progressive, 'transformation agenda', then current funding restrictions may need to be removed, otherwise, its empowering ideals may never be fully realised.

For example, as we have already hinted, the success of personalisation may ultimately depend upon the availability of good-quality, independent advocacy support. As Beresford (2008b) argues, *Direct payments don't work as a simple consumerist transaction; they need a proper developed infrastructure of information, advice, advocacy and ongoing support to be accessible and empowering to all*. It is not only service users with complex needs that require such support, which can provide training in managing care, as well as assistance with budgeting, accounting and payroll services. However, the current level of such support is woefully inadequate, mainly because of the significant costs involved in delivering it. In England, for example, only around half of those in receipt of direct payments access agencies providing advocacy support, yet caseloads in these agencies are *at the high end of the maximum recommended level* (Davey *et al.*, 2007). These organisations would be unable to cope with providing support for those currently receiving personalised services, let alone the future anticipated increase in the numbers receiving direct payments. This is just one example of where personalised services may involve additional necessary, but 'hidden' costs, that in the absence of sufficient funding, threatens their potential As Glasby and Littlechild (2009, p147) argue, *there is a growing consensus that financial concerns may be a major obstacle to the success and progress of direct payments, preventing some local authorities from promoting their schemes and potentially leaving recipients without sufficient funds to purchase adequate care.*

Finally, the huge public expenditure cuts introduced by the new Conservative-led coalition administration have exacerbated fears over government commitments to fully resource the personalisation agenda. At the time of writing, local authorities are announcing how they intend to deal with the first tranche of cuts that have been imposed upon them by central government. It is clear that funding for personalised services, like that for social care generally, is set to be slashed. Social workers across the country are reporting huge cuts in the resources they are able to devote to personalisation, as well as the imposition of tight constraints over what service users can spend their budgets on (Dunning, 2011). As Glasby has acknowledged, *many of the social workers I meet seem to feel very isolated and alienated – as if personalisation is giving them empowering language but that they are being set up to fail by a financial context that makes it impossible to deliver* (cited in Association of Directors of Adult Social Services, 2011, p9). Service user groups have also expressed their alarm at the scale of cuts, and have sought to mobilise their constituents in opposition to them.

> *Independent living, that is being able to meet our support needs in the way we choose so that we can be equal citizens in society, is in crisis! Everything we have gained as a movement over the last 30 years is now being put in jeopardy. If we cannot get our support needs met then we will become institutionalised in our own homes living in intolerable conditions and unable to take part in community life. We will be forced to be dependent on family, friends and volunteers who we have no control over. Just like the old days. We cannot allow this to happen! NCIL is actively campaigning against these draconian public expenditure cuts joining with other sections of our society who are also opposed.*
>
> (National Centre for Independent Living, 2011)

The impact of personalisation on 'traditional' forms of provision

Others have expressed concerns that as individual budgets are rolled out, the ability of local authorities to fund and organise good-quality collectivist services will be undermined, a process which will effectively confine many vulnerable adult service users to second-class, 'Cinderella' services. In a bizarre twist of fate then, service users reliant upon 'traditional' provision may find the quality of their social care needs are detrimentally affected by a process that purports to be about empowerment and social justice. As Beresford (2008a, p12) argues:

> There is an anxiety that the traditional menu of collective social care services – such as day centres and respite care – will wither away, leaving people adrift in a complex and inadequately regulated market: existing collective services may be closed without adequate alternative support provision being offered in replacement.

Many social workers share these concerns. In one recent survey, more than half of those questioned agreed with the statement that *Services such as day centres are being closed down in my area on the grounds that personal budgets will mean reduced use* (Dunning, 2010a, p15). Service user groups have also noted that 'traditional' services are being cut without any alternatives being made available for those who previously wished to continue to use them. A spokesperson for In Control, an organisation that itself has acted as a powerful advocate in favour of personalised services, has expressed concerns about such developments:

> The worst thing for personalisation is that it's used as an excuse to cut services. Personalisation is [supposed to be] about choice. We know a lot of people are still choosing day centres and, if day centres aren't there, people won't have a choice.

(Dunning, 2010a, p14)

Reluctance among social workers to embrace personalisation

The attitudes and knowledge of social workers have also been identified as potential barriers to the successful implementation of the personalisation agenda. Some surveys, for instance, have suggested that social workers have been distinctly reluctant to embrace personalisation. In part, the lack of enthusiasm is said to stem from legitimate anxieties surrounding some of the issues we have discussed above. Social workers have expressed concerns over the risks associated with allowing vulnerable people to manage their own budgets. The absence of sufficient funding and the potential threat personalisation poses to collectivist services have also contributed to scepticism within the profession about the transformatory potential of personalisation. In addition, the practical pressures associated with working in busy, poorly resourced social work teams can operate as an additional disincentive for front-line workers to embrace an agenda that (initially at least) is resource-heavy and time consuming. This was one of the findings of the Individual Budgets Evaluation Network (IBEN, 2008, p22), which conducted a detailed analysis into the provision of personalised services. As one adult services care co-ordinator told the IBEN researchers, *Care man-agers really do see the benefits but don't feel able to put in much time when they have such high caseloads*. On a more practical level, many social workers are said to lack knowledge about direct payments, which limits their ability to advise service users about the benefits of personalisation.

However, as Glasby and Littlechild (2009, p137) argue, *it may not just be a lack of knowledge that hinders implementation, but political and/or professional opposition*. There can, in fact, be little doubt that many social workers have misgivings about the impact of personalisation on their professional autonomy. It does involve *a radical rethink of the nature of modern social work*, and while many social workers have welcomed the challenge, others have interpreted it as a process which undermines their professional status and skills. The following comments, made by a care co-ordi-nator for adult services, illustrates the genuine concerns shared by many other social workers over the extent to which personalisation may lead to a dilution of the pro-fession's skill-base:

> *I just feel like I'm doing an office job most of the time now. You know, when you train to be a social worker, you get trained in counselling techniques and different therapeutic approaches. What I do is go out with a tick box form and read it out to somebody and then get somebody to come back to tell me how much money they are allowed and that's not a social worker. It's getting worse and worse.*

> (IBEN, 2008, p189)

In fact, there is evidence that personalisation may contribute to a process of de-skilling in local authority social service departments, as well as the social care sector generally. For example, many social work teams have reported a decline in qualified, experienced staff. Indeed, one recent survey found that one in eight social workers felt that personalisation had contributed to a reduction of social workers in their teams, while 16 per cent felt it had contributed to an increase in non-qualified staff (Samuel, 2010b). Regarding the social care workforce generally, early 'sceptics' of the trajectory of the personalisation agenda, such as Ungerson (1997), had argued that personalised care could lead to the development of an unregulated, low-paid, unskilled, potentially exploitative social care labour market. She was concerned that recipients of direct payments and individual budgets may be tempted to employ personal assistants informally, on an illegal, cash-in-hand basis, with no provision being made for employment rights of any kind. While Ungerson (2006, p217) accepts that her worst fears have not materialised, she continues to argue that the working conditions experienced by many personal assistants are *not wholly satisfactory* and at times are *deeply unsatisfactory*. Service user groups themselves have strenuously denied such claims (Morris, 1997), while others have highlighted the compensatory factors that, in practice, can mitigate what ostensibly appear to be poorer employment rights, such as more worthwhile, meaningful relationships with service users (Glasby and Little-child, 2009). That said, it is fair to say that recent research has warned about the possibility of the development of a 'two-tier' social care workforce, *with trained and regulated workers employed by agencies, possibly under better terms and conditions;*

and a less qualified and unregulated workforce employed directly by individual service users (Baxter *et al.*, 2011). Naturally, social work professionals and social care workers are concerned about such developments and this, partially, helps explain some of the professional resistance to personalisation that exists.

Finally, it is also important to bear in mind that opposition to personalisation within the social work profession can also stem from genuine concerns about the ideological underpinnings of the agenda. Put simply, many social workers fear that 'personalisation' is, to an extent, 'a wolf in sheep's clothing'; part of a skilful, ideologically motivated strategy to fundamentally retrench welfare and to transfer the burden of funding and administering care onto adult service users themselves. We examine some of the main elements of ideologically focused critiques of personalisation below.

Ideological concerns

As we have already outlined above, a number of academics and social workers have questioned the ideological motives of politicians who have embraced 'personalisation'. Politicians have, some argued, utilised the progressive language of personalisation to justify neo-liberal-inspired strategies to reduce state welfare provision. This critique shares much in common with the critique of postmodernism that we outlined earlier. While the personalisation agenda shares some of the appealing 'rhetoric of empowerment' of service user movements, ideologically, critics argue, it has very little else in common with it. It is, they insist, lacking any commitment to dramatically improve the state's funding of welfare services, as evidenced by the government's insistence that personalised services do not cost any more than 'traditional' services. It is, they argue, a market-led, consumerist approach, with the focus placed upon utilising the choices and preferences of service users to help drive up standards and secure efficiency gains. At best, this might lead to a greater element of participation and user input, but it will do little to address the issues related to discrimination and the underfunding of provision that acts to the detriment of adult service users.

This variant of personalisation, critics argue, in reality constitutes little more than a diversionary tactic – an 'ideological smokescreen' – designed to draw attention away from the more fundamental, costly reforms that are necessary to secure the economic and social well-being of adult service users. At the same time, social workers and service users are in danger of becoming unwitting, *compliant collaborators* in the residualisation of welfare, as governments seek to transfer responsibility for the delivery and oversight of welfare from the state (and social workers) to individuals themselves (Scourfield, 2007, p112). Again, there are links here to Taylor Gooby's critique of postmodernism outlined earlier. As Scourfield (2007, p108) argues:

> *the danger of using independence and choice as central organising principles is to forget how and why the public sector emerged in the first place – to ensure that those who are necessarily dependent are treated with respect and dignity, to ensure a collectivised approach to risk, and to ensure that secure and reliable forms of support outside of the market or the family are available.*

As we showed in Chapter 5, neo-liberals are ideologically opposed to state welfare and suspicious of the motives of state welfare workers, who are often dismissed as a self-serving cadre of bureaucrats. In this context, it is not hard to see the attraction of certain aspects of 'personalisation' to those wanting to reduce the state's role in the provision of social care and to encourage a greater role for the private sector.

In addition, on a practical level, personalisation could potentially make it less difficult, or less politically problematic, for ideologically motivated governments to reduce expenditure on welfare in the future. As we have seen on numerous occasions in the past, the threatened closure of large-scale, collectively provided services has frequently prompted large-scale, collectivist opposition on the part of service users and communities. Communities and service users have come together, in many cases successfully, to defend provision that they feel common ownership with. The organised, collective nature of such protests is hard for elected politicians to ignore, making it politically difficult for them to press ahead with widespread retrenchment. By contrast, individualising provision may reduce the potential for such opposition. Resistance to cuts may become more individualised, making it considerably more difficult to develop organised opposition to ideologically influenced reductions in social care funding and services. In the current cuts-driven political and economic climate, one can certainly see the political attraction of a strategy that inhibits the potential of collective resistance to reductions in funding for social care.

In summary, ideologically based critiques of personalisation do not reject the principles of user empowerment, or the idea that the views of service users themselves should be central in shaping the provision they receive. Indeed, many of those who are suspicious of the ideological influences underpinning personalisation are themselves passionate advocates of the concepts of user empowerment and 'independent living'. Their criticisms are based upon their belief that what we are seeing implemented is a very much diluted version of the kind of personalisation that has been demanded by user movements. They fear that the personalisation agenda has been driven primarily by neo-liberal principles, and that appealing rhetoric of empowerment is helping to disguise an ideologically influenced strategy that, in reality, is rapidly becoming synonymous with public expenditure cuts, reduced choice and increased privatisation. Many of those opposed to the current trajectory of policy would prefer to see a much greater level of prominence given to the promotion of social democratic principles within the personalisation agenda.

ACTIVITY 9.3

As we have argued, personalisation has been embraced by commentators, academics, politicians of all political complexions. Certainly, the 'language' of personalisation has been utilised by both social democrats and neo-liberals to criticise existing provision and to justify different policy prescriptions. In this activity, we want you once again to don your 'ideological spectacles' and to think critically how the concept can be used to justify different policy ends.

Continued

ACTIVITY **9.3** *continued*

- *What aspects of the 'personalisation' agenda might be appealing to social democrats?*
- *What might a social democratic approach to 'personalisation' look like, and how might it differ from one that is based upon neo-liberal principles?*

A social democratic vision of personalisation

One can certainly see the appeal of the rhetoric of personalisation to social democrats who, as we saw in Chapter 4, place considerable emphasis upon the need to secure social justice, equality and the promotion of human welfare. To the extent that personalisation is, to cite *Putting people first*, said to be *driven by a shared commitment to social justice* (HM Government, 2007, p5), it does seem very much in tune with key social democratic principles. So too does the promise personalisation holds out to empower service users, *enabling them to participate as active and equal citizens, both economically and socially* (p2).

However, while welcoming the principle of greater participation, a social democratic-influenced personalisation agenda would also insist upon the need to address wider structural problems that shape the living conditions and standards of care experienced by adult service users. Hence, alongside an assurance to ensure greater user involvement, social democrats would insist upon an accompanying commitment to, for example, guaranteeing financial security, and to ensuring that adequate funds are available to meet the health and social care needs of adult service users. Current funding for adult social care and social security, they argue, is woefully inadequate and governments – whatever their political complexion – should not be allowed to divest themselves of responsibility for this by seeking to locate the blame for inadequate provision solely upon the way services are organised and delivered.

Supporters of such a strategy argue that it would, in fact, have much in common with philosophies and programmes of various user movements, who for many years have been demanding greater participation in the formulation and delivery of services and more fair, equitable and adequate mechanisms of funding. Participation is obviously a key demand for such movements, but they have also been driven by a commitment to social justice and radical social change (Beresford, 2008a), sharing much in common with social democratic thought, and indeed Marxism. Thus, while the question of procedural rights to participate in the design and delivery of services are seen as extremely important aims, the need to ensure adequate resources and to tackle structural inequality is perceived to be equally crucial. This is the approach adopted, for example, by many disability activists. They welcome the recent emphasis placed by government on the need for welfare practitioners to listen to and engage with people with disabilities, but insist that this in itself is insufficient. As Barnes (2004) has argued, *to achieve a lifestyle comparable to non-disabled peers disabled people need far more than simply user-controlled services*:

> To attain 'Independent living' disabled people need equal access to mainstream schools, jobs, transport, houses, public buildings, leisure etc. or 'all the things that non-disabled people take for granted' ... It is a goal that is far from being achieved despite the introduction of the 1995 Disability Discrimination Act and subsequent amendments.

(Barnes, 2004, p13)

Beresford makes much the same point, drawing attention to the potential contradictions between the kind of user empowerment demanded by service-user movements and the personalisation model that he feels is currently being promoted by government. The former, he argues, grew out of positive, democratising, user-led collective campaigns which fought for the right for service-user control over welfare resources. These user-movement campaigns were designed to strengthen and improve the legitimacy and quality of collective state welfare provision. By contrast, the ideological origins of the government's personalisation model, he suggests, can be found in individualised, market/efficiency-driven neo-liberal agendas, the aims of which have ultimately been to weaken support for collective provision. Scourfield (2005, p473) agrees: politicians seeking to transfer responsibility for securing welfare from the state to individual citizens have, he argues, skilfully 'sat' their market-driven justifications for personalisation on top of service users' 'social rights' discourse, *producing a powerful hybridisation but one riddled with tensions*. Arguably, in what has until relatively recently been a fairly benign economic environment, the personalisation agenda has hitherto managed to reconcile these apparently contradictory ideological influences, with varying degrees of success. However, the early signs are that the election of the Conservative-dominated coalition government has led to a seismic 'neo-liberal turn' in economic and social policy, one which many commentators feel will bring to the fore the ideological tensions underpinning personalisation, and undermine the limited gains that have so far been achieved:

> *Sadly, current positive moves to personal budgets, self directed support and personalisation seem to be being undermined as they are being challenged by broader and bigger cuts leading to increased restrictions on eligibility criteria, cash ceilings and, of course, serious attacks on disability benefits. They are increasingly being seen as a cover for cuts rather than a real improvement.*

(Beresford, cited in Association of Directors of Adult Social Services, 2011, p11)

CHAPTER SUMMARY

We began this chapter by drawing attention to some of the factors that have contributed to the emergence of personalisation on the social policy agenda. As we saw, the 'universal' post-war welfare state's perceived failure to meet the particular needs of different groups of adult service users led to calls for the injection of greater heterogeneity and user empowerment in the organisation and delivery of welfare. Service users' needs, it was argued, had been stifled by a professionally led, 'one-size-fits-all' model of welfare that took little account of their own wishes and preferences. This had contributed to the development of unresponsive, inappropriate, even oppressive welfare interventions which, in practice,

Continued

CHAPTER SUMMARY *continued*

served to reinforce rather than alleviate the difficulties faced by many adult service users. Giving service users control over the collectively funded welfare resources they consumed was promoted by service-user groups themselves as being the most effective means of developing a more responsive, emancipatory model of delivering adult social care. As we have shown, an initial reluctance on the part of governments to embrace 'personalisation' has now given way to an unbridled enthusiasm for the concept, and its arrival on the social policy agenda has been welcomed by academics and politicians of all political shades. However, agreement over the basic principles underpinning personalisation – greater user empowerment and choice – should not be allowed to disguise the real differences in opinion that exist over the general trajectory of policy, or the growing questions that are being raised about the ideological and political imperatives that are driving the personalisation agenda. As Scourfield (2005, p470) argues, *the hegemonic character of the transformative discourse that has emerged around direct payments has largely led to the silencing of critiques, usually by the construction of such critiques as being reactionary*. However, the sheer volume of such concerns, together with the fact that they are emanating from some of the most passionate advocates of user empowerment and independent living, means that they warrant our close attention. As future welfare practitioners and social workers, it is, of course, crucial that you are aware of the emancipatory potential of personalisation. However, it is equally important that you are able to identify the potential contradictions underpinning the personalisation agenda, as well as some of the concerns that have been expressed by some of its most passionate advocates.

FURTHER READING

There are a number of sources that cover many of the issues examined in this chapter in greater detail. The following textbook provides an excellent summary of the history and nature of direct payments at what was a key stage in their development:

Glasby, J and Littlechild, R (2002) *Social work and direct payments*. Bristol: Policy Press.

This text has now been revised and updated to take account more recent developments in policy and practice:

Glasby, J and Littlechild, R (2009) *Direct payments and personal budgets: putting personalisation into practice*. Bristol: The Policy Press.

The following edited collection contains useful chapters on policy and practice, as well as service user perspectives on personalisation:

Leece, J and Bornat, J (eds) (2006) *Developments in direct payments*. Bristol: The Policy Press.

Gardner, A (2011) *Personalisation in social work*. Exeter: Learning Matters.
This Learning Matters' text also provides a good critical overview of the personalisation agenda and reflects on the legislation, history, theories, values and collective voices that have influenced it.

Chapter 10
Ageing, social policy and social work

This chapter will help you to meet the following National Occupational Standards.

Key Role 1: Prepare for, and work with individuals, families, carers, groups and communities to assess their needs and circumstances.

- Work with individuals, families, carers, groups and communities to enable them to assess and make informed decisions about their needs, circumstances, risks, preferred options and resources.
- Assess and recommend an appropriate course of action for individuals, families, carers, groups and communities.

Key Role 2: Plan, carry out, review and evaluate social work practice, with individuals, families, carers, groups, communities and other professionals.

- Apply and justify social work methods and models used to achieve change and development, and improve life opportunities.

Key Role 3: Support individuals to represent their needs, views and circumstances.

- Advocate for, and with, individuals, families, carers, groups and communities.

Key Role 4: Manage risk to individuals, families, carers, groups communities, self and colleagues.

- Balance the rights and responsibilities of individuals, families, carers, groups and communities with associated risk.

Key Role 5: Manage and be accountable, with supervision and support, for your own social work practice within your organisation.

- Monitor and evaluate the effectiveness of your programme of work in meeting the organisational requirements and the needs of individuals, families, carers, groups and communities.

Key Role 6: Demonstrate professional competence in social work practice.

- Review and update your own knowledge of legal, policy and procedural frameworks.
- Use professional and organisational supervision and support to research, critically analyse, and review knowledge based practice.
- Implement knowledge based social work models and methods to develop and improve your own practice.
- Identify and assess issues, dilemmas and conflicts that might affect your practice.

The chapter will also introduce you to the following academic standards which are set out in the 2008 QAA social work benchmark statements:

4.2 Defining principles.

4.3 Defining principles.

4.6 Defining principles.

4.7 Defining principles.

5.1.1 Subject knowledge, understanding and skills.

Introduction

In this chapter we examine a number of broad, policy-based issues that are of relevance to you as students of social work. Our intention here, as with other chapters in this book, is not to list and describe policies and strategies affecting older people. Nor is it our intention to provide a detailed description of day-to-day 'hands-on' work with older service users. There are other titles in the Learning Matters series that fulfil such functions (see, for example, Crawford and Walker, 2008). Rather, our aim is to examine a number of broad, interacting themes and debates, the outcome of which has a direct impact upon policy and practice affecting older service users. In particular, we seek to present a challenge to the dominant conception of older people as a burden, drawing attention to the extent to which ageist stereotypes impact negatively upon the life chances of older people, as well as the quality of services provided to them. We will show how a pervasive culture of ageism structures the lives of older people, leading them to experience inequality and discrimination across a whole range of areas of economic and social and life.

The policy background

Most of us are now living much longer than before. In 1901 males in the UK could only expect to reach the age of 45, and females 49. By contrast, life expectancy rates for males and females born in the UK in 2006 were 77 and 82 respectively. It is predicted these rates will continue to rise, and that by 2021 men born in the UK will, on average, live until they are 81, and women 84 (Office for National Statistics, 2009). Some commentators have predicted even more startling increases in life expectancy rates. A recent *Daily Mail* article, reporting on the purported discovery of what it termed a 'golden oldie gene', predicted an increase in the number of UK centenarians (people living to 100) from 10,000 today to 280,000 by around the middle of the century. Another estimate suggests that 22 per cent of males and 27 per cent of females born in 2001 will live to reach 100 (Office for National Statistics, 2009, p4). Contrast this to 1952, when the newly crowned Queen Elizabeth sent only 270 telegrams to people on their hundredth birthday (it has long been practice in the UK for personal 'royal' greetings to be sent to new centenarians) (Cayton, 1998). Of course, demands on future monarchs apart, population ageing should surely be seen as a cause for celebration: as a reflection of improved standards of living, and the achievements of welfare institutions such as the National Health Service and other branches of the welfare state.

However, despite the positive sentiments expressed in some official policy documents, population ageing is invariably seen as a problem for society, rather than something to be celebrated. Experts, academics, politicians, business leaders and media commentators all tell us that increased life expectancies and ageing populations will, in the near future, place an intolerable strain on the welfare states of nations such as the UK. We are said to be facing a 'demographic time bomb' of unprecedented proportions, and immediate action must be taken if we are to avoid a 'meltdown' in our social care, health and pension systems. To a certain extent, such claims are based upon factual statistical data, which does point to that fact that the UK's population (like that of other developed countries) is getting older. This is an issue which we examine later in this chapter, where we critically examine the 'demographic time bomb' thesis in greater detail. They are, though, also based upon a particular perception of ageing and older people; one which is shaped by age-based stereotypes which see older adults as 'helpless' and as a 'burden'. Put simply, older people are seen as unproductive and as drain on resources, and hence data suggesting there are likely to be more of them are deemed to point to a deeply problematic future.

ACTIVITY 10.4

This activity is designed for use in larger groups, and is similar to the activity we included in Chapter 8, where we sought to gauge your views of younger people. This time, we want to elicit your perceptions of older people and to encourage you to think about how these might impact upon your future practice. This is important, because working with and providing services to older people can constitute a significant part of a social worker's role, and you need to be aware of how your own perceptions of the ageing process might impact upon your practice. It is a fairly simple activity, and one that is based upon methodology that has been used to assess societal perceptions of older people.

- *Firstly, we want each of you to write down on a piece of paper half a dozen words or phrases that come to mind when you hear the terms 'older people' or 'pensioner'. It is important that you try to be as honest as possible, and in order to facilitate this we would suggest that you complete this exercise anonymously, without writing your name on the piece of paper.*

Once you have completed this, gather all the separate pieces of paper, shuffle them together, and nominate one person to read out the responses.

COMMENT

We have tried this exercise with cohorts of our own students and have, at times, been surprised at the generalised, stereotypical attitudes that some have about older people. They tend to associate 'older people' and 'pensioners' with negative words and phrases, such as 'dependent', 'ill', 'burden', 'past it', 'sad' and 'inactive', all of which tell us a lot

Continued

about how some of our students, many of whom will in future be responsible for providing services to older adults, view older people.

We suspect that some of your group's comments will not have been too dissimilar to those we describe above. As the research round-up below illustrates, this is hardly surprising – most members of the public seem to perceive older people in a negative light.

As we have already stated, the above task is based upon a commonly used methodology that has been utilised to gauge the public's views on older people. In 2006, for example, Age Concern published a survey entitled, *Ageism: A benchmark of public attitudes in Britain* (Ray et al., 2006). The survey questioned a representative sample of the population about their views of older people, seeking to assess the public's perceptions of their relative levels of capability. The results are summarised below.

- One in three people viewed those over 70 as 'incompetent' and 'incapable'.
- One in ten people feel that people over the age of 70 are 'unfriendly'.
- Twenty-seven per cent of people view 'older people' with 'pity'.
- One-half of respondents agreed with the statement that, 'employers don't like having older people on their workforce as it spoils their image'.
- Seventeen per cent felt that older people take out of the economy more than they have put in.
- One-third of people feel that population ageing will make life 'worse' for all.

In summary, the Age Concern study found compelling evidence of *patronising or benevolent prejudice, ranging from the more hostile image of a 'cantankerous old codger', to less overtly negative images ... whereby older people are perceived as ... 'doddery but dear'* (p53). Such interpretations, according to the report's authors, had a long historical pedigree and have become part of an inaccurate, yet deeply ingrained negative conception of older people. In the light of such views it is perhaps understandable why many view population ageing as a problem, and are susceptible to the claim that future demographic trends pose 'problems' for society.

Just how much of a burden do older people present to society? Clearly, large sections of the population seem to think that the burden is considerable, and that it is likely to become even more so as population ageing gathers pace. Once again, though, it is important for us to think critically about some of the assumptions that underpin this perception of older people, for they are often based on wildly inaccurate estimates as to the numbers in need of intensive residential and social care. They also underestimate the positive contribution millions of older citizens make to the economy and the communities within which they live.

- *How many people over 65 do you think receive social care?*

Continued

ACTIVITY **10.2** *continued*

- *How many people over 65 live in residential care?*

- *Is it right to describe older, retired people as 'unproductive' and as a burden? What contributions do older people make to the effective functioning of society?*

COMMENT

Many people tend to assume that old age is synonymous with dependency and decline. Consequently, when asked about the percentage of older people who need and receive social care, the answers given are often widely inaccurate. In fact, only a small minority of those over 65 – 15 per cent – receive social care, and only three per cent live in residential care. Among the over-80s, the percentage living in residential care is still a relatively low 18 per cent, considerably less than popular stereotypes would have us believe (Audit Commission, 2008, p18). Hence, the pervasive image of older people as helpless, dependent 'geriatrics' is a myth, albeit a very powerful and persuasive one.

Nor is it inevitable that people become 'unproductive' after they have reached retirement age. Contrary to popular perceptions, 1.42 million people over the retirement age (which at the time of writing is 60 for women and 65 for men) continue to work, thus making an important economic contribution to society (Office for National Statistics, 2010b). Older people also provide a whole range of crucial, unpaid caring and voluntary activities. It is estimated that 60 per cent of child care in the UK is provided by grandparents, saving the economy around £4 billion per year (Audit Commission, 2008, p18). Many others care for their partners or other aged relatives, receiving very little recognition or remuneration for their considerable efforts. Indeed, according to one estimate, people aged over 65 provide 35 per cent of caring for those above that age (Thane, 2000).

Nor should we underestimate the positive, meaningful contributions older people make to their communities through their volunteering activities. Almost one in three (28 per cent) of those aged between 65 and 74 participate in formal volunteering, while well over one in three (38 per cent) engage in some form of informal volunteering. For those aged 75 or over, the formal and informal volunteering rates are 21 per cent and 31 per cent respectively (Communities and Local Government, 2009, p8). Such activity is obviously beneficial for older people themselves, in that they remain engaged and embedded in their communities, while at the same time obtaining a sense of status and worth. However, the knowledge and expertise of older volunteers is also indispensable to many third-sector organisations, whose operations are dependent upon the efforts of reliable, conscientious volunteer workers. One survey suggests that those over 60 contribute around 18 million hours a week in unpaid work, which if paid at the minimum wage level, would cost £4.3 billion per year (Binyon, 2009).

Older people are also more likely to contribute to the political and democratic culture of the country. They are more inclined than their younger counterparts to vote in national and local elections and they are also often more likely to be actively involved in shaping decisions and policy at a community level. Indeed, those in the 65–74 age category are more likely to take part in direct decision-making about a local service or issue (through, for instance, taking on a role such as a councillor, school governor or magistrate) than any other age cohort (Communities and Local Government, 2009, p8).

All these trends serve to contradict popular conceptions of the ageing process, which see it as an inevitable period of decline, deterioration and 'disengagement' from useful economic and social functions. Indeed, they point to a highly engaged, politicised older citizenry who are as involved, or perhaps even more involved in shaping their communities than younger age groups. As one recent longitudinal survey of the ageing process concluded, the *myth of older age as uniformly characterised by decline and dependency is contradicted by the evidence of vigorous and active nonagenarians* (Banks et al., 2008). *As future practitioners, it is crucial that you bear this in mind when considering the support needs of older people.* As Qureshi and Walker argue, older people *do not give up their independence easily: with few exceptions they are reluctant subjects in caring and dependency ... elderly people desire, often more than anything else, the preservation of their independence* (cited in Thane, 2000, p431). However, as we saw earlier, people's perceptions of older people remain fixated on the notion that they are a 'problem' to be managed rather than an asset to be valued and respected. As a society we tend to view older generations through an explicitly ageist lens, which draws from inaccurate, though pervasive negative images of older people. This has a direct and adverse impact upon older peoples standards of living, as well as the quality of services that are provided to them.

RESEARCH SUMMARY

A Marxist interpretation of ageing and ageism

Some commentators have sought to provide a Marxist interpretation of ageing in capitalist societies. For Marxists, the origins of inaccurate, negative portrayals of older people lie with the capitalist system itself. In a system that is based upon production, efficiency and profit accumulation, 'unproductive' older, retired people are seen as an unnecessary drain on otherwise productive resources. They are, to put it bluntly, less essential to the needs of capital (Phillipson, 1982, p156). This is the reason why the state in capitalist societies has consistently failed to devote adequate funding to health and well-being of older citizens. As Phillipson (1982, p102) puts it:

> The need for the [capitalist] state to have a healthy workforce is one matter, whether it needs to have a healthy population of elders is quite another. The necessity for the former has been a major impulse in the creation of social policy. By comparison, the desirability of the latter has had only a marginal influence.

Consequently, Marxists argue that is in the interests of the bourgeoisie for the majority of the population to perceive older people as a growing, expensive burden. This provides capitalist governments with the justification they need to retrench public spending on welfare provision for 'unproductive' older people (Phillipson, 1982). Once convinced of the 'myth' that older people present a rapidly increasing and intolerable burden, citizens are far less likely to protest against miserly retirement incomes and inadequate caring

Continued

services, or actively resist cuts in social care and pensions budgets. In short, fewer demands will be made by older people, and their advocates, on the public purse. From this perspective, therefore, the 'problem' of ageing has been consciously 'manufactured' by the state in capitalist societies. It provides a powerful rationale for failing to address the poverty and exclusion experienced by many older people.

Capitalism benefits in other ways from the 'structured dependency' of older people. Mandatory retirement ages found in most capitalist societies are not, Marxists argue, 'natural', nor do they reflect the capabilities of many older workers. They are artificially imposed age categories, deliberately designed to fulfil the requirements of the capitalist economy. On the one hand, the removal of older people from the workplace provides employers with access to a younger, cheaper, more efficient, disciplined and conserva-tive workforce. The old are thus sacrificed in the corporation's drive for order and effi-ciency: speed-ups on the line, work-measurement techniques, etc., sealing the fate of the ageing worker *(Phillipson, 1982, p156). On the other hand, as we have seen above, retirement 'frees' older people up to provide crucial, unpaid caring functions, which capitalist societies cannot do without. In this way, the forced 'retirement' of older work-ers allows working-age parents to utilise the free domestic labour of older relatives, and to enter the labour market at no, or minimal, cost to business. Older people also provide extensive levels of care to older relatives, which would otherwise cost billions of pounds. The manipulation of retirement ages also allows capital to use older people, like women, as a 'reserve army of labour', which can be drawn into, or rejected from the labour market when economic conditions deem it necessary.*

In summary, therefore, Marxists dismiss overdeterministic assumptions about the uni-versality and inevitability of poor health and low status in old age *(Vincent, 1995, p15). Not only are they misleading, they serve to mask the extent to which capitalism benefits from the myth that older people are an unproductive burden upon societal resources. In reality, there is* no good reason to assume a priori that a chronologically old person is necessarily or significantly different in hopes, abilities and potential capacity from a chronologically middle-aged individual *(p22).*

Need and expenditure

So far, we have provided evidence to question the commonplace assumption that older people are necessarily a burden, who inevitably 'disengage' from society as they get older. However, it is clear than many older people in the UK are vulnerable to, for example, poverty, ill health and disablement. According to one estimate, around 900,000 older people in the UK are considered to have high levels of need, in that they are unable to carry out one of the main activities associated with daily living, such as washing, dressing or eating (Wanless, 2006, pxxiii), while around almost one in five older people are thought to be living in poverty (Work and Pensions Committee, 2009). It is, of course, the role of social policy and welfare practitioners, such as social workers, to provide various forms of welfare support to help address these issues.

Indeed, the principle of cradle-to-grave security, whereby the state accepted responsibility for the welfare of citizens, from birth and through old age, was perhaps the defining, underpinning theme of the welfare state that emerged after 1945. However, doubts have been raised about the extent to which older people's welfare needs are adequately met. For although older people do consume a higher proportion of welfare resources than other age cohorts, many of the services they receive remain underfunded and inadequate to meet need. As we show below, the resources that we as a society devote to the welfare needs of older people are far from sufficient, and the economic and social problems they face are tolerated to a far greater extent than they would be if they affected other groups.

Poverty, age discrimination and disadvantage

Older people's incomes in the UK

Older people are not a homogenous group, and many older people have incomes which are more than sufficient to meet their needs. Numerous surveys, however, have drawn attention to the extent to which many older people are likely to be living in poverty. As we have argued elsewhere, as future social workers you need to be aware of the extent to which poverty structures the lives of the service users that you will be working with, impacting upon their social, economic and psychological well-being (Cunningham and Cunningham, 2008). With regard to older people specifically, poverty provides the context that can increase the likelihood of them coming into contact with social services. It can, as we will show, lead older people to cut back on food, heating, clothing and other essentials, which in turn can adversely affect their ability to live healthy, independent lives. It is therefore important that you, as future practitioners, are aware of the extent of poverty in old age, as well its consequences.

Regarding the extent of poverty, in 2007/08 almost one in five (18 per cent) pensioners were living on incomes below the government's official poverty line (this was £115 per week for single pensioners and £199 for pensioner couples, after housing costs) (Work and Pensions Committee, 2009). The incomes of many pensioners actually fall well below these levels. The Office for National Statistics (2009) has estimated that 23 per cent of single pensioners have incomes of less than £4,000 pa and 28 per cent of pensioner couples have incomes of less than £6000 pa. Given such low incomes, it is hardly surprising that many older people are unable to afford the basic goods and services they require. The inability to afford essentials, such as food, clothing, transport and fuel, means that many older people simply 'do without', detrimentally impacting upon both their physical and mental health and well-being. According to one survey, one in five UK pensioners feel anxious or depressed about their financial situation. Almost one-quarter of those surveyed stated that concerns about money had led them to cut back on buying new clothing and more than one in ten had reduced spending on food (Osbourne, 2005). Other surveys show that more than one in three older people in the UK are anxious about their ability to afford fuel bills over winter, a far higher figure than that found in countries with comparable climates. As the following study found, pensioners in the UK are far more likely than their counterparts in other countries to dread the onset of winter and to reduce spending on heating:

> *UK respondents are more likely than those in Germany and Sweden to have rationed their heating last winter. Indeed, they are four times more likely than those in Sweden to have avoided heating room in their home and to have turned off their heating even when they were cold because they were worried about the cost ... UK respondents are also more likely to ... worry about getting out and about in winter, and about being vulnerable to hypothermia, heart attacks and strokes.*

(MORI, 2006, pp3, 8)

These fears are well founded, for in 2004/05 there were 31,600 excess winter deaths among older people in the UK, a far higher level than that found in countries such as Sweden, which have colder winters than the UK. This shocking statistic serves to illustrate the very real impact poverty can have on the lives of older people. When compounded with the other crises that are often encountered in later life, such as bereavement, isolation, illness and the onset of disability, poverty can literally mean the difference between life and death for many older people.

One of the main causes of poverty in old age is the inadequate level of financial support provided by the UK's state pension system. As the all-party Work and Pensions Committee (2009, p12) notes, it fails to provide an income sufficient to meet the *minimal costs for healthy living in respect of requirements including nutrition, physical activity, housing, psychological relations, mobility and medical care*. Certainly, there can be little doubt that UK pensioner incomes from state provision have fallen well behind those of their European counterparts. The UK system delivers to the average UK pensioner a replacement rate of less than 37 per cent of previous earnings in retirement, compared with 72 per cent in Sweden, 70 percent in the Netherlands and 54 per cent in France. The UK system is even less generous than residual US social security, which delivers a gross replacement rate of 45 per cent to its retired older people (Pensions Commission, 2004, p58).

Indeed, the real value of the basic state pension in the UK has fallen considerably and consistently since 1980, when a decision was taken by Margaret Thatcher's Conservative government to increase it annually in relation to prices rather than earnings. Claiming to be concerned about the 'burden' of providing for increasing numbers of 'dependent' older people, successive Conservative governments introduced this, and a range of other policies, designed to reduce the state's obligations to provide financial security in old age, and to transfer responsibility on to individuals and families themselves. As we will see, although population ageing was cited as justification for this shift, a number of commentators argue that Conservative ministers were influenced primarily by neo-liberal, ideological concerns. In short, they were ideologically committed to rolling back the state and reducing welfare provision across the board, and 'apocalyptic demography' was used to justify ideologically influenced reductions in provision for older people (Cunningham, 2006). Irrespective of their motives, as a consequence of the cuts, by the time the Conservatives lost the General Election in 1997 almost one in three pensioners (29 per cent) had incomes below the official poverty line (Work and Pensions Committee, 2009, p12). In addition, as the value of the basic state pension has continued to fall, many more pensioners have become reliant upon means tested support to top up their incomes to what is deemed an 'acceptable' level.

Pensioner poverty has fallen somewhat since 1997 due to Labour's improvement in the value of means-tested support (the Pension Credit), but as outlined above, poverty among older people still remains at unacceptable levels. One of the main issues has been the previous Labour government's continued reliance upon means-tested strategies to distribute financial support to vulnerable older people. As is often the case with means-tested benefits, there has been a significant problem of non-take-up.

ACTIVITY **10.3**

As social workers, one of your roles will be to ensure that older people receive the financial support that they are entitled to. As we have just seen, even when in receipt of their full entitlements, in many cases pensioners will still be lacking an income that is sufficient to meet their needs. However, many older people in the UK are failing to receive even these minimal levels of support. After reading through the data presented below, try answering the questions that follow.

- *In 2007/08, between 30 and 39 per cent of older people eligible for the means-tested income support via the Pensions Credit failed to claim their entitlement, saving the government £1.900–£2.930 million per year (DfWP, 2009). Just to put this in perspective, this was considerably more than the £830 million that was estimated to have been lost through benefit fraud for the same period.*

- *In 2007/08, 40–47 per cent of pensioners eligible for means-tested Council Tax Benefit failed to claim their entitlement, saving £1,240–£1,690 million (DfWP, 2009, p83). There has been a downward trend of take-up of some 13 per cent since 1997/8.*

- *In 2007/08, 13–19 per cent of pensioners eligible for Housing Benefit did not claim their entitlement. The amount saved amounted to £440–£820 million.*

In Chapter 2 we looked briefly at the issue of non-take-up of means-tested benefits and provided some hints there as to why people may fail to claim support they are entitled to. Why do you think there is a particular problem of non-take-up among pensioners?

COMMENT

Research suggests that there are a number of crucial factors that contribute high levels of non-take-up among older people. Firstly, many are simply not aware that they are eligible for means-tested support, assuming (incorrectly) that they would be informed about any benefits to which they are entitled. As Moffatt and Higgs (2007, p455) note, a

Continued

significant proportion of older people have only a vague idea about the welfare benefits system and very little idea about what they were entitled to.

Secondly, among those who are aware of their eligibility, a sizeable proportion are deterred from claiming because of the complexity of the process. The 2011 version of the Pension Credit form, for instance, is a voluminous 23 pages, and there are an additional 20 pages of guidance to 'help' applicants fill in the form. The form itself asks complex, detailed questions about finances that many potential claimants find confusing, and it requires applicants to send in original copies of proof of evidence for any sources of income. Faced with such obstacles and requirements, many older people view the claiming process as too onerous and simply fail to submit claims.

Finally, many associate claiming with the intrusive, stigmatising means tests of the inter-war years, and they resent having to reveal detailed financial information in order to claim benefits that they feel they should be entitled to as a right. Hence, research shows that significant numbers of non-claimants are actually aware of their entitlements, but decline to claim because of the stigma associated with the process. One Department for Work and Pensions (DfWP) survey found that up to 5 per cent of non-claimants would still refuse to claim even if they received an extra £40 per week (cited in DfWP, 2005, p22). These were the conclusions of another DfWP-funded study:

> Respondents across the sample raised the issue of stigma and described feeling like they were 'begging' when making a claim for Pension Credit ... Some recipients and non-recipients of Pension Credit found application forms in general to be complex and confusing. Specific fears were raised about filling them out incorrectly and, consequently, being accused of fraud and/or having to pay money back.
>
> (Kotecha et al., 2009, p16)

These surveys draw into question the current chosen method for distributing financial support for older people – means-tested assistance. As Goodman et al. (2003) note, if means-tested benefits are not taken up, then increases in entitlements, no matter how large, will not make a significant contribution to ending pensioner poverty. The evidence suggests that many of those failing to claim are the poorest pensioners and that hundreds of thousands are falling below this means-tested safety net and remaining in poverty due to missing out on their benefits (Goodman et al., 2003). Just to reiterate, the issue is not simply one of complexity or lack of awareness. Research shows that significant numbers of non-claimants are actually aware of their entitlements, but decline to claim because of the stigma associated with the process. Hence, organisations representing older people, such as the National Pensioners Convention and Age UK, argue that the only effective way of getting additional resources to those pensioners who need them most is to introduce a truly universal citizens' basic state pension, which guarantees all older people an income above the official poverty line.

Age discrimination

In the light of our earlier discussions about societal perceptions of older people, it should come as no surprise to learn that older people face discrimination across a whole range of different walks of life. The prejudice older people face can take a number of forms. As consumers, older people face difficulty in accessing various financial products, such as loans, mortgages, and health, travel and car insurance, all of which can impact upon their ability to participate fully in society. In the labour market, we find that employers often discriminate against older candidates for jobs, assuming (incorrectly) they will be less motivated and more unreliable than younger applicants. Perhaps of more relevance to you as future social workers, is the discrimination that older people often face in accessing welfare services.

Ageism and health care

The difficulties that older people often experience in accessing health care services are now well documented. The following examples of discrimination in health services were outlined in a 1999 Age Concern report entitled, *Turning your back on us*.

- A 75-year-old women, suffering from a build-up of cholesterol, was told by her GP that the cut-off age for cholesterol treatment was 70. She was declined treatment on the NHS.
- A 71-year-old man with gallstones was told by a doctor *we wouldn't consider surgery at your age.*
- An elderly man with dementia had been placed on the floor with no bedclothes because he was being *demanding*. A sign had been placed next to him saying *good luck for tonight*, warning staff he was *troublesome*.

Turning your back on us illustrated the extent to which the prejudicial, stereotypical attitudes we outlined earlier were influencing the views of health professionals, leading to inferior standards of care for older patients. Often this discrimination was inadvertent, based upon subtle, covert, often unconscious, ageist assumptions and attitudes. Practitioners had unwittingly internalised societal age stereotypes, and it was this, rather than any conscious malicious intent, which led them to assign older people a lower priority status than younger people.

However, Age Concern found evidence of more direct discrimination, whereby discriminatory practices were formally enshrined in policy. Thus, women aged over 70 were, as a matter of policy, not offered breast-screening opportunities, despite a clear risk, and in many areas there was an arbitrary cut-off of 60 operating for heart transplants and some other forms of care, including accident and emergency treatment, kidney dialysis and knee replacements (Lourie, 2001, p13). As we have already noted, an ageing population was one of the NHS's crowning achievements of the twentieth century, yet by the end of the century the NHS was being criticised for failing to meet older people's needs. As Harry Cayton (1998), head of the Alzheimer's Society, argued, the health service seemed to have responded to demographic change *not by redirecting resources to the old but by trying to ration care for them.*

The publication of the *National Service Framework for Older People* (NSFfOP) in 2001 was prompted by then Labour government's acknowledgement that older users of health (and social care and social work services) were not being offered the same standards of care as other citizens. As the Health Minister, Alan Milburn, frankly admitted, services often *fail to meet older peoples' needs – sometimes by discriminating against them, by failing to treat them with dignity and respect* (Department of Health 2001a, pii). There was, the NSFfOP stated, *evidence of poor, unresponsive, insensitive, and in the worst cases, discriminatory, services*, and the first of its eight framework standards pointed explicitly to the need for health and social care services to be geared towards *Rooting out age discrimination*:

> *NHS services will be provided, regardless of age, on the basis of clinical need alone. Social care services will not use age in their eligibility criteria or policies, to restrict access to available services.*

(Department of Health, 2001a, p12)

Some eight years after the publication of the NSFfOP, the Department of Health commissioned the Centre for Policy on Ageing (CPA) to undertake a review of discrimination on the health and social care sectors. One of the resulting reports, *Achieving age equality in health and social care*, provides a summary of the progress made in tackling ageism since 2001 (Carruthers and Ormondroyd, 2009). Some improvements have occurred, particularly in relation to overt age discrimination, and the report noted that a number of useful strategies had been introduced. Some of these are intended to tackle problems across the adult social care sector, but many are explicitly targeted at ensuring older people are able to access the same opportunities as other citizens. These initiatives include:

- the National Service Framework for Older People (2001);
- the Opportunity Age Strategy (2005);
- the Dignity in Care campaign (2006);
- Putting People First (2007);
- the End of Life Care strategy (2008);
- Public Service Agreement 17 – to Tackle Poverty and Promote Greater Independence and Well-being in Later Life The Building a Society for All Ages initiative (2009);
- the National Dementia Strategy (2009);
- Building a Society for All Ages (2009).

However, despite these potentially positive policy campaigns and developments, the CPA found *clear evidence that discrimination remains* (p6). Once again, subtle, unconscious ageist attitudes of welfare organisations and professionals were highlighted as the major issue. Most examples of age discrimination, the report points out, *appear to be matters of thoughtlessness and misplaced assumptions, often reflecting those in wider society and are not the product of avowed prejudice* (p40). In one sense, this is a relief, since it suggests that the problem is not one of deeply held prejudice against older people. On the other hand, it is worrying, in that it implies that many individual practitioners and welfare institutions are largely oblivious to their own discriminatory behaviour. The CPA called for professional bodies such as the General Social Care Council and the Nursing and Midwifery Council to redouble their efforts to ensure that all health and social care workers, through their training, are made aware of the need to identify and challenge ageism, and to base their practice *upon peoples actual needs, preferences and aspirations, not assumptions about them derived from age* (p41).

Ageism and social care

Health care is not the only area of welfare that is characterised by differential levels of treatment. Age-related inequalities in standards of provision are also a characteristic feature of the social work and social care sectors and practices that would be deemed as wholly unacceptable for other groups, such as children, young people and disabled adults, are routinely tolerated when it comes to older service users.

Funding and social care

Firstly, there is the question of funding for social care services. Unlike the National Health Service, which provides free health care on a universal basis to all people irrespective of their incomes, the provision of social care (residential and home care) in England is subjected to stringent eligibility criteria and means tests. Regarding the means test, in 2008/09 individuals in England with assets of over £22,250 (including their homes) received no public support for social care, irrespective of the level of need identified. Those with assets of between £13,000 and £22,250 are also expected to make significant contributions to the costs of their care. Worryingly, one survey found that 31 per cent of the population are unaware of this obligation, assuming that free social care will be available to them when they need it. This is a concern, and it epitomises the ignorance that surrounds social care funding, which in reality is heavily dependent upon private contributions. In 2006, for instance, it was estimated that total private expenditure on social care by older people, including user charges, top-up payments and privately purchased care, amounted to around £5.9 billion, which was roughly the same amount spent by local authorities (King's Fund, 2009). Of those in residential care, around 39 per cent (146,000) are forced to pay their care fees privately, without any assistance from the state or the local authority (National Pensioners Convention, 2009, p4).

However, being in receipt of a low income is in itself no guarantee that support will be provided. This will ultimately be determined by a complex assessment of needs, which is governed by the *Fair Access to Care Services* (FACS) guidance. Introduced by the Department for Health in 2002, FACS categorises individuals into four bands of 'risk':

- critical;
- substantial;
- moderate;
- low (for a more detailed description of these risk categories see Crawford and Walker, 2008).

FACS was intended to ensure that services were needs led and would be driven by a non-discriminatory, human-rights approach, though recent investigations by the Commission for Social Care Inspection (CSCI, now called the Care Quality Commission) has revealed widespread variations in practice.

One of main problems identified by the CSCI is the artificial rationing of services by local authorities. Concerned about their own dwindling resources for meeting their social care responsibilities, and in the absence of any political will to increase funding, many local authorities have increased eligibility thresholds. So whereas previously service users with low or moderate needs may have been entitled to care, only those with substantial or critical levels of need might now be eligible. This may seem harsh, but it is perfectly legal. Although the four categories of need are set nationally, individual local authorities are able to choose themselves which categories should be used as a gateway to support. Also, under FACS guidance local authorities are allowed to take into account their own financial resources when making decisions about entitlement, which in itself makes something of a mockery of the claim that social care is distributed on a service user needs-led basis (CSCI, 2009, p20). Put simply, as demands on local authorities have increased, many of them have responded by 'changing the goalposts', increasing the level of need required to access care in order to ration provision and save resources. As the CSCI (2009, p26) found:

> In 2006–07, the proportion of councils who set their eligibility at 'substantial' or 'critical' level of risk increased from 53 per cent to 62 per cent. In 2007–08, 72 per cent of councils were operating at 'substantial' or 'critical' level. (70 per cent of councils set the threshold at 'substantial' and 2 per cent at 'critical'). Formally this means most people with 'moderate' or 'low' needs are not eligible for publicly funded support.

The CSCI has identified a 'postcode lottery', whereby services may be available to people with particular needs in one area, but those with the same levels of need in neighbouring local authorities are ineligible for support. Inevitably, this *generates confusion and dissatisfaction among service users and carers, who do not understand how a system called 'fair' can result in the same level of need being met by provision of social care in one local authority and not another* (CSCI, 2009, p34). The resentment is, of course, compounded by the fact that those who do not meet these (often somewhat arbitrary) thresholds are expected to organise and pay for their own care.

Of course, it is front-line social workers who are tasked with the responsibility of managing the increasingly stringent eligibility criteria adopted by local authorities, a role that many naturally feel uncomfortable with. Many social workers are motivated to join the profession out of a profound sense of social justice and a desire to affect positive change in the lives of marginalised, vulnerable people. However, many feel that much of their time and energy is devoted to doing precisely the opposite, preventing vulnerable people from accessing services that will be of benefit to them. Assessments are, to cite one CSCI report (2008a, p23), *more concerned with using standardised procedures to screen people out of support rather than to assess their needs.* This inevitably affects morale among practitioners, many of whom believe such 'screening' contravenes the social work value base that they signed up to and passionately support. More concerning, however, is its impact upon those denied services who, according to a CSCI (2008b, p47) review into eligibility for social care, are simply *lost to the system*:

> *Without support people still had needs (and often, it appeared, significant needs that were simply overlooked) and they managed as best they could, but often at great cost in financial, emotional, personal and physical terms.*

Nor should we underestimate the broader climate of fatalism and resignation that such a system engenders among potential beneficiaries of services, many of whom are deterred from applying for assistance that they desperately need. As the Parkinson's Disease Society have argued:

> *The system is overly budget-driven with eligibility criteria being used to save money. People report that they feel social services are looking for excuses to exclude them, not to meet their needs ... The word of mouth impact of this is that other potential users are put off even trying to get help.*

> (cited in CSCI, 2008a, p37)

Clearly, all service user groups are affected by these shortcomings, but as the CPA (2009) argue, the failings we have identified often work to the particular detriment of older service users. For example, the fact that 72 per cent of local authorities restrict access to support to the two highest categories of need means that 'low' or 'moderate' levels of support, which can be crucial in enabling older people to live independently in the community, are not provided, leaving residential care as the only option for many. What is clear is that local authorities using 'substantial' risk as a threshold to care provide a far inferior range of community services for older people than those that use a 'moderate' threshold, spending on average £62 less per individual older person (CSCI, 2008b, p48). Paradoxically, of course, this can lead to increased rather than lower levels of expenditure in the long run. As the CSCI (2008a, p31) argue, not only the current strategy socially unjust, it is *simply storing up problems for the future*.

What type of care for older people?

Despite the rhetorical emphasis placed upon 'choice', 'empowerment' and the psychological benefits of providing services in users' own homes, the underlying assumption that shapes practice still seems to be that 'residential care' is the most appropriate option for older people. This conclusion is supported by data which show that fewer older people per 1,000 population were receiving community-based council services in 2006 than in 2002 (CSCI, 2008a, p25). It is also reinforced by data on social care expenditure, which illustrate that spending on residential care home placements has risen at a faster rate than that on home care (Wanless, 2006). Worryingly, the evidence suggests that this trend has been driven less on the service users' needs or wishes, but more upon the limited resources available to fund older people's care. As the CPA (2009) argue, *In practice, cost ceilings for packages of care can trigger reviews which might lead older people being pressured to accept residential care that*

177

is considered more cost effective for local authorities at an earlier point than younger adults.

Certainly, the cost ceilings on care for older people are far more stringent than those for other groups. This, it seems, is a reflection of the assumption that they do not require, or deserve the same level of provision as others. Thus, in 2007–08, the average 'spend' on the residential and health care needs of individual older people was £465 and £467 per week respectively. By contrast, the equivalent 'spend' for adults with learning disabilities was £1,059 and £845 per week, whereas for adults with physical disabilities it was £780 and £706 per week (CPA, 2009, p35). The following comments were made by professionals responsible for providing care services for older people, and they serve to illustrate the inferior treatment received by older service users.

> *The limit for younger disabled is much higher ... The market for older people is more 'pile em high, sell 'em cheap'. But also ... there's a notion of 'it's more important to keep a young person at home'.*

> *There have been people who have been forced into care because we've refused to fund them any further [with domiciliary care packages]. They are told 'So you take your risk and stay at home or you go into care'.*

> *Generally ... there's less per head for older people ... [Older people are] placed in residential care homes so we don't overspend. It's discrimination because it's not how we would treat ... children, then it's 'hang the cost'.*

> *So you could have an older person in the early stages of dementia or whatever it might be, who really wants to stay in their own home, but their package is going to be absolutely massive and you have got a spend ceiling for older people, so they can't have it. They have to go into residential care unless somebody tops them up, you know, their family. You could have a person with learning disability with dementia in their later stages of life being supported, and massively, to stay at home. Now that's the tension.*

> *We expect to pay significantly higher amounts for residential care for younger adults. It's historical, based on lower expectations ... Some of that will be realistic and some is 'that's the way we've always done it'.*

(CPA, 2009, pp19 and 34–5).

The quality of care for older people

There is also the question of the variable quality of care provided to older people. As the above quotations imply, inferior levels of spending inevitably equate to inferior standards of care. Thus, in some residential care homes, often little is done to ensure that residents benefit from social, recreational and community activities. Inadequate funding is clearly a contributory factor here, though ageist stereotypes about what is an appropriate package of care for older people also plays their part. As one recent inquiry into the conditions found in care homes concluded, the *prevalent model in care emphasises the debilitating effects of old age where staff take on the role of custodians who 'do things to' residents* (Owen, 2006, p68). Residential care for older adults is, therefore, frequently seen by welfare professionals as a 'last refuge' rather than as a potentially positive, empowering experience. The CSCI has also commented on the comparatively poor standards of residential care provided to older people. Its report to Parliament on the state of social care in the England in 2007/08 stated the following:

> There are marked differences in terms of quality ratings between care homes for younger adults and those for older people. 76 per cent of homes for younger adults were rated 'good' or 'excellent' compared with 67 per cent of homes for older people.

(CSCI, 2009, p76)

Of course, this is not to suggest that residential care is an inappropriate choice for many service users, or that many residential care homes do not provide an excellent standard of care to their older service users. Nor is it to belittle the hard work and professionalism of social care workers working in many residential homes, the over-whelming majority of whom are dedicated to providing their service users with dignified, person-centred appropriate care. However, residential care for older people is often under-resourced and based upon a qualitatively different set of assumptions about the type of support that is needed. As Scourfield (2006, p1136) argues, *In both popular and professional discourses, people living in residential care are often homo-genized, being defined in terms of 'complex needs' and 'dependency'*, and too little attention is paid to the possibility that they may wish to remain 'active' and 'engaged' citizens.

Even where home care packages are provided for older people, they tend to be focused upon personal care needs, rather than seeking to support them in participat-ing in useful, engaging, empowering activities, such as education or voluntary work. Different assumptions therefore seem to be made about what is an 'appropriate' quality of life for older people, and this is reflected in both the levels of financial resources devoted to their care, as well as the standard of care provided. As we discussed earlier, the assumption that old age is a time of decline, mental and physical deterioration and dependency is widely held, and this, as the CPA (2009, p40) state, *can lead to assumptions about how older people should lead their lives ... with an emphasis on managing dependency and decline.*

In summary, there is widespread evidence pointing to age discrimination in both health and social care provision in the UK, a problem that is in many cases com-pounded by the income poverty that many older people face. Utilising this evidence, groups representing older people argue that there is a clear, compelling case, based upon moral and social justice grounds, for enhancing the funding and quality of welfare provision for older people. However, the voices of those advocating such a policy shift are increasingly drowned out by the protestations of what we shall refer to here as 'demographic pessimists'.

Demographic 'pessimists'

Demographic pessimists accuse those calling for improved levels of provision for older people of naive sentimentalism, and of ignoring demographic and economic realities. The position of the pessimists is fairly unequivocal. They argue that ageing populations in developed countries such as the UK are going to impose steep, unsustainable, health, social care and pensions costs, and immediate action is needed if we are to avoid a looming 'demographic timebomb'. The 'solutions' advocated by the pessimists vary. On the extreme end, we have those such as the author Martin Amis, who advocate voluntary euthanasia. He predicts a 'silver tsunami':

> There'll be a population of demented very old people, like an invasion of terrible immigrants, stinking out the restaurants and cafes and shops. I can imagine a sort of civil war between the old and the young in 10 or 15 years' time.

> (cited in Chittenden, 2010, p7)

This 'silver tsunami', he suggests, can be avoided by the setting up of voluntary euthanasia booths on street corners, and those choosing to do the 'decent thing' can be offered a Martini and a medal for their trouble! Of course, not all pessimists agree with Amis's crude, unsophisticated musings on the implications of population ageing. Most focus upon what they see as the need to reduce public funding for older people's services. From this perspective, rather than improving public provision, governments should slash their obligations. They should increase retirement ages, cut the value of publicly funded health, social care and pensions, and state unambiguously that they cannot and will not meet the welfare requirements of future older people. Governments should also make it clear that today's workers must take more responsibility for their own future financial needs. The post-war 'cradle to grave' settlements, whereby states accepted responsibility for the welfare of citizens, from birth and through old age, must therefore be 'reformed'. The alternative – intergenerational conflict and economic stagnation – is, we are told, too frightening to consider. The implications of this kind of agenda for social work practice are serious. Eligibility criteria for accessing publicly funded support will be tightened still further, and the social worker's role may become concerned with little more than rationing resources that are woefully inadequate to meet older people's needs.

As we saw at the start of this chapter, some of the statistical evidence presented to support this 'pessimistic' position is compelling. The perception of an imminent crisis is also reinforced on an almost daily basis in the media. Predictions of a looming demographic time bomb and intergenerational conflict provide newspaper editors with 'catchy' headlines, and for this reason they are more than happy to uncritically promote the view that there is an imminent crisis at hand. This has given the claims made by pessimists an aura of respectability and an unquestionable appearance of 'fact'. The uncritical manner in which certain politicians and official government publications utilise demographic data also serves to reinforce the 'pessimist case'. The outgoing Labour government's White Paper, *Building the national care service*, is a good example of this. While acknowledging that there was widespread popular support for a much improved, taxpayer-funded, comprehensive public system of social care in the UK, it explicitly rejected such an approach, citing concerns about ageing population trends. Significantly improving funding for social care would, it argued, be *unfair between generations*. It would *place a large burden on the working-age population – and this burden would increase significantly over time as the proportion of working-age people decreases, and the number of older people grows* (HM Government, 2010, p127).

Criticism of the 'pessimists'

However convincing the pessimistic case seems, as students of social policy we need to be aware that the questions raised by the 'sceptics' are not simply economic, or for that matter demographic. As Vincent (1999) argues, debates over the most appropriate means of funding retirement incomes, like other aspects of social policy, are profoundly influenced and shaped by ideological principles. In this sense, it is important to acknowledge that the research bodies, academics, politicians and commentators warning us of the dangers posed by a 'demographic time bomb', are not ideologically or politically neutral. However, the ideological bias of these 'voices' are rarely, if at all, mentioned in the reporting of their claims. Their statements regarding the funding of the health, social care and income needs of older people are invariably portrayed as objective, authoritative and 'factual'. A largely uncritical media reports their 'findings' and recommendations, and little or no consideration is given to whether there is actually a 'crisis' that needs addressing. The question invariably posed is not, 'is there a problem', but rather, 'how can we cope with the imminent, looming catastrophe'? The voices of 'optimists', who argue that society is more than capable of meeting the financial, health and social care needs of future retired workers, are swept aside by an overwhelmingly sceptical discourse.

'Optimists' point out that ageing populations are not a particularly new phenomenon. They note that Britain's population has been ageing right throughout the twentieth century, and although 'crises' relating to dependency ratios have been predicted throughout this period, they have never materialised. Mullan (2000, p. 74) argues that Britain *coped with a tripling in the proportion of over-64s between 1911 and 1991* and *in comparison a further 50 per cent rise over the next 50 years does not seem that onerous*. From this perspective, there is no demographic time bomb, nor will Britain's ageing population cause any insurmountable problems. The key to this argument is the acknowledgement that economic growth and growing tax revenues have historically been more than sufficient to ensure the increasing levels of resources needed to fund more costly public services for older people. This point was supported by the influential Wanless Review into the future of social care services for older people. It concluded that future projected levels of economic growth were more than sufficient to pay not just for current levels of care, but for a *much improved* social care system for older people. A movement towards a system which delivered *the highest levels of personal care*, and which guaranteed older people were *socially included, able to participate socially, achieve a sense of well-being* was, it argued, eminently affordable, involving only a slight increase in the percentage of resources devoted to social care spending, from 1.4 per cent to 2 per cent of GDP by 2026 (Wanless, 2006, p180).

In the light of such projections, it is important to consider why, as a nation, we continue to be transfixed by the notion that decent, publicly funded social care for older people is becoming an increasingly unaffordable aim. As hinted at earlier, 'optimists' have linked the propagation of what they sometimes refer to as 'apocalyptic demography' in the UK to the rise of the neo-liberal right and its attempts to undermine state welfare. Thus, for Vincent (2003, p. 86), the notion that population ageing will create a demographic time bomb is a myth, constructed by neo-liberals, who share a particular agenda and specific way of seeing the world. Put simply, they are seeking to heighten and exaggerate fears about population ageing in order to undermine support for otherwise popular publicly funded social care and pensions. From this perspective, many sceptics are actually ideologically motivated, and are deliberately seeking to create a (false) sense of inevitability and certainty that public funding for older people's services is unaffordable.

In fact, numerous government-sponsored commissions of inquiry have confirmed that the UK is not facing a looming demographically induced financial meltdown. For example, the Royal Commission on Long-Term Care for the Elderly (1998) concluded that *there is no demographic 'timebomb'*. The UK, it argued, *has already lived through its 'time bomb' earlier this century. The future is much more manageable.* Confirming Mullan's (2000) analysis, the Commission noted that the UK's elderly population has always grown, and society has proven to be more than capable of finding the additional necessary resources to fund retirement incomes. On this specific point, a House of Lords (2003) inquiry offered further encouragement. It points out that projected productivity gains mean that per capita income will more than double over the next half century, delivering more than enough revenue to cope with the UK's ageing population. *We conclude*, the inquiry's report stated, *that population ageing does not pose a threat to the continued prosperity and growth of the United Kingdom economy; in this sense, therefore, there is no looming 'crisis' of population ageing in the United Kingdom* (House of Lords, 2003, p15).

However, the UK policy debate about funding welfare for older people continues to be dominated more by apocalyptic predictions about the 'unsustainable' nature of current levels of public expenditure than it does concern over the economic and social well-being of older people themselves. As 'optimists' such as Alan Walker argue, it is filled *by a demography of despair, which portrays population ageing not a triumph for civilisation, but something of an apocalypse* (cited in Dean, 2004).

The personalisation agenda

Rather than spending more on social care, governments seem to have chosen the route of changing the way services are delivered, with the personalisation agenda now at the forefront of social care reform. We examined the advantages and disadvantages of the current policy shift towards personalisation in Chapter 9, where we discussed it in relation to provision for adult services. Certainly, one can see the possible advantages of such an agenda for older service users. As the government document *Putting people first* argued, personalised services, which allow older people themselves to determine the shape of the provision they receive, has the potential to liberate them from the ageist 'straitjacket' that has shaped many of the services they have received in the past. As we have seen, too often the assumption has been that residential care is the best option for older people, when other, more empowering and personalised packages of support would have been more appropriate. Hence, few would disagree with *Putting people first*'s aim to *replace paternalistic, reactive care of variable quality with a mainstream system focussed on prevention, early intervention, enablement, and high quality personally tailored services* (HM Government, 2007, p2). Likewise, the principle that older people should be seen and empowered to be *active and equal citizens, both economically and socially* – another key objective of *Putting people first* – should command widespread, universal support, particularly in the light of existing levels of exclusion. The promises personalisation holds out to older users of social care services, therefore, seem inherently progressive. They will no long-er be treated as second-class citizens, and like those who privately fund their own provision, they will increasingly have *maximum choice, control and power over the support services they receive*.

As Lymbery (2010, p13) argues, it is difficult to marshal criticisms against an approach which seems so *warmly persuasive*. Those that do question the trajectory of policy can easily be portrayed as representing the *forces of paternalism, conservatism or reaction*. Who, after all, could possibly be opposed to the principles of empowerment and choice for older service users? However, some have questioned both the motives underpinning the personalisation agenda for older people, as well as its practical impact it may have upon the quality of services received (Ferguson, 2007). As was the case with 'community care' in the 1980s and 1990s (Cunningham and Cunningham, 2008), they argue that the benevolent rhetoric surrounding personalisation has the potential to mask a number of less than progressive developments.

On a practical level, questions have been raised about the willingness and ability of some older service users to exercise significant elements of choice over the care they receive. Clearly, a large number of older service users will want to embrace some of the initiatives encompassed by personalisation, but at the same time many *may not wish to undertake the activities upon which self-directed support depends – nor indeed be capable of undertaking them* (Lymbery, 2010, p17). As Ferguson (2007, p396) puts it, many older service users do not conform to the 'typical' personalisation profile of the *choosing, deciding, shaping human being who aspires to be the author of their life*. A Department of Health-sponsored analysis of the trajectory of policy concurred with this view, pointing out that *the personal capacities of some very old people are inadequate to the challenge of orchestrating their own care* (Askham, 2008). Another government-funded review of the impact of personalisation on service users came to much the same conclusions. Indeed, it found that the introduction of individual budgets – a key part of personalisation strategies – led to *lower levels of well-being* and increased levels of anxiety and stress for older people:

The evaluation indicates that a potentially substantial proportion of older people may experience taking responsibility for their own support as a burden rather than as leading to improved control. Older people satisfied with their current care arrangements – particularly when this involved an established relationship with a current care worker – were reported to be reluctant to change.

(Individual Budgets Evaluation Network, 2008, p238)

The National Pensioners Convention (NPC), a user-led movement that seeks to promote the welfare and interests of older citizens, agrees. Expecting *some of our most vulnerable older people to take on the responsibility of micro-employers – recruiting, dealing with payroll matters, contracts, discipline, employment rights, paying tax and national insurance – is*, it argues, *simply unrealistic* (2009, p12). It also states that policies that promote independence and choice have implications for the protection of vulnerable adults, particularly physical and financial abuse, which advocates of personalisation have failed to address.

Of course, the NPC and others who are cautious about the impact of personalisation on older people are not suggesting that personalised services should not be available, but just that such an approach may sometimes be unwelcome or inappropriate, representing a hindrance rather than a benefit. They are also concerned that in the current climate, where personalisation is seen to represent the magical panacea to the shortcomings in social care, the social care needs of those who do remain 'dependent' will be marginalised and overlooked, and that those who make a considered choice not to opt for personalised services may be pathologised.

Others have questioned the assumptions underpinning the personalisation agenda for older people, as well as the motives that have driven it. One of the key criticisms centres on the fact that the difficulties that older people face in accessing decent quality social care are seen to result from failings in the *style of delivery* of care, rather than one of *a lack of adequate funding* for care. They are seen to be a consequence of the 'old' paternalistic approach to organising provision, rather than a failure to guarantee the resources needed to meet older people's needs. *Putting people first,* for instance, made it clear that any reformed system *must be constrained by the realities of finite resources*, and emphasis was placed upon the need to *spend existing resources differently* (HM Government, 2007, p5). Clearly, spending existing resources differently may well lead to improved outcomes from some, or indeed many older people, and to the extent that it does it is to be welcomed. The problem is, it is unlikely to address the significant relative underfunding of welfare and care services that works to the detriment of millions of older people, who are forced to live in hardship and to depend upon chronically underfunded social care provision. This has led some to question whether the promotion of the 'personalisation' agenda in relation to older citizens is motivated by less altruistic intentions than is commonly thought. Certainly, there are those who believe that one of the real objectives is to divert attention away from the costly, genuinely progressive, fundamental social care reforms that are desperately needed (Ferguson, 2007; Lymbery, 2010). From this perspective, changes in the style of delivery alone will be unable to bring about the significant improvements that are needed in social care for older people, unless they are matched by huge improvements in funding.

This is the approach adopted, for example, by the NPC. It welcomes the recent emphasis placed by government on the need to listen to and engage with older service users, but insists that this in itself is insufficient. If older people are to be treated with dignity and respect, the state needs to do much more than simply change the way existing resources are delivered. It must reaffirm the state's commitment to ensuring cradle-to-grave security, and significantly improve funding with a view to establishing a free, universal, taxpayer-funded National Care Service. This model of delivery of social care can be found in Sweden, where approximately 97 per cent of services are publicly funded from taxation and national insurance (CSCI, 2008b).

CHAPTER SUMMARY

The overarching theme to emerge from the discussion in this chapter is our failure as a society to meet the welfare needs of older citizens. Despite the introduction of a number of ostensibly progressive initiatives and developments, all the evidence seems to suggest that older people continue to suffer from a high incidence of hardship, and that the welfare services they receive are inadequate to meet their needs. As we have argued, these trends are undoubtedly reinforced by inaccurate, but pervasive negative societal perceptions of older people, which portray them as an 'unproductive burden'. This pejorative conception of older people, coupled with demographic arguments depicting Britain's ageing population as a threat to the nation's long-term economic and social well-being, provides justification for unequal, discriminatory treatment which, for other social groups, would be seen as unacceptable.

Our main aim in this chapter has been to challenge this negative conception of older people. We hope that our discussion will encourage you to exercise caution when considering issues relating to ageing and social care, and to treat some of the more alarmist claims made about population ageing with a degree of healthy scepticism. As we have intimated, predictions of a looming demographic time bomb can be, and often have been, prompted by ideological concerns rather than any genuine fears about the sustainability of supporting older people. The utilisation of 'apocalyptic demography' to justify ideologically influenced cuts in expenditure on older people is not a particularly novel phenomenon, but its apparent basis in 'statistical fact' gives it continued appeal to those wishing to implement policies that transfer the burden of responsibility for supporting older people from the state to the individual.

For the same reasons, we should perhaps exercise caution when analysing the trajectory of the current personalisation agenda for older people. Of course, few would disagree with the notion that the services older people receive should be based around their needs and preferences. However, as we pointed out in the previous chapter, the rhetoric of personalisation can also potentially be used to justify ideologically motivated strategies that, ultimately, will do little to advance the economic and social well-being of older service users. Improving user input and providing personalised packages of care are clearly important aims. However, the overarching focus on personalisation should not be allowed to obscure what for many is the pressing issue facing the provision of welfare services to older people – chronic, systematic underfunding. Unless this issue is addressed, then the rhetorical, progressive aims of personalisation may never be realised.

185

FURTHER READING

Those of you wanting to read a good history of ageing and social policy, that makes links between past and present debates, will find the following book useful:

Thane, P (2000) *Old age in English history: Past experiences and present issues*. Oxford: Oxford University Press.

The following text, written by Chris Phillipson, provides a critical, Marxist analysis of ageing and social policy:

Phillipson, C (1982) *Capitalism and the construction of old age*. London: Macmillan.

For an accessible critique of what the author refers to as the 'myth' of population ageing, see:

Mullan, P (2000) *The imaginary time bomb: Why an ageing population is not a social problem*. London: IB Tauris & Co.

If you are interested in a practice-focused account of social work with older people we would recommend:

Crawford, K and Walker, J (2008) *Social work with older people*. Exeter: Learning Matters.

At the time of writing, much of the literature looking critically at the personalisation agenda for older people is confined to academic journal articles. Among these, we would recommend:

Lymbery, M (2010) A new vision for adult social care? Continuities and change in the care of older people. *Critical Social Policy*, 30(1), 5–26.

In addition, we would recommend the texts listed in the 'Further reading' section of the previous chapter.

Conclusion

Throughout this book we have emphasised the important contribution social policy can make to your social work education. As we have shown, governmental responses to social and economic problems – their social policies – impact directly upon the life chances and opportunities of services users, and they can hinder as well as enhance the welfare of vulnerable, marginalised individuals and groups. Having read the book, we hope that you are now able to appreciate how the social and economic well-being of citizens is intrinsically linked to the social policy decisions that politicians make.

We have also seen how social work practice itself is shaped and circumscribed by legislation, policy and guidance that determine and constrain the levels, nature and quality of support that social workers are able to provide. As academics who have taught social work students for many years, we are well aware of the motivations that have led many of you to decide to become social workers. Some of you will have been driven by your own personal experiences of the social welfare system (good or bad) and a desire to support others who are experiencing similar circumstances to those that you faced. Others of you will have been motivated by a more general sense of social justice: you want to combat discrimination, 'help people', or ensure that vulnerable groups receive adequate support and are able to reach their full potential. However, as we have pointed out throughout this text, on occasions it is likely that you will not be able to provide service users with the support that you know they need. This will not be due to any professional incompetence on your part, but to the wider political and policy environments that restrict the decisions you are able to make. We hope, therefore, that we have succeeded in helping you to understand the limitations of social work and the barriers you will face in providing service users with the support they need. Of course, in drawing attention to the limits of social work practice, it has certainly not been our intention to disillusion or demotivate you before you embark upon your social work careers. On the contrary, we hope that a knowledge of such constraints might encourage you to become more critical, active and engaged practitioners, who are prepared to advocate and campaign on behalf of your service users.

We have also sought to draw attention to the way in which the ideological predispositions of politicians often influence the welfare policies they introduce when they are in government. Chapters 4 to 6 of the book provided a 'timeline' of influence of the three main ideological perspectives, social democracy, neo-liberalism and Marxism, assessing the respective influence of each. These, and subsequent chapters, point to a strong neo-liberal undercurrent in recent social policy developments. Conservative-led governments have tended to be more enthusiastic adherents to neo-liberalism than their Labour counterparts, but the social policies of all governments since 1979 have, to varying degrees, been influenced by neo-liberal ideals. In this very real sense then, political ideas and values do matter, and it is for this very reason that we have devoted a considerable amount of attention to analysing different ideological approaches to social problems and issues. In doing so, we have tried to provide you with an adequate understanding of not only the values that have been most influential in shaping the policy process, but also those of competing ideological perspectives. Our intention here has been to encourage you to think critically about alternative potential interpretations for (and solutions to) the economic and social problems experienced by the people that you will be working with.

Finally, we would like to end the book by briefly reiterating once more the importance of embracing a social policy dimension to your studies. As academics who have taught social policy for many years, we are passionate in our belief that it is crucial for social workers to develop an appreciation of the wider social policy environment within which social work takes place. As future social workers, it is vital that you are encouraged at this early stage to develop your critical faculties and to be able to assess the underlying influences that shape welfare policy. The QAA (2008, p7) Benchmarks for Social Work state that you should be able to *think critically about the complex social, legal, economic, political and cultural contexts in which social work practice is located.* Hopefully, this text will have provided you with an appreciation of the causes of the problems and difficulties experienced by service users, and equipped you with some of the intellectual tools you require to critically analyse social policies.

Appendix

Subject Benchmark for Social Work

4 Defining principles

4.3 Contemporary definitions of social work as a degree subject reflect its origins in a range of different academic and practice traditions. The precise nature and scope of the subject is itself a matter for legitimate study and critical debate. Three main issues are relevant to this.

- Social work is located within different social welfare contexts. Within the UK there are different traditions of social welfare (influenced by legislation, historical development and social attitudes) and these have shaped both social work education and practice in community-based settings including residential, day care and substitute care. In an international context, distinctive national approaches to social welfare policy, provision and practice have greatly influenced the focus and content of social work degree programmes.

- There are competing views in society at large on the nature of social work and on its place and purpose. Social work practice and education inevitably reflect these differing perspectives on the role of social work in relation to social justice, social care and social order.

- Social work, both as occupational practice and as an academic subject, evolves, adapts and changes in response to the social, political and economic challenges and demands of contemporary social welfare policy, practice and legislation.

4.4 Honours graduates in social work should therefore be equipped both to understand, and to work within, this context of contested debate about nature, scope and purpose, and be enabled to analyse, adapt to, manage and eventually to lead the processes of change.

4.6 Honours degree programmes in social work involve the study, application of, and critical reflection upon, ethical principles and dilemmas. As reflected by the four care councils' codes of practice, this involves showing respect for persons, honouring the diverse and distinctive organisations and communities that make up contemporary society, promoting social justice and combating processes that lead to discrimination, marginalisation and social exclusion. This means that honours undergraduates must learn to:

- recognise and work with the powerful links between intrapersonal and interpersonal factors and the wider social, legal, economic, political and cultural context of people's lives;

- understand the impact of injustice, social inequalities and oppressive social relations;

- challenge constructively individual, institutional and structural discrimination;

- work in partnership with service users and carers and other professionals to foster dignity, choice and independence, and effect change.

4.7 The expectation that social workers will be able to act effectively in such complex circumstances requires that honours degree programmes in social work should be designed to help students learn to become accountable, reflective, critical and evaluative. This involves learning to:

- think critically about the complex social, legal, economic, political and cultural contexts in which social work practice is located;

- acquire and apply the habits of critical reflection, self-evaluation and consultation, and make appropriate use of research in decision-making about practice and in the evaluation of outcomes.

5 Subject knowledge, understanding and skills

Subject knowledge and understanding

5.1 During their degree studies in social work, honours graduates should acquire, critically evaluate, apply and integrate knowledge and understanding in the following core areas of study.

5.1.1 **Social work services, service users and carers**, which include:

- the social processes (associated with, for example, poverty, migration, unemployment, poor health, disablement, lack of education and other sources of disadvantage) that lead to marginalisation, isolation and exclusion, and their impact on the demand for social work services;

- explanations of the links between definitional processes contributing to social differences (for example, social class, gender, ethnic differences, age, sexuality and religious belief) to the problems of inequality and differential need faced by service users;

- the nature of social work services in a diverse society (with particular reference to concepts such as prejudice, interpersonal, institutional and structural discrimination, empowerment and anti-discriminatory practices);

- the focus on outcomes, such as promoting the well-being of young people and their families, and promoting dignity, choice and independence for adults receiving services.

5.1.2 **The service delivery context**, which includes:

- the location of contemporary social work within historical, comparative and global perspectives, including European and international contexts;

- the changing demography and cultures of communities in which social workers will be practising;

- the complex relationships between public, social and political philosophies, policies and priorities and the organisation and practice of social work, including the contested nature of these;

- the issues and trends in modern public and social policy and their relationship to contemporary practice and service delivery in social work;

- the significance of legislative and legal frameworks and service delivery standards (including the nature of legal authority, the application of legislation in practice, statutory accountability and tensions between statute, policy and practice);

- the current range and appropriateness of statutory, voluntary and private agencies providing community-based, day-care, residential and other services and the organisational systems inherent within these;

- the significance of interrelationships with other related services, including housing, health, income maintenance and criminal justice (where not an integral social service);

- the development of personalised services, individual budgets and direct payments.

5.1.3 **Values and ethics,** which include:

- the nature, historical evolution and application of social work values;

- the moral concepts of rights, responsibility, freedom, authority and power inherent in the practice of social workers as moral and statutory agents;

- the complex relationships between justice, care and control in social welfare and the practical and ethical implications of these, including roles as statutory agents and in upholding the law in respect of discrimination.

5.1.4 **Social work theory,** which includes:

- the relevance of sociological perspectives to understanding societal and structural influences on human behaviour at individual, group and community levels;

- social science theories explaining group and organisational behaviour, adaptation and change;

- user-led perspectives;

- knowledge and critical appraisal of relevant social research and evaluation methodologies, and the evidence base for social work.

5.1.5 The nature of social work practice, which includes:

- the characteristics of practice in a range of community-based and organisational settings within statutory, voluntary and private sectors, and the factors influencing changes and developments in practice within these contexts;

- the processes that facilitate and support service user choice and independence;

- the place of theoretical perspectives and evidence from international research in assessment and decision-making processes in social work practice;

- the integration of theoretical perspectives and evidence from international research into the design and implementation of effective social work intervention, with a wide range of service users, carers and others;

- the processes of reflection and evaluation, including familiarity with the range of approaches for evaluating service and welfare outcomes, and their significance for the development of practice and the practitioner.

5.4 Social work honours graduates should acquire and integrate skills in the following areas.

Problem-solving skills

5.5.1 Managing problem-solving activities: honours graduates in social work should be able to plan problem-solving activities, i.e. to:

- think logically, systematically, critically and reflectively;

- manage processes of change, drawing on research, theory and other forms of evidence.

5.5.3 Analysis and synthesis: honours graduates in social work should be able to analyse and synthesise knowledge gathered for problem-solving purposes, i.e. to:

- assess human situations, taking into account a variety of factors (including the views of participants, theoretical concepts, research evidence, legislation and organisational policies and procedures);

- analyse information gathered, weighing competing evidence and modifying their viewpoint in light of new information, then relate this information to a particular task, situation or problem;

- consider specific factors relevant to social work practice (such as risk, rights, cultural differences and linguistic sensitivities, responsibilities to protect vulnerable individuals and legal obligations);

- assess the merits of contrasting theories, explanations, research, policies and procedures;

- synthesise knowledge and sustain reasoned argument;

- employ a critical understanding of human agency at the macro (societal), mezzo (organisational and community) and micro (inter and intrapersonal) levels;

- critically analyse and take account of the impact of inequality and discrimination in work with people in particular contexts and problem situations.

5.5.4 Intervention and evaluation: honours graduates in social work should be able to use their knowledge of a range of interventions and evaluation processes selectively to:

- negotiate goals and plans with others, analysing and addressing in a creative manner human, organisational and structural impediments to change;

- support service users to take decisions and access services, with the social worker as navigator, advocate and supporter.

Communication skills

5.6 Honours graduates in social work should be able to communicate clearly, accurately and precisely (in an appropriate medium) with individuals and groups in a range of formal and informal situations, i.e. to:

- listen actively to others, engage appropriately with the life experiences of service users, understand accurately their viewpoint and overcome personal prejudices to respond appropriately to a range of complex personal and interpersonal situations.

191

Skills in working with others

5.7 Honours graduates in social work should be able to work effectively with others, i.e. to:

- involve users of social work services in ways that increase their resources, capacity and power to influence factors affecting their lives;

- act with others to increase social justice by identifying and responding to prejudice, institutional discrimination and structural inequality;

- challenge others when necessary, in ways that are most likely to produce positive outcomes.

Skills in personal and professional development

5.8 Honours graduates in social work should be able to:

- challenge unacceptable practices in a responsible manner;

- use research critically and effectively to sustain and develop their practice.

6 Teaching, learning and assessment

6.2 The learning processes in social work at honours degree level can be expressed in terms of ... inter-related themes.

- **Awareness raising, skills and knowledge acquisition** – a process in which the student becomes more aware of aspects of knowledge and expertise, learns how to systematically engage with and acquire new areas of knowledge, recognises their potential and becomes motivated to engage in new ways of thinking and acting.

7 Benchmark standards

Knowledge and understanding

7.3 On graduating with an honours degree in social work, students should be able to demonstrate:

- acknowledgement and understanding of the potential and limitations of social work as a practice-based discipline to effect individual and social change;

- an ability to use research and enquiry techniques with reflective awareness, to collect, analyse and interpret relevant information;

- a developed capacity for the critical evaluation of knowledge and evidence from range of sources.

Subject-specific and other skills

7.4 On graduating with an honours degree in social work, students should be able to demonstrate a developed capacity to:

- integrate clear understanding of ethical issues and codes of values, and practice with their interventions in specific situations.

References

Abbott, E and Bompas, K (1943) *The woman citizen and social security*. London: Women's Freedom League.

Abel Smith, B and Townsend, P (1965) *The poor and the poorest*. London: G Bell and Sons.

Addison, P (1994) *The road to 1945*. London: Pimlico.

Age UK (2011) Spending on older peoples care to be cut by 8.4 per cent. Press release. 27 June. **www.ageuk.org.uk/latest-press/spending-on-older-peoples-care-to-be-cut-by-84/**

Appleyard, M (2010) The steriliser. *The Sun*, 6 March.

Askham, J (2008) *Health and care services for older people: Overview report on research to support the national service framework for older people*. London: Department of Health.

Attlee, CR (1920) *The social worker*. London: G Bell and Sons.

Baginsky, M, Moriarty, J, Manthorpe, J, Stevens, M, MacInnes, T and Nagendran, T (2010) *Social workers' workload survey: Messages from the frontline*. London: Social Work Taskforce.

Bailey, R and Brake, M (1975) *Radical social work*. London: Edward Arnold.

Bailey, R and Brake, M (1980) *Radical social work and practice*. London: Edward Arnold.

Banks, J, Breeze, E, Lessof, C and Nazroo, J (2008) *Living in the 21st century: Older people in England*. London: Institute for Fiscal Studies.

Barnes, C (2004) *Independent living, politics and implications*. Leeds: Centre for Disability Studies.

Bartholemew, J (2006) *The welfare state we're in*. London: Politicos.

Baxter, K, Wilberforce, M and Glendenning, C (2011) Personal budgets and the workforce implications for social care providers: Expectations and early experiences. *Social Policy and Society*, 10 (1), 55–65.

Beresford, P (2008a) Whose personalisation? *Soundings*, (40), 8–17. **www.lwbooks.co.uk/journals /soundings/articles/02 per cent20S40 per cent20beresford.pdf**

Beresford, P (2008b) Personalisation of social care can't be done on the cheap. *Guardian Online*, 22 October 2008. **www.guardian.co.uk/society/joepublic/2008/oct/22/social-care-personalisation-individual-budgets**

Beveridge, W (1942) *Social insurance and allied services*. London: HMSO.

Beveridge, Sir W (1944) *Full employment in a free society*. London: George Allen and Unwin.

Binyon, M (2009) Hunt for the inspirational Britons age cannot wither. *The Times*, 1 October.

Blair, T (1999) Why we should stop giving lone teenage mothers council homes. *Daily Mail*, 14 June 1999.

Boyson, R (1978) *Centre forward: A radical Conservative programme*. London: Temple Smith.

Bradford District Infant Mortality Commission (2006) *Summary report*. **www.bradford.nhs.uk/ ebm/BDIMC/Documents/Infant_Mortality_Report.pdf**

Brindle, D (1999) Media coverage of social policy: A journalist's perspective. In Franklin, B (ed.) *Social policy, media and misrepresentation*. Florence, KY: Routledge.

Brindle, D (2011) Police investigate abuse at private care home. *The Guardian*, 11 June.

Brown, M (1969) *Introduction to social administration in Britain*. London: Hutchinson University Library.

Brown, M (1983) The development of social administration. In Loney, M, Boswell, D and Clarke, J (eds) *Social policy and social welfare: A reader*. Milton Keynes: Open University Press.

Burton, M and Kagan, C (2006) Decoding valuing people. *Disability and Society*, 21 (4), 299–313.

Butterworth, E and Holman, B (1975) *Social welfare in modern Britain*. Glasgow: Fontana/Collins.

Byron, T (2009) We see children as 'pestilent'. *The Guardian*, March 17.

Cabinet Office (2010) Building the big society. **http://www.cabinetoffice.gov.uk/sites/default/files/resources/building-big-society_0.pdf**

Cameron, D (2006) Chamberlain lecture on communities, Balsall Heath, Birmingham, 14 July 2006. **www.cforum.org.uk/blog/wp-content/uploads/2006/07/DavidCameronChamberlainlecture.doc**

Cameron, D (2007) *Civility and social progress*: Speech to the Royal Society of Arts, 23 April 2007.

Cameron, D (2010) *Speech on supporting parents*, 11 January 2010. **www.conservatives.com/News/Speeches/2010/01/David_Cameron_Supporting_parents.aspx**

Carruthers, I and Ormondroyd, J (2009) *Age equality in health and social care*. London: Central Office for Information.

Carter, J (1998) Postmodernity and welfare: When worlds collide. *Social Policy and Administration*, 32, (2), 101–115.

Case Con Manifesto (1975). In Bailey, R and Brake, M (1975) *Radical social work*. London: Edward Arnold.

Cater, S and Coleman, L (2006) *Planned teenage pregnancy: Perspectives of young parents from disadvantaged backgrounds*. York: JRF.

Cayton, H (1998) Over 65? The NHS couldn't care less now. *The Independent*, 5 July.

Centre for Policy on Ageing (2009) *Ageism and age discrimination in social care in the United Kingdom: A Department of Health-commissioned review from the literature*. London: CPA.

Checkland, SG and Checkland, O (1974) *The Poor Law Report of 1834*. Harmondsworth: Penguin.

Children Now (2011) The month's key stories in 10 minutes. 1 June.

Chittenden, M (2010) Amis calls for euthanasia booths on street corners. *The Sunday Times*, 24 January.

Cohen, S (2006) *Folk devils and moral panics*. 3rd edition. London: Routledge.

Colwill, J (1994) Beveridge, women and the welfare state. *Critical Social Policy*, 14 (41), 53–78.

Commission for Social Care Inspection (2008a) *Analysis of evidence submitted to the CSCI review of eligibility criteria*. London: CSCI.

Commission for Social Care Inspection (2008b) *Cutting the cake fairly: CSCI review of eligibility criteria for social care*. Newcastle: CSCI.

Commission for Social Care Inspection (2009) *The state of social care in England, 2007/08*. London: CSCI.

Commission on Big Society (2011) *Powerful people, responsible society*. London: ACEVO.

Commons Hansard: Various dates

Communities and Local Government (2009) Citizenship survey: April-September 2008, England. **www.communities.gov.uk/documents/statistics/pdf/1133115.pdf**

Cook, B (2011) Families near to breaking point. *Community Care*, 16 June.

Cook, D (1989) *Rich law, poor law: Differential responses to tax and supplementary benefit fraud*. Milton Keynes: Open University Press.

Cooper, J (2011) News. *Community Care*, 5 May.

Crawford and Walker (2008) *Social work with older people*. Exeter: Learning Matters.

Cunningham, J and Cunningham S (2008) *Sociology and social work*. Exeter: Learning Matters.

Cunningham, S (2006) 'Demographic time bomb', or 'apocalyptic demography': The great pensions debate, in Lavalette, M and Pratt, A (eds) *Social policy: A conceptual and methodological introduction*. Sage: London.

Davey, V, Snell, T, Fernández, J-L, Knapp, M, Tobin, R, Jolly, D, Perkins M, Kendall, J, Pearson, C, Vick, N, Swift, P, Mercer G and Priestley, M (2007) *Schemes providing support to people using direct payments: A UK Survey*. London: PSSRU/LSE.

Davies, C (2010) £200 vasectomy fee to addict 'immoral'. *Guardian*, 19 October.

Dean, H (2004*) Growing older in the 21st century*. London: ESRC.

Department for Education and Skills (2005) *Youth matters. Cm 6629*. London: HMSO.

Department for Education (2010) Government sets out new vision for ending child poverty. Press release, 21 December 2010. **www.education.gov.uk/childrenandyoungpeople/families/child poverty/a0071184/government-sets-out-new-vision-for-ending-child-poverty**

Department for Work and Pensions (2005) *Income related benefits: Estimates of take-up*. London: DfWP.

Department for Work and Pensions (2008) *Fraud and error in the benefit system, April 2007 to March 2008*. **http://www.dwp.gov.uk/asd/asd2/fem/fem_apr07_mar08.pdf**.

Department for Work and Pensions Select Committee (2009) *DWP's commissioning strategy and the flexible new deal: Volume 1*. London: HMSO.

Department for Work and Pensions (2009) *Income related benefits: Estimates of take up: 2007/08*. **http://research.dwp.gov.uk/asd/income_analysis/jun_2009/0708_Publication.pdf**

Department of Health (2001a) *National service framework for older people*. London: HMSO.

Department of Health (2001b) *Valuing people: A new strategy for learning disability for the 21st century. Cm5086*. London: HMSO.

Department of Health (2005) *Independence, well-being and choice: Our vision for the future of social care for adults in England. Cm6499*. London: HMSO.

Department of Health (2007) *Implementation plan for reducing health inequalities in infant mortality: A good practice guide*. London: Department of Health.

Department of Health (2010) *A vision for adult social care: Capable communities and active citizens*. London: Department of Health.

Domokos, J (2011) Jobseekers tricked out of benefits to meet staff targets. *The Guardian,* 2 April.

Doughty, S (1999) Hostel scheme to help teenage mothers work. *Daily Mail*, 1 February.

Doward, J (2010) Anti-drugs campaigner who pays addicts to be sterilised brings her crusade to the UK. *The Observer*, 20 May.

Dunning, J (2010a) Councils deny social care support to all but the most needs. *Community Care*, 15 September.

Dunning, J (2010b) Cuts threaten transformation agenda. *Community Care*, 20 May.

Dunning, J (2011) Personalisation is being undermined by budget cuts and reduced choice and control, say social workers and service users. *Community Care*, 3 February.

Engels, F (1845) *The condition of the working class in England*. Frankfurt: Literarische Anstalt.

Esping Anderson, G (1990) *The three worlds of welfare capitalism*. London: Polity Press.

Evans, EJ (1978) *Social policy 1830-1814: Individualism, collectivism and the origins of the welfare state*. London: Routledge and Kegan Paul.

Every Disabled Child Matters (2011) Disabled children's benefits cut by 50 per cent under the new proposals. Press release. 5 April. **www.ncb.org.uk/edcm/news/press_releases/press_releases _2011/4_apr_11_premiums.aspx**

Ferguson, I, Lavalette, M and Mooney, G (2002) *Rethinking welfare: A critical perspective*. London: Sage.

Ferguson, I (2007) Increasing user choice or privatizing risk? The antinomies of personalization. *The British Journal of Social Work*, 37 (3), 387–403.

Ferguson, I (2008) *Reclaiming social work*: *Challenging neo-liberalism and promoting social justice*. London: Sage.

Ferguson, I and Woodward, R (2009) *Radical social work in practice: Making a difference*. Bristol: Policy Press.

Field, F (1989) *Losing out: Emergence of Britain's underclass*. Oxford: Blackwell.

Field, F (2010) *The foundation years: Preventing poor children becoming poor adults*. London: HM Government.

Field, F and White, P (2007) *Welfare isn't working: New deal for young people*. London: Reform.

Forrester, D and Harwin, J (2007) Parental substance misuse and child welfare: Outcomes for children two years after referral. *The British Journal of Social Work*, 38 (8) 1518–35.

Franklin, B (1999) *Social policy, media and misrepresentation*. Florence, KY: Routledge.

Fraser, D (1984) *The evolution of the British welfare state*. London: Macmillan.

Furedi, F (2002) *Paranoid parenting: Why ignoring the experts might be best for your child*. Chicago: Chicago Review Press.

Furlong, A and Cartmel, F (2007) *Young people and social change: New perspectives*. Maidenhead: Open University Press.

Garrett, PM (2007) 'Sinbin solutions': The 'pioneer' projects for 'problem families' and the forgetfulness of social policy research. *Critical Social Policy*, 27 (2), 203–30.

General Social Care Council (2002) *Codes of Practice for Social Care Workers and Employers*. London: GSCC.

Gentleman, A (2010a) Anger and alarm as Tory minister attacks benefit claimants who have large families. *Guardian*, 8 October.

Gentleman, A (2010b) Minister calls for more social work volunteers. *Guardian*, 30 November.

George, V and Wilding, P (1994) *Welfare and ideology*. Hemel Hempstead: Harvester Wheatsheaf.

Gilbert, BB (1973) *The evolution of national insurance in Britain: The origins of the British welfare state*. London: Michael Joseph.

Glasby, J and Littlechild, R (2002) *Social work and direct payments*. Bristol: Policy Press.

Glasby, J and Littlechild, R (2009) *Direct payments and personal budgets: Putting personalisation into practice*. Bristol: Policy Press.

Golding, P and Middleton, S (1981) *Images of welfare: Press and public attitudes to poverty*. Oxford: Martin Roberts and Company.

Goodman, A and Gregg, P (eds) (2010) *Poorer children's educational attainment*. York: Joseph Rowntree Foundation.

Goodman, A, Myck, M and Shephard, A (2003) *Sharing in the nation's prosperity? Pensioner poverty in Britain*. London: Institute for Fiscal Studies.

Gough, I (1979) *The political economy of the welfare state*. London: Macmillan.

Gove M (2009) *Residential academies could help disadvantaged children*. Speech, 9 March 2009. Conservative Party. **www.conservatives.com/News/Speeches/2009/03/Michael_Gove_Residential _academies_could_help_the_most_disadvantaged_children.aspx**

Green, D (1999) *An end to welfare rights: The rediscovery of independence*. London: CIVITAS.

Gregg, P (2010) *Family intervention projects: A classic case of policy based evidence*. London: Centre for Crime and Criminal Justice Studies.

Hackett, S, Kuronen, M, Matthies A-L and Kresal, B (2003) The motivation, professional development and identity of social work students in four European countries. *European Journal of Social Work*, 6 (2), 163–78.

Hall, S (1984) The rise of the representative/interventionist state 1880s–1920s. In MacLennan *et al*. *State and society in contemporary Britain*. Cambridge: Polity Press.

Hall, S (1998) The great moving nowhere show. *Marxism Today*, November/December, p14.

Halsey, K and White, R (2008) *Young people, crime and public perceptions: A review of the literature*. London: Local Government Association.

Harris, J (2004) Consumerism: Social development or social delimitation? *International Social Work*, 47 (4), 533–42.

Harris, R (1971) A gift horse. In Boyson, R (ed.) *Down with the poor*. Middlesex: Churchill Press Ltd.

Healthcare Commission and Commission for Social Care Inspection (2006) *Joint investigation into the provision of services for people with learning disabilities at Cornwall Partnership NHS Trust*. London: Commission for Healthcare Audit and Inspection. **http:www.cqc.org.uk/_db/_documents/ cornwall_investigation_report.pdf**

Helm, T and Boffey, D (2011) Lib Dems in mutiny over benefit cap. *The Observer*, 27 March.

Heywood, A (1998) *Political ideologies: An introduction.* London: Macmillan Press.

Hillyard, P and Watson, S (1996) Postmodern social policy: A contradiction in terms? *Journal of Social Policy*, 2 (3), 321–46.

HM Government (2007) *Putting people first. A shared vision and commitment to the transformation of adult social care.* London: HMSO.

HM Government (2010) *Building the national care service. Cm7854.* HMSO: London.

HM Treasury and Department for Children, Schools and Families (2007) *Aiming high for young people: A ten year strategy for positive experiences.* London: HMSO.

House of Commons Library (2009) *Welfare Reform Bill: Social security provisions.* Research paper 09/08. London: HMSO.

House of Commons Library (2011) *Localism Bill: Local government and community empowerment.* London: HMSO.

House of Lords (2003) *Select committee on economic affairs: Aspects of the economics of an ageing population. HL Paper 179-I.* London, HMSO.

Hughes, S (2009) Sin bins for scum families. *Daily Star*, 23 July.

Independent Commission on Youth Crime and Anti-Social Behaviour (2010) *Time for a fresh start.* London: The Police Foundation.

Individual Budgets Evaluation Network (2008) *Evaluation of the individual budgets pilot programme.* York: University of York Social Policy Research Unit.

Inland Revenue (2009) *Child tax credit and working tax credit: Estimates of take up rates in 2006/ 07.* **www.hmrc.gov.uk/stats/personal-tax-credits/cwtc-take-up2006-07.pdf**

Ipsos MORI (2006) *Attitudes towards teenagers and crime.* **www.ipsos-mori.com/researchpub lications/researcharchive/poll.aspx?oItemId=287**

Ipsos MORI (2010a) Policing anti-social behaviour: The public perspective. **http://ipsos-rsl.com/ DownloadPublication/1378_sri-crime-hmic-policing-anti-social-behaviour-september-2010.pdf**

Ipsos MORI (2010b) Youth aspirations in London. **http://ipsos-rsl.com/DownloadPublication/ 1374_sri-third-sector-youth-aspirations-in-london-march-2010.pdf**

Johnston, J (1909) *The wastage of child life: As exemplified by conditions in Lancashire.* London: Fabian Society.

Jones, C (1976) *The foundations of social work education: Working papers in sociology, No. 11.* Durham: University of Durham.

Jones, C (1983) *State social work and the working class.* London: Routledge.

Jones, C (2005) The neo-liberal assault: Voices from the front line of British state social work. In Ferguson, I, Lavalette, M and E. Whitmore (eds) *Globalisation, global justice and social work.* London: Routledge

Jones, C (2011) The best and worst of times: Reflections on the impact of radicalism on British social work education in the 1970s. In Lavalette, M (ed.) *Radical social work today: Social work at the crossroads.* Bristol: Policy Press.

Jones, C and Novak, T (1999) *Poverty, welfare and the disciplinary state.* London: Routledge.

Jones, C, Ferguson, I, Lavalette, M and Penketh, L (2004) *Social work and social justice: A manifesto for a new engaged practice.* www.socialworkfuture.org/index.php/swan-organisation/manifesto?84e4966ffb2a94832870f77fe3157220=20f4f975c2a709187cb009e189e08fa1

Jones, C, Burstrom, B, Martilla, A, Canvin, K and Whitehead, M (2006) Studying social policy and resilience to adversity in different welfare states: Britain and Sweden. *International Journal of Health Services*, 36 (3), 425–42.

Jones, G (2002) *The youth divide: Diverging paths to adulthood.* York: JRF.

Kerrigan Lebloch, E and Beresford, P (2010) Volunteers must not take the place of professional social workers. *Guardian*, 1 December.

King's Fund (2009) *Funding adult social care in England.* London: King's Fund.

Kleeman, J (2010) This woman thinks drug addicts should not be allowed to have children. *Weekend Guardian*, 12 June.

Kotecha, M, Callanan, M, Arthur, S and Creegan, C (2009) *Older people's attitudes to automatic awards of Pension Credit, Department for Work and Pensions Research Report No 579.* London: HMSO.

Laming, Lord (2009) *The protection of children in England: A progress report. HC 330.* London: HMSO.

Langan, M and Lee, P (1989) *Radical social work today.* London: Unwin Hyman.

Lavalette, M and Ferguson, I (2009) Social work after 'Baby P'. *International Socialism*, 122, March 2009.

Lawrence, S, Lyons, K, Simpson, G and Huegler, N (2009) *Introducing international social work.* Exeter: Learning Matters.

Lawton, A (2009) *Personalisation and learning disabilities: A review of evidence on advocacy and its practice for people with learning disabilities and high support needs.* London: SCIE.

Leece, J and Bornat, J (eds) (2006) *Developments in direct payments.* Bristol: The Policy Press.

Leonard, P (1975) Towards a paradigm for radical practice. In Bailey, R and Brake, M (eds) *Radical social work.* London: Edward Arnold.

Levitas, R (2005) *The inclusive society: Social exclusion and New Labour.* London: Macmillan.

Lloyd, CM (1923) Industrial welfare work. *Manchester Guardian*, 17 May.

Lords Hansard 6 March 1996, c372.

Lourie, J (2001) *Age Equality Commission Bill, House of Commons Research Paper 01/100.* London, HMSO.

Lowe, R (1993) *The welfare state in Britain since 1945.* London: Macmillan.

Lymbery, M (2010) A new vision for adult social care? Continuities and change in the care of older people. *Critical Social Policy*, 30 (1), 5–26.

Lumley, R (2011) *Campaigners to rally against cuts to adult social care in West Sussex. The Argus*, 13 May.

Macnicol, J (1986) The effect of the evacuation of schoolchildren on official attitudes to state intervention. In Smith, HL (ed.) *War and social change: British society and the second world war.* Manchester: Manchester University Press.

Macnicol, J (1987) In pursuit of the underclass. *Journal of Social Policy*, 16 (3), 293–318.

Malthus, TR (1973) *An essay on the principle of population*. London: Dent.

Marsden, D (1969) *Mothers alone: Poverty and the fatherless family*. London: Penguin.

Marshall, TH (1967) *Social policy*. London: Hutchinson University Library.

Marsland, D (1991) *Beyond the welfare state*. London: Libertarian Alliance.

Marsland, D (1996) *Welfare or welfare state: Contradictions and dilemmas in social policy*. New York: St Martin's Press.

Marsland, D (2010) *Iconclasts*. Radio 4 broadcast, 28 August.

Marx, K and Engels, F (1969) *Manifesto of the communist party*. Moscow: Progress Publishers.

McKinstry, L (2011) Young offenders are mollycoddled by justice system. *Express* 11 February.

McLennan, G (1986) *Beliefs and ideologies*. Maidenhead: Open University Press.

Miliband, R (1973) *The state in capitalist society*. London: Quartet.

Miliband, R (1977) *Marxism and politics*. Oxford. Oxford University Press.

Mishra, R (1977) *Society and social policy: Theoretical perspectives on welfare*. London: Macmillan.

Moffatt, S and Higgs, P (2007) Charity or entitlement? Generational habits and the welfare state among older people in north-east England. *Social Policy and Administration*, 41 (5), 449–64.

Mooney, G (1998) Remoralizing the poor? Gender, class and philanthropy in Victorian Britain. In Lewis, G (ed.) *Forming nation, framing welfare*. London: Routledge.

MORI (2006) *A Comparative Study of Attitudes and Behaviours in the UK, Germany and Sweden*. www.centrica.co.uk/files/pdf/iposos_mori.pdf

Morris, J (1993*)* *Independent lives: Community care and disabled people*. Basingstoke: Macmillan.

Morris, J (1997) Care or empowerment? A disability rights perspective. *Social Policy and Administration*, 31 (1), 54–60.

Moseley, T (2011) Lancashire social services legal battle takes new twist. *Lancashire Telegraph*, 21 May.

Mullan, P (2000) *The imaginary tme bomb: Why an ageing population is not a social problem*. London: Tauris and Co. Ltd.

Murray, C (1999) *Charles Murray and the underclass: The developing debate*. London: CIVITAS.

National Centre for Independent Living (2011) *We must preserve independent living*. Press release, 16 February 2011. www.ncil.org.uk/show.php?contentid=71&categoryid=16

National Pensioners Convention (2009) *Shaping the future of care together: Response to the green paper*. London: NPC.

The Observer (2009) The killers of Baby P came from decades of abuse and dysfunction. Can the state ever reach these families? 16 August.

OECD (2007) *Babies and bosses: Reconciling work and family life*. Paris: OECD.

O'Flynn, P (2009) How government policy led to the death of Baby P. *Express*, 12 August.

Office for National Statistics (2008) *Pension trends*. www.statistics.gov.uk/downloads/theme_compendia/pensiontrends/Pension_Trends_ch15.pdf

Office for National Statistics (2009) *Social trends, No. 39, 2009 edition*. London: Palgrave Macmillan.

Office for National Statistics (2010a) *Infant and perinatal mortality in England and Wales by social and biological factors, 2008*. **www.statistics.gov.uk/pdfdir/ipm1109.pdf**

Office for National Statistics (2010b) Labour market statistics, April 2010. **www.statistics.gov.uk/pdfdir/lmsuk0410.pdf**

Osbourne, H (2005) Scale of pensioner poverty revealed. *Guardian*, 9 December.

Owen, T (2006) *My home life: Quality of life in care homes*. London: Help the Aged.

Pearson, C (2000) Money talks? Competing discourses in the implementation of direct payments. *Critical Social Policy*, 20 (4), 459–77.

Pearson, G (1975) Making social workers: Bad promises and good omens. In Bailey, R and Brake, M (eds) *Radical social work*. London: Edward Arnold.

Pearson, G (1983) *Hooligan: A history of respectable fears*. London: Macmillan.

Pensions Commission (2004) *Pensions: challenges and choices: The first report of the Pensions Commission*. London, HMSO.

Phillips, M (2008) Shannon's mother, a crude culture of greed and why we must abolish child benefit. *Daily Mail*, 8 December.

Phillipson, C (1982) *Capitalism and the construction of old age*. London: Macmillan.

Project Prevention (2010) Objectives. **www.projectprevention.org/objectives/**

Pye, J, Lister, C, Latter, J and Clements, L (2009) *Young people speak out: Attitudes to and perceptions of full time volunteering*. London: Ipsos MORI.

QAA (2008) *Social work benchmarks*. **www.qaa.ac.uk/academicinfrastructure/benchmark/statements/socialwork08.pdf**

Ray, S, Sharp, E and Abrams, D (2006) *Ageism: A benchmark of public attitudes in Britain*. London: Age Concern.

Redwood, J (1995) Single mothers: Should the state always play nanny. *Daily Mail*, 13 August.

Respect (2006) *Family intervention projects*. London: Respect Agenda.

Rose, ME (1971) *The English Poor Law: 1780–1930*. Newton Abbot: David and Charles.

Royal Commission on Long-Term Care for the Elderly (1998) *With respect to old age: Long-term care – rights and responsibilities*. Cm4912-I. London, HMSO.

Samuel, M (2010a) Social care news. *Community Care*, 21 October.

Samuel, M (2010b) The doubts remain. *Community Care*, 20 May.

Saunders, T, Stone, V and Candy, S (2001) The impact of the 26 week sanctioning regime. London: DfWP. **http://webarchive.nationalarchives.gov.uk/+/http://www.dwp.gov.uk/jad/2001/esr100rep.pdf**

Scourfield, P (2005) Implementing the Community Care (Direct payments) Act: Will the supply of personal assistants meet the demand and at what price? *Journal of Social Policy*, 34 (3), 469–88.

Scourfield, P (2006) Helping older people in residential care remain full citizens. *The British Journal of Social Work*, 37 (7), 1135–52.

Scourfield, P (2007) Social care and the modern citizen: Client, consumer, service user, manager and entrepreneur. *The British Journal of Social Work*, 37 (1), 107–22.

Skott-Myhre, HA (2005) Captured by capital: Youth work and the loss of revolutionary potential. *Child and Youth Care Forum* 34 (2), 141–57.

Smith, R (2008) *Social work with young people*. London: Wiley.

Smith, R (2010) High case loads hitting practice. *Community Care*, 9 September.

Social Exclusion Unit (1999) *Teenage pregnancy*. Cm 4342. London: HMSO.

Social Work Action Network (2009) *A radical campaigning network within social work*. http://www.socialworkfuture.org/

Spandler, H (2004) Friend or foe? Towards a critical assessment of direct payments. *Critical Social Policy*, 24 (2), 187–209.

Spandler, H and Vick, N (2005) Enabling access to direct payments: An exploration of care coordinators decision-making practices. *Journal of Mental Health*, 14 (2), 145–55.

Sparrow, A (2011) Ministers hid evidence over benefits cap. *The Observer*, 4 July.

Stainton, T, Boyce, S and Phillips, CJ (2009) Independence pays: A cost and resource analysis of direct payments in two local authorities. *Disability and Society*, 24 (2), 161–72.

Starkey, P (1998) The medical officer of health, the social worker, and the problem family, 1943–1968: The case of family service units. *Social History of Medicine*, 11, (3), 421–41.

The Sun: Various dates.

Swaine, J (2010) Project prevention: Controversial US charity pays drug addicts to be sterilised. *Ottawa Citizen*, 25 October.

TARKI Social Research Institute (2010) *Child poverty and child well-being in the EU: Report for the European Commission*. www.tarki.hu/en/research/childpoverty/report/child_poverty_final per cent20report_jan2010.pdf

Tawney, RH (1964) *Equality*. 4th edition. London: George Allen and Unwin.

Taylor, SD (2008) Obstacles and dilemmas in the delivery of direct payments to service users with poor mental health. *Practical Social Work in Action*, 20 (1), 43–55.

Taylor, W (1904) Memorandum for the physical deterioration committee on the state on army recruits. In *Inter-departmental committee on physical deterioration: Volume 1: Report and Appendix*. pp95–6. Cm 2175. London: HMSO.

Taylor Gooby, P (1994) Postmodernism and social policy: A great leap backwards? *Journal of Social Policy*, 23 (3), 385–404.

Thane, P (1996) *Foundations of the welfare state*. London: Longman.

Thane, P (2000) *Old age in English history: Past experiences and present issues*. Oxford: Oxford University Press.

Thatcher, M (1983) Speech to Glasgow Chamber of Commerce (bicentenary), 28 January 1983. www.margaretthatcher.org/speeches/displaydocument.asp?docid=105244

Thompson, EP (1972) *The making of the English working class*. Harmondsworth: Penguin.

The Times (2008) Poverty and dignity: Editorial. 21 November.

The Times (2011) The shrinking idea. 8 February.

The Times: Various dates.

Timmins, N (1996) *The five giants: A biography of the welfare state*. London: Fontana Press.

Titmuss, RM (1950) *Problems of social policy*. London: HMSO/Longmans.

Titmuss, RM (1966) *Essays on the welfare state*. London: Unwin University Books.

Titmuss, RM (1973) *Commitment to welfare*. London: George Allen and Unwin.

Townsend, P (1962) The meaning of poverty: *British Journal of Sociology*, 13 (3), 210–27.

Toynbee, P (2008) This frenzy of hatred is a disaster for children at risk. *Guardian*, 18 November.

Toynbee, P (2011) Big society's a busted flush. *Guardian*, 8 February.

Travis, A (2009) New powers allow take over of failing youth offending teams. *Guardian*, 23 July.

Tunstill, J (2007) *Volunteers in child protection: Executive summary*. CSV. **http://edit.csv.org.uk/NR/ rdonlyres/CA57869D-88CD-4D76-98DA-1809AA64534D/87634/ExecutiveSummaryFinalVersion. pdf**

Ungerson, C (1997) Give them the money: Is cash the route to empowerment? *Social Policy and Administration*, 31 (1), 45–53.

Ungerson, C (2006) Direct payments and the employment relationship: Some insights from cross-national research. In Leece, J and Bornat, J (eds) *Developments in direct payments*. Bristol: Policy Press.

UNICEF (2000) *A league table of child poverty in rich nations*. Florence: UNICEF.

UNICEF (2005) *Child poverty in rich countries*. Florence: UNICEF.

UNICEF (2007) *An overview of child well-being in rich countries*. Florence: UNICEF.

UNISON (2011) Private practices for social workers: Big con trick. UNISON briefing and advice to branches. **www.unison.org.uk/acrobat/briefing_on_social_work per cent20practices.pdf**

Valios, N (2010) A job for volunteers? *Community Care*, 22 July.

Vincent, J (1995) *Inequality and old age*. Florence, KY: Routledge.

Vincent J (1999) *Politics, power and old age*. Buckingham: Open University Press.

Vincent, J (2003) *Old age*. London: Routledge.

Wanless, D (2006) *Securing good care for older people: Taking a long term view*. London: King's Fund.

Welshman, J (1999) The social history of social work: The issue of the problem family, 1940–1970. *British Journal of Social Work*, 29 (3), 457–76.

Whelan, R (2001) *Helping the poor: Friendly visiting, dole charities and dole queues*. London: CIVITAS.

White, C, Warenner, M, Reeves, A and La Valle, I (2008) *Family intervention projects: An evaluation of their design, set up and early outcomes: Research report No. DCSF-RW047*. London: Department for Children, Schools and Families.

Wilding, P (1983) The evolution of social administration. In Bean, P and MacPherson, S (eds) *Approaches to welfare*. London: Routledge and Kegan Paul.

Wilkinson, R and Pickett, K (2010) *The spirit level*. London: Penguin.

Williams, F (1989) *Social policy: A critical introduction*. Cambridge: Polity Press.

Williams, F (1992) Somewhere over the rainbow: Universality and diversity in social policy. In Manning, N and Page, R (eds) *Social Policy Review 4*. Canterbury: Social Policy Association.

Williams, R (2011) We are being committed to radical, long-term policies for which no one voted. *New Statesman*, 9 June.

Wilson, H (1971) *The Labour government, 1964–1970: A personal record*. London: Weidenfield and Nicolson.

Women's Group on Public Welfare (1943) *Our towns: A close up*. London: Oxford University Press.

Wootton, B (1959) *Social science and social pathology*. London: George Allen and Unwin.

Work and Pensions Committee (2009) Tackling pensioner poverty. London: HMSO.

World Bank (2011) *Health expenditure*. **www.data.worldbank.org/indicator/SH.XPD.TOTL.ZS**

World Economic Forum (2010) Global competitiveness report, 2009–10. **www.weforum.org/documents/GCR09/index.html**

Wyn, J and White, R (1997) *Rethinking youth*. London: Sage.

Young, AF and Ashton, ET (1956) *British social work in the nineteenth century*. London: Routledge and Kegan Paul.

Younghusband, E (1978) *Social work in Britain, 1950–1975: A follow up study*. London: George Allen and Unwin.

Index